Entertainment & Politics

PETER LANG
New York • Washington, D.C./Baltimore • Bern
Frankfurt am Main • Berlin • Brussels • Vienna • Oxford

David J. Jackson

Entertainment & Politics

The Influence of Pop Culture
on Young Adult Political Socialization

SECOND EDITION

WITH CONTRIBUTIONS FROM NEAL G. JESSE

PETER LANG
New York • Washington, D.C./Baltimore • Bern
Frankfurt am Main • Berlin • Brussels • Vienna • Oxford

LIBRARY OF CONGRESS CATALOGING-IN-PUBLICATION DATA

Jackson, David J. (David James).
Entertainment and politics: the influence of pop culture
on young adult political socialization / David J. Jackson. — 2nd ed.
p. cm.
Includes bibliographical references and index.
1. Popular culture—Political aspects—United States.
2. United States—Social life and customs—1971–
3. Young adults—United States—Political activity.
4. Mass media and youth—United States.
5. Mass media—Political aspects—United States.
6. Political socialization—United States. I. Title.
E169.12.J25   302.230973—dc22   2009018348
ISBN 978-1-4331-0655-2 (hardcover)
ISBN 978-1-4331-0643-9 (paperback)

Bibliographic information published by **Die Deutsche Bibliothek**.
Die Deutsche Bibliothek lists this publication in the "Deutsche
Nationalbibliografie"; detailed bibliographic data is available
on the Internet at http://dnb.ddb.de/.

Table of Contents

Tables

Preface

This book is a substantially revised version of the first edition of *Entertainment and Politics*. As such, a significant number of substantial improvements have been added.

The most significant of these is the inclusion of the analysis of the relationship between popular culture and politics in three additional countries: English-speaking Canada, the U.K., and Ireland. With regard to the data and analysis for two of these countries, the U.K. and Ireland, a bit of explanation about authorship is necessary.

The surveys upon which those analyses are based were written by me and my B.G.S.U. colleague Neal G. Jesse. He administered the surveys in Great Britain, and we co-authored the material in this book regarding the U.K. and Ireland.

Other significant changes include the addition of more advanced statistical analysis of the influence of celebrity endorsements of ideas on their likelihood of being agreed with in each of the places we study. These consistent and significant findings across four countries may be the most important results of the revised work.

Significantly as well, additional theoretical perspective is added by a consideration of cultural imperialism and anti-Americanism theory as lenses through which to view how American popular culture is received in other countries.

Acknowledgments

I gratefully acknowledge the support I received from a number of individuals and institutions in writing this work. I am thankful to the professors and universities who allowed access to their students for the surveys upon which much of this work is based. I am also especially thankful to Wayne State University's political science department for contributing so strongly to my education in the noble science of politics. I am especially grateful for the assistance I have received over the years from Dr. John Strate.

A number of individuals connected with Bowling Green also have been especially helpful to me with regard to this project. These include the former chairman of the political science department, Marc Simon, and several individuals who have subsequently departed B.G., including Rob Alexander, Dale Thomas, Bill Rose, Glen Biglaiser, and John Sislin. The department's secretary, Becky Lentz-Paskvan, contributed valuable assistance to the project as well, as did my colleague Neal G. Jesse. A number of other current B.G.S.U. political science colleagues have provided valuable insights over the years. These include Candace Archer, Shannon Orr, Dion Farganis, Jeff Peake, Rob Mominee and Stefan Fritsch. Without their help and encouragement, I would never have completed this work.

Friends and family have been especially supportive as well. I thank my mom Barb and Dad Jim for all of their help over the years. My brother Jim and sister Jean have been good friends as well, as has my sister-in-law Kendra. Other friends especially deserving of thanks for tolerating me during the writing of this book include Stuart Tucker, Steven Engel, J.P. Faletta, Eric Rader, Alec Thomson, Harry Chapin, Tom Strong, Marty Schramm, Moira Fracassa, Jim Fracassa, Julie Jozwiak, Steve Florek, Elena Fracassa, Paul Sternberg, Chuck Beaubien, Ed Lebowsky, Amy Lebowsky, Mark Jakubowski, Fred Sampson, Sherri Cherry, Randy Krajewski, Margaret Dramczyk, and Phil Ochs.

While I happily acknowledge the support of these friends and institutions, the credit for any errors in the work belongs exclusively to the author.

Some sections of this book were previously published in the following articles:

Jackson, David J. 2007. Selling Politics: The Impact of Celebrities' Political Beliefs on Young Americans. *Journal of Political Marketing* 6(4):67-83.

Jackson, David J. and Thomas I.A. Darrow. 2005. The Influence of Celebrity Endorsements on Young Adults' Political Opinions. *The Harvard International Journal of Press/Politics* 10: 80-98.

1

Introduction

Political Socialization
and the Entertainment Media

Why did President Ronald Reagan visit the University of Notre Dame twice during his two terms in office and occasionally try to persuade Congress to pass legislation by asking them to "win one for the Gipper?" Just what did Vice-President Dan Quayle hope to accomplish in 1992 when he attacked the television character Murphy Brown's decision to have a baby out of wedlock? What did President George H.W. Bush hope to achieve when he asserted that the U.S. needed more families like the *Waltons* and fewer like the *Simpsons*? Did presidential candidate Bill Clinton hope to woo conservative voters in 1992 with his attack on rapper Sister Souljah? Did he hope to sway young voters with his appearances on the *Arsenio Hall Show* and MTV? Why does Irish rock superstar Bono meet with presidents and prime ministers to discuss his ideas on alleviating the debt of developing countries? How did Ken Dryden, a former goalie for the Montreal Canadiens manage to get elected and reelected to Canadian federal Parliament in 2004 and 2006? Why did so many people immediately respond to the 11 September 2001 terrorist attacks on the World Trade Centers and Pentagon by saying, "it seemed just like a movie?" Were there no other images or metaphors from real-life that seemed to apply?

    Whatever one might think of these and the myriad other connections between the popular culture and the political life of politicians, candidates, and average citizens, two things are certain: first, for good or ill, politics and entertainment media are becoming increasingly intertwined (Combs, 1991).[1] In addition, along the theme of the decreasing distinction between news and entertainment media, Nimmo and Combs (1990) argue that both the news and entertainment media spin political reality into fantasy and melodrama, at the expense of facts. People experience both kinds of media, of course. Also, at some level these office seekers and holders mentioned earlier, and their consultants, must have recognized the possibility that some people's political beliefs may be influenced by the entertainment media, or star status of a politician derived from their participation in entertainment. This book investigates that possibility.

This work presents a theory of the political socialization process that includes the entertainment media as important agents of socialization in the United States, English-speaking Canada, the United Kingdom, and Ireland. Data gathered from surveys of undergraduate college students at universities in each country is used to demonstrate a number of political effects of the entertainment media, defined here as entertainment television, movies, and music. These effects are important because they are linked with the ongoing conflict over the basic values that define the political community—a debate that has become known in the U.S. as the "culture wars" debate, but which exists in a more muted form in other nations as well. These effects are also examined through the lens of cultural imperialism theory and anti-Americanism, because so much of the world's popular culture is produced in the U.S.

This chapter argues that political socialization should remain a worthwhile subject for both academic and general study. However, political scientists and other social scientists must enlarge the scope of their research on the potential agents of political socialization to include the entertainment media, if for no other reason than the fact that young people are targeted by the entertainment media and spend astronomical amounts of their time engaged with it.

Of course, before studying a concept it is important to define it, so in this chapter some definitions of the concept of political socialization are examined, and one is selected and modified for the value it offers as a means of understanding how popular culture might work to influence young people's beliefs. The traditionally researched agents of political socialization and several general theories of the process are considered as well. Finally, the surveys used in this study are described, including the individuals sampled, the methods used to analyze the data, and then an outline of the chapters to follow is presented.

Scholars generally believe that parents, schools, peers, churches, and the news media influence the political socialization of children, and roughly in that order of importance. While each of these has an impact, researchers who focused exclusively on these agents of socialization at times came up with very tenuous results, or no sig-

---

1   For an argument about the ills of this see Morgan (1993). Also, Street (2004) presents the
      argument against celebrities as politicians, and politicians as celebrities, and ultimately defends
      the practices as within the conventions of representative democracy. "The point," he claims, is
      to "acknowledge the aesthetic character of the representative relationship, in which notions of
      'authenticity' or 'credibility,' style and attractiveness, are legitimate terms" (p. 449).

nificant results at all. For example, Jennings and Niemi (1974, 1981) in their classic panel study demonstrated that the correlation of parent and child ideology peaks at a tau value of .34, and then declines as both cohorts age. If parents have so little enduring significance, it suggests that there may be no answer to the question of how young people learn about politics. Moreover, Jennings and Niemi believe that one of their most important findings is the potential for change in political attitudes. Also, there plainly is no easy way to study the process in detail from beginning to end and thus sort out the myriad influences. However, methodological limitations are not the only reason for our lack of knowledge about this subject.

This book argues that in general social scientists thus far have ignored a veritable goldmine of agents of socialization by not investigating the influence of popular culture. In other words, the error may be one of omission. Scholars should increase the number of agents examined by considering the influences of the entertainment media. If these influences are sizeable researchers will have a better understanding of why the influence of parents is limited. Even if the effects are not sizeable, our understanding of a very important aspect of political behavior will be increased. In other words, the work presented here is not designed to tear down previous research, so much as to add to it.

Definitions of Socialization

As with many concepts in political science, political socialization is not an easy term to define. Weintraub-Austin and Nelson (1993, 420) defined socialization as, "a process by which individuals obtain relevant knowledge, skills, and dispositions that enable them to function competently in the socio-political structure." A similar definition was offered by Sigel (1970, 1), who wrote, "Political socialization refers to the learning process by which political norms and behaviors acceptable to an ongoing political system are transmitted from generation to generation." Dodson (1990, 1112) constructed a similar definition of socialization in the context of political parties and other organizations when she wrote, "(t)he socialization process provides individuals with information regarding the attitudes, values, norms, behaviors, and knowledge customary or desirable within an organization" Liebes and Ribak (1992, 619) operationalized socialization as, "the measured similarity between agent and subject, taking relevant social trends into account."

There are almost as many definitions of socialization as there were researchers in the past who were interested in the issue. However, these definitions share a number of important similarities. First, socialization is always defined as *a process*. It is not something that happens quickly or that is due to the influence of a single important agent or experience. Complex developmental processes are at work that can be expected to vary from person to person and environment to environment. Some developmental processes are commonplace. Social scientists believe that individuals emulate those with whom they have intimate contact, and for the overwhelming majority of persons this means the individual's mother or father. The first inklings of belief are referred to by Knutson (1974) as "pre-political ideologies," and they are the base upon which new beliefs are built. For children beyond a certain age/stage of development, what occurs next is that a new model, belief, or image to emulate enters the child's frame that either complements or contradicts the base. The individual then links the new and old beliefs together in a coherent way. Naturally the process builds outward and away from the family when the child first begins to become aware of actors other than parents. It is doubtful that individuals are aware of these developmental processes, how they work, and what impact they have had on their own beliefs. This lack of awareness by the individual of the processes he or she is undergoing makes the study of the process through survey research more difficult, but not impossible.

After parental influence, political scientists think that the school is the next most important. It is thought that schools are most effective at transmitting relatively objective "textbook" knowledge about government and politics, but there are other effects also detailed below. In recent years, more attention has focused upon the mass media, and especially television. Television watching is so prevalent in homes today that it has very nearly a simultaneous influence along with parents. Also, some of the first important images of the outside world that a child experiences are from television, rather than real, firsthand experiences. Of course, television has long been known to present a distorted picture of the world.

One of the underpinnings of this research is that the television programs children and young adults actually watch are not only the nightly news but entertainment. Ever since Plato, it has been common to assume that children have trouble differentiating the fictional from the real. Of course, the former dominates the entertainment media. Because the political significance of entertainment media may not be obvious, this does not mean that it is nonexistent. The presence of television in the overwhelming majority of homes, if we find that it has any political content, means it may be an integral element of political socialization.

The second shared characteristic of the definitions of socialization is that the individual obtains *knowledge*. Now, certainly, parents teach their children massive amounts of information and impart important skills. In terms of political knowledge, most parents probably do not spend a great deal of time explaining federalism, the three branches of the U.S. national government, or the electoral impact of single-member districts. This sort of knowledge is likely gained through the schools and news media, if at all. However, very politically active parents may impart such knowledge directly. Further, general knowledge about politics is something that churches and news and entertainment media impart as well.

It is unclear what to expect from the entertainment media in terms of the gaining of political knowledge among young people. Take for example the movie *13 Days*, a lightly fictionalized tale of the Cuban Missile Crisis of 1962. In that film President Kennedy and a number of fictionalized versions of very real characters play out the U.S. decision making process during the time when most observers believe the U.S. and U.S.S.R. came the nearest to nuclear confrontation. How much ought we to expect a young person to learn from viewing such a film? The fact that John F. Kennedy was U.S. president in 1962? One would hope a high school student would already know this. That the president decides when the U.S. goes to war? While constitutionally incorrect, Kennedy says this in the film. The obvious nature of much information in popular culture and its frequently incorrect nature are two of the difficulties associated with expecting the entertainment media to inform its audiences.

The next important shared element of the definitions is that socialization is a process that imparts political *beliefs, values,* or *norms.* Of course, parents occasionally try to influence their children's politics directly by encouraging certain beliefs. More often, however, parents influence the attitudes of their children indirectly. For example, children witness a parent's reaction to being stopped by a police officer (the child witnesses a reaction to coercion and authority—the essence of government), and they see whether or not the parent votes, writes letters to the editor concerning political issues, attends a community meeting, and so on. Teachers generally claim that they do not attempt to teach beliefs, values, or norms in the classroom, but teaching about a state's political system undoubtedly endorses its salient features. Aside from schools, other organizations, such as churches, frequently offer prescriptive rather than merely descriptive information about the political system. Commentators and experts on news broadcasts try to influence people's opinions.

Increasingly, the entertainment world is filled with celebrities making political comments, monetary contributions, or political statements with their work. Certainly, they do this not simply to express their opinions, but also to influence public opinion. Political scientists must discover whether or not these activities have any impact on political orientations. The 2000 U.S. presidential election appears to have been a turning point for celebrities' endorsing candidates and/or contributing money to them. For example, Eddie Vedder (lead singer of phenomenally popular rock band *Pearl Jam*), actors Paul Newman, Susan Sarandon, Tim Robbins, and Danny Glover, and singers Bonnie Raitt and Willie Nelson endorsed the Green Party candidacy of Ralph Nader. Vice-President Al Gore received the support of actors Robert de Niro, Harrison Ford, Gwyneth Paltrow, Sharon Stone, Kevin Costner, Michael Douglas, Tom Hanks, Jack Nicholson, Jerry Seinfeld, Tommy Lee Jones, Nicholas Cage, Candice Bergen, and Richard Dreyfuss, among many others. Gore also received the support of a number of musicians, including Sheryl Crow, Herbie Hancock, Quincy Jones, and Barbra Streisand. Actor Chuck Norris endorsed George W. Bush, as did singers Loretta Lynn and Pat Boone. The trend continued in 2004 and 2008, with even more celebrity endorsements, along with films made to sway voters, and concerts performed to raise money for candidates.

In 2008, U.S. rock legend Bruce Springsteen performed several free concerts in support of Barack Obama, and he was joined by folk icon Pete Seeger when he performed Woody Guthrie's "This Land is Your Land" at the inauguration concert in Washington, D.C. Not to be outdone, John McCain earned the support of country and western greats such as Hank Williams, Jr., Aaron Tippin, and Gretchen Wilson, each of whom performed at McCain/Palin campaign events.

Internet video played a role in the 2008 election as it never had before. For example, rapper will.i.am of the group *Black Eyed Peas* released a collage video of a song called "Yes We Can," the lyrics of which consist of Obama speeches as spoken by Obama himself and sung simultaneously by a number of performers. The video quickly went viral and has been viewed more than 25 million times. John Legend and will.i.am performed the song at the Democratic National Convention as well.

Feelings and emotions are outcomes of socialization as well because it is feelings and emotions, rather than just cognition and reasoning that motivate individuals to acquire political beliefs and to act on those beliefs. Because popular entertainment trades in feelings and emotions, I believe it has not been taken seriously by some scholars as an agent of socialization worthy of academic study. We can overcome this problem if we recognize that an agent can have an impact, even if it expresses mere feelings rather than reasoned arguments.[2] To illustrate this point, whereas the works of Karl Marx make a far more intellectually compelling argument for socialism than the music of *The Clash*, a British punk band with socialist leanings, the written words of Marx do not muster the sensual and emotional wallop that results from hearing the angry music of *The Clash*, Billy Bragg, or a myriad of other passionate socialist singers.

As the field of psychology has demonstrated, reason does not exist apart from emotion (e.g., Zajonc, 1980; Zajonc and Markus, 1984). Rather, reason is itself a product of emotion. For example, patriotism is a curious blend of reason, based on self-interest (adherence to the nation-state for the protection it provides) and emotion (love for a country and its symbols) (Johnson, 1986). The entertainment industry does not exist to transmit information. Its purpose is to engage the audience emotionally, but in so doing the ideas that it does transmit may be more deeply learned and retained.

Definitions of Politics and Ideology

It is important to note the definition *of politics* that will be utilized in this research and its link to beliefs, values, and norms. Political scientists define politics to include activities within a society relevant to the acquisition, use, and retention of power. In the public arena, politics includes activities of members of the various branches of government; it includes processes like elections and policy making; and it includes the activities of nongovernmental actors such as parties and interest groups. All individuals acquire attachments, beliefs, knowledge, and values with respect to politics as a result of learning processes that span from early childhood throughout the adult lifespan. One of the most important of these is partisanship. Partisanship is a clear

---

2   Petty and Cacioppo (1986) suggest that, "attitude changes that result mostly from processing issue-relevant arguments," which they call the central route to persuasion, are more likely to endure and influence behavior than are attitude changes that result from peripheral cues, which would include emotion based influence from the entertainment media. While this suggests pop culture's influence may not be long enduring, it is worthy of study nonetheless.

enough construct when used in reference to individuals that it need not be discussed here (see Campbell et al. 1960). Political ideology, however, has taken on many different meanings, so that how it is used in this research must be discussed in some detail at the outset.

Political ideology commonly is defined as a set of coherent beliefs about politics. Ball and Dagger (1998, 5) offer a more elaborate definition when they write, "an ideology is a fairly coherent and comprehensive set of ideas that explains and evaluates social conditions, helps people understand their place in society, and provides a program for social and political action." Historically, the polar opposite terms *liberal (left)* and *conservative* imply choices between conflicting positions on issues such as the scope of governmental activity, the responsibilities of the federal versus the state and local governments, regulation of the economy, isolationism versus intervention in the affairs of other nation-states, and domestic social welfare spending. Young adults do not often think of these terms in this way (Campbell and Strate, 1981).

Political ideology for the young includes a host of "life-style" issues: attitudes toward religion, abortion, affirmative action, civil rights, conformism, gay rights, promiscuity, marriage, violence, women's role, and others not clearly demarcated by the traditional definitions of liberal and conservative. Interestingly, it is also over these issues that entertainment television, films, and music are likely to take conflicting positions. It is uncommon to hear a song with lyrics that endorse lower taxes. It is far from uncommon to hear lyrics that attack religion, endorse promiscuity, or promote violence or social tolerance. Taking Ball and Dagger's definition in the broadest sense, lifestyle issues are not strictly social, but inevitably political because of their relevance to the acquisition, use, and retention of political power.

The moral precepts that should guide a community are inevitably a matter of contention and politics. For example, a traditional moralist will oppose the presentation of characters on television soap operas who "sleep around" and participate in sexual relations before and/or outside marriage, and utilize artificial birth control or abortion. Clearly, this individual is saying that sex without the public commitment to marriage and family and the possibility of procreation is immoral. The same person then is also implying that television writers and actors ought not to condone such behavior by creating characters who engage in it. Whereas traditional morality is not political ideology in its usual sense, it does comprise a set of beliefs about how people should behave in civilized society and what the government should do to support such beliefs.

Models of Socialization

What about the general and theoretical works on socialization? Jennings and Niemi (1981, 20–22) discuss four models of socialization. These are the "classic" models of socialization and they guide this research. Their first model, the *lifelong persistence* model, holds that what children learn early in their lives endures and that individuals become more resistant to change as they age (for confirmation of the persistence model see Sears and Funk, 1999). The *lifelong openness* model holds that there is little or no effect of childhood learning on adult political values. Individuals are open to influences throughout their lives. The *life-cycle* model holds that persistence of early learning is the rule, but that at certain life-states people are more open to change. For example, the classic claim that young people are more liberal might simply mean that young people are more open to political influence. Finally, the *generational* model asserts that, although persistence is the rule, there are certain social and political movements, epochs or periods of upheaval and change, and that these influence individuals' political beliefs. It is fair to say that the research presented here is most influenced by the likelihood of the validity of the *life-cycle* model.

Setting out a generational model, Inglehart (1990a) argues that very profound value changes have been taking place in industrial societies in recent decades. He calls the shift one of movement from "materialism" to "post-materialism." He believes that system level changes translate into individual level changes that then have system level consequences. He outlines four system level changes: satisfaction of sustenance needs for larger proportions of populations because of technology changes; rising levels of education; the absence of total war during most recent generations; and, finally, the expansion of mass communications leading to increased penetration of mass media into people's lives. These system level changes have triggered changes in people's values (including increasing emphasis on needs for belonging, esteem, and self-realization) and skills (including an increased proportion of population with skills to handle politics on a national scale). Most importantly for this research, these changes in values lead to system level consequences.

First, conflict based on lifestyle issues increases relative to conflict based on social class. Second, there is a decrease in legitimacy of national institutions and a rise in supranational concerns. Third, there is a change in participation away from party politics and a greater focus on specific issues.

These theoretical pieces are important to the research presented in this work for a number of reasons. First, with the exception of the *lifelong openness* model, each of Jennings and Niemi's theories of continuity and change holds that early learning is important. Early learning is more likely to occur through connections to the popular culture because young people take popular music, movies, and television much more seriously than do adults. Moreover, each of these theories of continuity are really theories of change as well, as Niemi and Jennings point out later in their classic work. The research reported on here, derived as it is from snap-shot style questionnaires of political attitudes of young people at a given moment, is not the longitudinal study necessary to demonstrate real persistence. However, as Jennings and Niemi indicate, not demonstrating persistence need not trouble us. This research will demonstrate that young people have been influenced by the popular culture at some time in their lives, just as it will demonstrate that young people are currently being influenced by the popular culture. Perhaps most importantly, this work demonstrates that popular culture is an agent of socialization likely to change the beliefs of young people or reinforce recent changes away from the beliefs of parents and parentally selected agents of socialization.

Inglehart's work concerning the shift to postmaterialism in industrial society is important for this work because it helps explain how the young conceive of politics, how they define political ideology, and with which political issues expressed in the popular culture they agree or disagree and by which they are influenced. It is not, however, a theory from which the hypotheses tested are derived. Rather, it is a useful framework for helping shed light on why young people might perceive politics in the personalistic and individualistic ways the data indicate that they do. It may help to explain levels of patriotism and nationalism felt by young people. It may assist in explaining increased attention to environmental and other supranational concerns. It may explain why young people conceive of politics as related with how individuals make moral choices, rather than how collectives make public choices. It may shed light on the origins of the importance of lifestyle and culture wars issues among the young.

Agents of Socialization

Much research on socialization, especially the early U.S. literature, has focused on the family as a primary agent (Hyman 1959; LeVine, 1963; Sigel 1970; Jennings and Niemi, 1981; Liebes and Ribak, 1992; Beck and Jennings, 1991; Acock and Bengston 1978; Dash, 1992; Weintraub-Austin and Nelson 1993; Tedin 1974; Moore et al., 1985; Greenstein 1965; Jennings and Niemi ,1974; Knutson, 1974). Canadian studies have stressed the importance of the family as well (Belovari et al., 1976, Martinez 1984), as did early studies of socialization in Great Britain (Butler and Stokes, 1969; Dowse and Hughes, 1971).

Schools in the U.S., as a parentally selected agent of socialization, have been considered as well (Hess and Torney 1967; Ehman 1980; Muller, Seligson, and Turan 1987, 27; Seefeldt 1989; Berti 1988; and Knowles 1993). Canadian scholarship has established the influence of schools as agents of socialization too (Pammett 1971; Tompkins, 1977: 87–91; Lambert et al., 1988), with some polemicists arguing the schools do nothing but produce consumers and mindless supporters of cultural diversity (Emberley and Newell 1994). Early British research found support for the school as an agency of socialization as well (Dowse and Hughes 1971)

Churches, another parentally selected, agent have received some scholarly attention also (Huckfeldt, Plutzer and Sprague 1993; Wald, Owen and Hill 1988; Peterson 1992).

Research on agents less likely to have been selected by parents, such as peers, the news media, entertainment television, pop music, and movies deserve greater attention in this book.[3]

---

3   It is simply impossible to present a comprehensive review of all the literature concerning the various agents of socialization. The review here presents important findings in each of the countries studied in this book, but also recognizes and supports the implicit assumption of

Peers

The influence of peers on political socialization has always presented a chicken-and-the-egg dilemma. If young people learn political beliefs from their peers, then where did the peers learn them in the first place? The consensus among political scientists on peer influence is that it is generally weak, but that there is a relationship between youths' and their peers' sociopolitical beliefs (see Hess and Torney 1967; Langton 1967; Jennings and Niemi,1981; Campbell 1980; and Tedin 1980).

The News Media

The news media have been considered as agents of socialization as well. Early U.S. studies asserted that mass media were secondary agents of socialization that merely reinforced existing views (Klapper 1960; for a review of work up to that point see Kraus and Davis, 1976). Chafee et al. (1970) supported the view of Greenstein's that children do not really have ideological or political views before a certain age, so there is nothing for the media to reinforce. Children may acquire information from news media (see Conway et al., 1981), but it is less clear what impact the media have. According to early U.S. research, boys and girls prefer different content: "Girls like music and non-conflictual themes, while boys prefer adventure and action fantasy content" (Roberts 1973). Conway et al. (1981) also found that news media use among children positively correlates with political knowledge, and Delli Carpini, Keeter, and Kennamer (1994) found similar results among American adults. Newhagen and Reeves (1992) found that respondents remember television news based in part on the degree of negatively compelling images and sounds. Burriss (1987) found that as the complexity of a story increases, the ability of Americans to recall the story declines. Furthermore, as story complexity decreases, positive evaluations of the story increase. Graber (1990, 153) found that the pictures shown during television news broadcasts expand knowledge of the human aspects of stories, but that pictures do not increase knowledge for stories that defy illustration. Robinson and Davis (1990) found that television news viewing actually corresponds with lower levels of comprehension of issues.

According to Valentino and Sears (1998), "the dominant models of mass media effects emphasize agenda-setting, priming, and framing effects." All three of these concepts, "assume a potent role for standing pre-dispositions" (128). According to Entman (1993), "to frame is to select some aspects of a perceived reality and make them more salient in a communicating text" (52). For Iyengar (1991), framing can be either "thematic" or "episodic," and that generally the episodic framing of issues makes location of responsibility more difficult for citizens. Episodic framing encourages viewers to hold individuals responsible for problems, while thematic framing encourages viewers to hold social and political institutions responsible (Streich 2000).

---

much one-country research: namely, that findings in one English-speaking country may in most cases safely be generalized to the others.

In terms of elections coverage, Patterson argues that the news media utilize a "game" schema to explain the process while voters use a "governing" schema (in Streich 2000). A "game" schema focuses on the horserace aspects of an election or policy debate, while a "governing" schema looks at the impact of candidates' beliefs and policies. The U.S. media's reliance on the "game" schema induces cynicism and a belief among the electorate that "politics (is) a strategic game played by political elites" (63).

McCombs and Shaw (1972) defined agenda setting as media control over what people think about, but not necessarily control over how people think. They have demonstrated the existence of agenda setting through correlations between content of newspaper reports of the 1968 U.S. presidential campaign and survey data about what issues people consider important. Shaw and Martin (1992), in a follow-up to the previous study, added controls for race, class, gender, and education. They found that increased newspaper reading results in less variation of opinion within categories of these demographic variables, and smaller differences of opinion across categories. Increased television viewing results in less variation of opinion within categories as well. Pan et al. (1994) demonstrated through comparison of samples before and after the Persian Gulf War that exposure to newspaper, CNN, and PBS coverage of the war led to higher levels of knowledge about the war among Americans. Watching CNN reduced differences in knowledge about the war between persons with different levels of education. Watching network news correlated with increased image-oriented information, whereas cable coverage correlated with learning abstract information about the war.

Priming is the ability of the news media to change public opinion or behavior, not by changing people's beliefs, but by changing the relative weight people assign to different components of the decision making process (Iyengar and Kinder 1987) Mendelsohn (1996) has shown that voters exposed to more media coverage of campaigns tend to make up their minds based on candidate evaluations, because that is how the media have framed the contest. Krosnick and Brannon (1993) have shown that media attention to the first U.S.-led war against Iraq influenced Americans to evaluate President George H. W. Bush based on his handling of that situation, instead of other foreign and domestic policies. Mutz (1993) has demonstrated that the news media influence how much weight the U.S. public places on economic matters, and in fact have been more influential than personal experience. Krosnick and Kinder (1990) have shown that the media coverage of the Iran-Contra scandal primed Americans' judgment of President Reagan.

Just as interesting as who watches the news is the question of who does not. Poindexter (1980, 64) demonstrated, not surprisingly, that the young avoid the news, adults with larger incomes and more education are less likely to watch local news, while those with smaller incomes and less education are less likely to view network news. Finally, Page, Shapiro, and Dempsey (1987) have demonstrated that the content of network television news generates a high proportion of overall change that occurs in the U.S. public's policy preferences. Particularly influential are news commentators, experts (retired generals who moved the public against SALT II), and popular presidents.

Belovari et al. (1976, in Tomkins 1977) found that young Canadians relied heavily on television for political information, while teachers were a key source of information only in the early grades, and even then ranked behind parents. Siegel (1986) argued the familiar claim that francophone and Anglophone media present very different perspectives on news and may be partly responsible for cultural differences between the two groups. Lambert et al. (1988) demonstrated that newspapers and newsmagazines contributed significantly to Canadians' knowledge of politics, while the effect of news television was substantially weaker. Buckingham (1999) conducted in-depth interviews of 11–17 year old British youths and found that young people were at least somewhat critical viewers of the news, and also tended to be very cynical about politicians.

Entertainment Television

There has been relatively little study of the popular media as agents of socialization. Fluck (1987) has argued that much of the interpretation of the popular media's influence errs on either the side of overestimating its manipulating and indoctrinating effects, or on the side of the media's ability to meet the legitimate needs of the user.

Miller and Reeves (1976) have shown that television characters help shape children's sex-role perceptions in the U.S. Boys select aggressive characters to emulate, whereas girls choose characters based on their physical attractiveness. The authors contend, however, that increased exposure to counter-stereotypical characters causes modifications in real sex-role perceptions. Baran (1976) has demonstrated that young Americans who perceive characters on television as sexually more capable than themselves and experiencing more enjoyment report less satisfaction with their own initial coital experiences. Those who have enjoyed their first sexual encounter perceived as accurate the portrayal of sex on television.

In terms of sex, family, quality of life, and basic values, entertainment television seems to influence viewers. Smaragdi (1983, 198) has demonstrated that television watching by children does not impede family life, isolate children from peers, or hinder enjoyment of preferred leisure activities. Neuman (1982) has found that television has a homogenizing effect on American viewers. Controlling for education, he has concluded that respondents' analytic and interpretive responses to entertainment television are the same. Potter and Ware (1989) have found that there are 20.2 prosocial acts per hour of U.S. prime-time TV. Prosocial acts are rewards given to characters for positive behavior. Selnow (1986) has shown that in most entertainment programming problems are presented as solvable in short timespans by hard work, truth, righteousness, and ingenuity. Fictional women find solutions to romantic dilemmas, whereas men find aggressive solutions to their problems. Morgan (1984) has found that watching more entertainment television correlates with a negative perception of the quality of one's life. High-use viewers are less likely than lower use viewers to rate their life as "great."

In terms of influence with regard to more traditional political beliefs, Meyer (1976) argued that the situation comedy *All in the Family* reinforces political attitudes among American adults, but the moral/ethical lessons of the show have no impact on children. Ball-Rokeach et al. (1981) demonstrated that the mini-series *Roots II* had little impact on viewers' beliefs; Feldman and Sigelman (1985) have shown that news coverage and discussion related to *The Day After*, a fictitious drama about a nuclear attack on the U.S., have been more influential on viewers' beliefs about nuclear war than the actual program. Utilizing focus groups, Delli Carpini and Williams (1996) have shown that entertainment television's coverage of issues related to toxic waste influenced public opinion as much as news coverage did. Lenart and McGraw (1989) have demonstrated that those who watch a television miniseries depicting the consequences of a takeover of the United States by an enemy state a more hawk-like in their foreign policy attitudes than those who have not viewed the series.

Roberts (1997) has demonstrated that MTV's *Choose or Lose* and *Rock the Vote* campaigns have had little influence on voter registration levels, actual votes of young people, partisanship, or ideology. Her findings clearly contradict the expectations of the nonacademic press (Hammer and Wolfberg 1992). Gerbner et al. (1984) have demonstrated that those Americans who watch more television (both news and entertainment) are more likely to identify themselves as political moderates and to avoid the extremes of the ideological spectrum.

Recently, a Comedy Central program has captured much media and some scholarly attention. *The Daily Show with Jon Stewart* boasts that it is a "fake news" show, but it mixes interviews with politicians and office seekers, odd-ball news segments, and decidedly left-leaning commentary to produce a half-hour program watched by millions of predominantly young people five nights a week. The program spawned a spin-off called the *Colbert Report*, wherein Stephen Colbert pretends to be a right-wing populist a la Bill O'Reilly as a means of lampooning such over the top "commentary in the guise of news" broadcasts.

The Pew Research Center for the People and the Press found that regular viewers of Colbert and Stewart were the most knowledgeable about politics. While not claiming that reliance on these shows caused high levels of political knowledge, such research helps refute the claim that such shows are bad for the polity ("Public Knowledge"). Perhaps more interestingly, Baumgartner and Morris (2006) investigated the impact of *The Daily Show* on young viewers' political beliefs. Utilizing an experimental design, they found that young people exposed to the program's jokes about George W. Bush and John Kerry tended to evaluate both more poorly than a control group did. Respondents exposed to the show also exhibited more cynicism toward the political system and news media.

Some British research has suggested that entertainment television use may correlate with behavior. Belson (1978) interviewed 1,500 London boys and their mothers and concluded that boys who see large amounts of violence on TV commit more serious acts of violence than those who watch lower amounts of violent television. Hargrave (2003) studied U.K. children aged nine to 13 years, and found them quite capable of differentiating between television violence and real violence, and reacted in appropriately different ways to TV news violence and entertainment TV violence. Wober and Gunter (1982) found that people who feel less in control of their lives and hold a fateful outlook watch more television, and in turn express more fearful attitudes about crime (cited by Gauntlett 2005). A comprehensive review of what he argues are the very meager findings of research into the effects of film and television's anti- and pro-social effects is provided by Gauntlett (2005: 23–142). Jones (2003) surveyed fans of the U.K. version of *Big Brother* and found that the "reality" show did not blur fact and fiction in viewers' minds, but because the show's artificiality was so transparent viewers could willingly suspend their disbelief and "look for the reality created within the artifice," (418).

Pop Music

Broadly, three kinds of research exist on the influence of popular music on young people's political values: scientific survey research; lyrical analysis; and experimental designs. An example of scientific survey research is Schwartz and Mannella's 1972 work. They are concerned with young people's perceptions of the political content of popular music and the correlations of those perceptions with self-reported ideology and issue positions. Their data derive from a survey of 610 suburban New Jersey high school students. They found that a sizeable proportion of teenagers perceive that their favorite music contains political statements or ideas. Teenagers who listen more to music and become more emotionally involved with it are more likely to perceive it as political and to have higher political interest and attentiveness to politics, and lower political alienation.

Another good example of broad survey research is Fox and William's 1974 work. They surveyed 730 University of Iowa students' ideology and music preference and found relationships between ideology, music preference, and listening to music on the radio, from one's own collection and at live performances. "Liberal students tend to attend rock and popular music concerts more frequently, buy more record albums and tapes, and spend more time listening to records and tapes than do their conservative peers," they reported (370). Interestingly, ideology was the independent variable in the research, while music preference was the dependent. This is odd, but the authors concluded that, "the causal connections between music and socio-political attitudes and behavior should be explored" (371).

Peterson and Christenson (in Christenson and Roberts 1989) hypothesized that music preference and political beliefs would not be as strongly related during the 1980s due to the de-politicization of music and young people in general during the era. Instead they found liberal youths tended to prefer music performed by black musicians, or heavily political music such as punk and new wave.

Denisoff (1972) pioneered lyrical analysis, examining the history of folk and protest music in the twentieth century. More recently, Pratt (1990) conducted a lyrical analysis of popular music. He argued that it afforded listeners a means of resisting the messages of the dominant culture. Conversly, Scheurer (1991), utilizing lyrical analysis as well, reached the opposite conclusion. He argued that popular music in America served to reaffirm the belief in America as a land of good and plenty. Bernard-Donals (1994), relying on the theories of Andrew Ross, argued that as older forms of music (specifically rap, rock 'n' roll, and jazz) moved from the margins to the main-stream, newer forms on the margins, as the voice of subversion, arose to replace them. He further argued that the academy (and especially left-leaning intellectuals) should examine critically the music of the margins, and not merely lionize or dismiss it.

Of the various forms of music with political content to which young people lis-ten, rap has been the most thoroughly studied. Zillmann et al. (1995) found that after exposure to radical political rap music, white U.S. high school students gave more support to a hypothetical African American liberal candidate for public office than to a white and anti-affirmative action candidate. The radical rap had no detectable influence on the choices of African American students, and the authors reported that, "rap—radical rap, in particular—appears to be a momentary, fleeting delight for African-American audiences" (21). These are counterintuitive findings, to say the least. It is commonly assumed that African American youths will prefer radical rap to nonpolitical rap (the reverse is true) and will be motivated politically by it (they do not appear to be). It is also assumed that white youths will be turned off by radical messages in rap music, while research indicates just the opposite is true. We still have much to learn about the political significance of rap.

Johnson, Jackson and Gatto (1995) found that African American males aged between eleven and sixteen exposed to violent rap videos indicated a greater accep-tance of violence compared to those exposed to nonviolent videos. Moreover, the sub-jects exposed to the violent videos in a decision simulation expressed greater acceptance of violence toward women and were more likely to want to emulate a materialistic young man than one trying to get an education. These findings are consistent with recent arguments about young men of low social standing and their proclivities toward crime and violence (Wrangham and Peterson 1996; Ghiglieri 1999). Boyd (1994) analyzed the lyrics of rappers Public Enemy, Sister Souljah, Ice Cube, KRS-One, and Arrested Development. These rappers opposed misogyny, racism, and a lack of respect and control among some in the African American community. They opposed police violence, and the tendency to place blame on the white community for problems in the African American community.

Some recent anecdotal evidence has been used to examine the political signifi-cance of other types of music. Bindas (1993) analyzed the lyrics of the English punk band *The Clash*. This band in the middle 1970s reacted against the residual narcis-sistic echo that was all that remained of the 1960s idealistic and revolutionary coun-tercultural spirit. Its message was based on a working class-derived ideology of "freedom, equality, opportunity, an end to imperialism, and a recognition of cultural pluralism" (78). Thompson (1993) showed that not only was there still a great deal of politics in the lyrics of popular music after the turbulent 1960s but that performers were increasingly putting their politics into practice. Examples in Britain included concerts for the Labour Party and against racism, and, globally, the Live Aid phenomenon of the mid 1980s. Even more recently in Canada, the *Rolling Stones, Blue Rodeo, AC/DC* and a number of other major bands performed at a benefit concert for the Toronto economy after it was devastated by the Severe Acute Respiratory Syndrome (SARS) outbreak.

Goldsmith (1996) reviewed dozens of recordings from the Folkways record label and demonstrated that American folk music has often carried political themes. Leymarie (1993) argued that certain kinds of music, but not lyrics, may engender violence and other social pathologies, but this view remains controversial. Thompson (1993) argued that popular music and politics are linked; however, his conclusion was based only on unsystematic observations of liberation bands that rejected the right-wing governments of the 1980s in the western democracies. Perkinson's (1996) interviews with Emily Saliers and Amy Ray of the alternative folk/rock act *The Indigo Girls* demonstrated their commitment to liberal causes and their belief in activism and educating their fans about political matters. Oumano (1996) asserted that most popular music "aspires no further than accommodating itself to the world in which it lives. Rather than acting as an agent for progressive change, American pop music reflects and, in some cases, even promotes the cynicism of our huckster society" (79). She seemed to contradict herself, however, by citing numerous counterexamples, like Amy Ray, *Rage Against the Machine*, Ani DiFranco and Billy Bragg. Hendrickson (1997) made a similar point in an interview with the members of *Rage Against the Machine*. Jackson (2005) demonstrated how the lyrics of long-time Canadian band *Blue Rodeo* reinforce a distinctive identity in English-speaking Canada. Perhaps the most valid conclusion that follows from the observations of these authors is that there is still much politics in popular music. The question is what sort of effect we ought to expect it to have, and whether or not it, in fact, has that effect.

Increasingly, there is systematic and scientific evidence to suggest that political statements made by musicians outside of their lyrics but in public statements may influence young people's beliefs. Bono, the lead singer of the Irish rock band U2, in particular has drawn significant scholarly attention (Jackson 2007). More specifically, Jackson and Darrow (2005) have shown that musicians' endorsements of specific political statements lead to greater agreement with already popular statements and less disagreement with unpopular positions among Anglophone Canadian youths. Jackson (2007) found similar results with regard to American musicians' influence over U.S. youths.

Movies

There has not been much study of movies as an agent of political socialization. One important study of movies, however, is Powers, Rothman, and Rothman's 1996 work. Through a content analysis of 159 of the top grossing films from 1946 to 1990, they demonstrated that Hollywood moviemakers are more liberal than most Americans, and more critical of the military, business and religion. Also, Adams et al. (1985) demonstrated through surveys of U.S. moviegoers that viewing the astronaut film *The Right Stuff* reinforced positive images of former astronaut and then presidential candidate Senator John Glenn.

Much of the academic and popular work on movies is not particularly relevant here, for it does not examine the effects of movies on young people in any systematic, scientifically rigorous way. Most of the research focuses on cinematic presentations of race (see Lyman, 1990), gender issues in general (see Powers, Rothman, and Rothman 1993a and 1993b), violence against women (see Adelman, 1989), positive portrayals of women in film (see Powers, Rothman, and Rothman 1993b), political leaders as "simpletons," "saviors," or "sleazeballs" (Larson 2000, 107–111) and other general political issues either in the plots of movies or in the industry itself (Christensen 1987; Phelps 1985; Williams 1979; Giglio 2000; Parenti 1992 (which also examines television); Combs 1993 and 1990 (an annotated filmography of political movies through the 1980s); Crowdus 1994 (a veritable encyclopedia of political movies, actors, and directors). While this body of work is very interesting and necessary because it demonstrates that movies contain socio-political values (for example, Phelps shows that citizens are usually presented as dupes in Hollywood movies), it tells us less about the *influence* of movies on the political attitudes of young viewers.

One filmmaker deserves special attention, however. Michael Moore has produced controversial documentaries since his premier film *Roger and Me* in 1989. He created a huge controversy during the 2004 presidential election with his film *Fahrenheit 9–11*, among the goals of which was the defeat of President George W. Bush. Because Bush was re-elected does not mean the film was a total failure. Its domestic box office is estimated at close to $120,000,000, which if a typical movie ticket cost $10.00, then 12 million people may have seen the film in theaters. Many more will have seen it at home on DVD. Watch parties were organized by local Democratic parties and liberal groups, which used the events to inform and register voters.

Other Agents

Some other agents of socialization that have been examined include political cartoons, children's literature, and third-party presidential candidates. Medhurst and Desousa (1981) argued that before we can consider political cartoons' persuasive effect, we have to create a taxonomy of categories into which the form fits. This they did by examining 749 cartoons from the 1980 presidential campaign. In terms of children's literature, Marshall showed that children's literature and television depicts political and other leaders frequently. Leaders are shown as being competent, not constrained by the institutions with which they interact, and also benevolent (1981, 396–97). Cook (1983, 333) rejected Marshall's argument that children's literature always presents leaders as omnipotent by pointing out that L. Frank Baum and Dr. Seuss show leaders as distinctly fallible.

Research Methods

Methodologically, the studies of political socialization have been very diverse. The two most common approaches are content analysis and survey research. Much of the media research focuses on the content of popular culture. If research identifies political content, the possibility exists that such content influences young people's political attitudes, even though the research may not demonstrate it directly. Survey research looks at correlations as indicators of the similarities between the political orientations of agents of socialization and those of youths, but is susceptible to criticism as well. Correlations do not establish causality. For example, if white youths who like rap music can be shown to be more progressive and less racist than their counterparts, how do we know that the beliefs are caused by the music preference and not vice versa? That is, perhaps there is some common cause of youth preferences for rap music and progressive views—such as African American friends. Further, other potential causal variables must be accounted for and controlled. Nevertheless, survey research is superior to content analysis because it does observe the political orientations of youths, rather than just inferring them. Although we can determine that the entertainment media and performers express political views, to assess influence we must also show that young listeners are exposed to the message. Plainly, a combination of the two methods will produce the most convincing findings.

The analysis of the influence of popular culture on youths in this book will be based upon data from questionnaires distributed to classes at large public universities in the U.S., the U.K., Anglophone Canada, and the Republic of Ireland. The U.S. questionnaire was distributed to Introduction to American Government courses at Bowling Green State University in the fall of 1997. Bowling Green State University is a state supported coeducational university, with then about 18,000 students (16,000 of whom are undergraduates) located in a small town in Northwest Ohio. The overwhelming majority of students are white, born and raised in rural or suburban Ohio, and reside on or near campus.

The U.S. questionnaire was also administered to Introduction to American Government classes at Wayne State University in the fall of 1997 and again in the winter of 1998. At the time approximately 30,000 students attended Wayne State University, an urban research university located in Detroit, Michigan. Of these, 13,000 were graduate students. About 23 percent of W.S.U.'s students are African American. Almost all of W.S.U.'s students came from Michigan and commuted to classes. All of the classes in which the questionnaire was administered were mass lecture courses not taught by the author. The total sample size is 709, and the response rate was nearly 100%, with only a handful of students refusing to complete the surveys.

A survey similar to the U.S. version was distributed to undergraduate students during course time at the University of Manchester and Keele University in the United Kingdom and at National University of Ireland-Galway during the period of September-October 2006. Survey distribution in the U.K. occurred in six courses,

covering first-, second-, and third-year classes.[4] These courses were comprised mainly
of students from the social science majors at these universities, with a heavier representation of political science majors in the third-year courses. Response rates varied
by course from 59% to 99%. Overall, the response rate was 463 collected out of 519
distributed, or 89.2%. Two instructors distributed the surveys in the U.K. without
one of the authors present. In both instances, the response rate (58.6% and 65.7%)
was lower than for the other four courses (95.3%). At NUI-Galway, the surveys were
distributed and collected by the course instructor, without either author present.[5]

    Canadian surveys were administered to students enrolled in introductory politi-
cal science classes at seven universities: Dalhousie in Nova Scotia; McGill University
in Quebec; University of Windsor and University of Western Ontario in Ontario;
University of Manitoba; University of Calgary in Alberta; and University of British
Columbia. The 456 completed questionnaires draw from all regions of Canada and
come from universities with varied academic reputations and admissions standards.
Response rates for the surveys administered in classes by the researchers ran at nearly
100%, while those administered by faculty members on our behalf (this includes only
those administered at the University of British Columbia) were returned at a substantially lower rate—about 25%. This produced an overall response rate of about 70%.

    While the use of only respondents enrolled in university is less than ideal if the
goal is to generalize about the entire youth population, recent socialization and public opinion projects have done so, especially when testing new theories (Dolan 1995;
Huddy and Terkildsen 1993).

    The generalizations we draw are appropriately constrained by the limits of our
samples. A positive argument may be made for examining the attitudes of university
students as well. Political science scholarship demonstrates that likelihood of voting
increases with the attainment of higher levels of education (Wolfinger and Rosenstone
1980). Henn, et al, (2005) show that obtainment of higher levels of education correlate with youth in Britain having more faith in voting as a positive vehicle of political
change. Therefore, in examining the attitudes of young people enrolled at university
we are learning about the beliefs of those most likely to vote, and therefore to influence the political process. Moreover, scholars have also found that elites, defined
mainly as those who work full-time in politics or public affairs, such as the U.S.
President, governors, members of Congress and so on, but sometimes defined more
broadly to include prominent members of communities such as corporate CEOs or
community leaders, influence the opinions of others (Paul and Brown 2001; Mondak

---

4   Five courses were at the University of Manchester: POLI10200 (Introduction to Comparative
    Government), POLI10801 (Social Problems and Social Policy), POLI20801 (British Public
    Policy), POLI30031 (European Union Politics), and POLI30121 (American Political
    Development). One course was at Keele University (West European Politics).

5   At NIU-Galway the surveys were administered in three courses: Public and Social Policy, and
    two sections of Political Science and Sociology. Specific response rates are not known for these
    sections, but there is no reason to believe they are any lower than those for courses in the
    U.K.

1993). Those with a university education are more likely to be found among the elite, and therefore to influence the beliefs of others.

Demographic Characteristics of the Samples

The average age of the U.S. sample is 19.17 years. African Americans make up 21.7% of the sample, while whites make up 65%. Just over 59% of respondents are female. Just under 70% attended Wayne State University.

The average age of the Canadian respondents is 20.24 years. In terms of gender, 54.6% of the sample is male. Because regional variation is such an important element of Canadian politics, a brief discussion of it is in order.

Table 1.1: Regional Distribution of Canadian Respondents

Region	n	Percent
Atlantic Canada	39	8.7
Quebec	57	12.7
Ontario	195	43.5
Prairies	69	15.4
Alberta	37	8.3
British Columbia	51	11.4
Totals	448*	100

There were 456 total respondents, but eight did not indicate in what province they live.

Atlantic Canada consists of the provinces of Newfoundland and Labrador, Prince Edward Island, Nova Scotia, and New Brunswick. The Prairies include Manitoba and Saskatchewan. Based on figures from the most recent Canadian census, Atlantic Canada is slightly over-represented in the sample (8.7% to 7.4%). Quebec is slightly under-represented (12.7% to 24%). This is not a problem because Quebec's percentage of Anglophone Canadians, who form the basis of this study, is lower than their proportion of the entire country. Ontario is slightly over-represented (43.5% to 39%). The Prairies are slightly over-represented (15.4% to 7%) and the West (Alberta and British Columbia) is under-represented too (19.7% to 23%). We do not believe these minor misdistributions are a problem because each region is represented by enough respondents to influence the results.

The U.K. sample consists of 443 respondents, of whom 52% are male, and the average age is 19.79. The Irish sample consists of 74 respondents, of whom 77% are female and the average age is 18.89. We are well aware of the extremely small size of the Irish sample and the relative lack of gender diversity, and so perform and present only statistical results that are appropriate for these extreme conditions.

The surveys included questions about television, music, and movie use (including quantity of time spent with each medium, and favorite performers and productions); political attitudes of the respondents and their perceptions of their parents' political attitudes; the respondents' perceptions of the political attitudes of favorite pop stars; and various issue positions. The questions were a mixture of open-ended and closed-ended items. See Appendix 1 for complete text of the questionnaires.

Analysis will be conducted using marginals, cross-tabulations, and a variety of multivariate methods such as regression analysis and logistic regression. To ascertain the statistical significance of relationships, alpha, the largest acceptable probability of a Type I Error, is set at .10. While this may seem high, the exploratory nature of this research requires greater latitude in terms of significance so that important relationships are not missed.

Chapter 2 outlines the broad theories of socialization used in the work, and takes a first look at some youths of unusual interest in the study: those who define themselves as more liberal/left than both parents. Chapter 3 examines the size and scale of the culture industries in the four countries studied, and looks at patterns of agreement and disagreement with political themes in the pop culture. Chapters 4–9 each look at the influence of specific elements of the pop culture on political socialization, with chapters 4–6 looking at the broad effects of movies, TV, and music, respectively. Chapters 7–9 more deeply investigate specific forms of music, with chapter 7 looking at rap, chapter 8 looking at alternative rock, and chapter 9 investigating classic rock and country music. Chapter 10 revisits the theoretical underpinnings of the work, summarizes the findings, and suggests directions for future research into this very important subject.

2

Culture Conflict, Learning Theory, and Cultural Imperialism

The review of previous research in political socialization, media studies, and public opinion demonstrates a number of important points. First, political socialization research has declined in terms of quantity in the past thirty years. The main reason for this is that a consensus exists that the family, peers, school, church and news media exhaust the important agents of socialization. This consensus, however, has failed to solve the puzzle of how children acquire and hold political values. The relative lack of research by political scientists on the entertainment media as possible agents of socialization clearly leaves a fundamental gap in knowledge relevant to that puzzle.

Conversations with students in classes and other settings and the review of the responses of students to open-ended survey questions demonstrate that young people today think about politics in ways that traditional political science terminology does not account for. As myriad scholars, politicians, and demagogues have argued, there is a culture war occurring in the U.S. (see Bork 1997; Gitlin 1995; Medved 1993, 1998). The war occurs on many fronts, but primarily it is a battle for the hearts and minds of American youths over competing positions on a wide variety of sociopolitical issues including abortion, homosexuality, violence, women's role, drug use, promiscuity, single parenting, and many other related issues. Conservatives tend to believe that permissive attitudes on these issues are prevalent in the entertainment media. For example, a great deal of rap music is concerned with threatening violence to others, expressing one's sexual prowess, or extolling the virtues of a life drunk on malt liquor or high on drugs. Daytime soap operas on television have long been filled with premarital sex, extramarital sex, and all sorts of other shenanigans. Because children are assumed to be in bed when prime-time soap operas such as *Desperate Housewives* are broadcast, they are often more explicit than their daytime equivalents. They are also phenomenally popular with young audiences.

Moreover, several episodes of television situation comedies and dramas have drawn the ire of (primarily conservative) critics. None was more controversial than when the character played by comedian Ellen Degeneres announced her homosexuality during an episode of her eponymous situation comedy in 1997. Gay rights activists lauded the actress's and network's courage for airing the episode. Conservative critics and fundamentalist Christian organizations attacked the network. Not surprisingly, the episode received the show's highest ratings, but nonetheless it was subsequently cancelled. Degeneres asserted that this was because the network perceived the program as "too gay."

Since Ellen's coming out, other homosexual characters have been placed front and center of situation comedies and dramatic television series. *Will and Grace* was a situation comedy that aired from 1998 to 2006 and featured four main characters, two of whom were gay men. During its eight years on the air it won 16 Emmy awards. Interestingly, while the show earned some criticism from the religious right (nothing compared with what *Ellen* received), it was also criticized by gay activists for presenting stereotypical images of gay men. One significant difference between *Ellen* and *Will and Grace* is that while Ellen Degeneres and her TV character came out as gay, Eric McCormack, who played Will, is heterosexual. This caused some to compare his performance to white characters in "black-face" who played African-Americans by blackening their faces with make-up—a phenomenon referred to as "gay-face" (Kanner 2003).

Movies also have included controversial content. As always, the greatest concern about movies is the effect that screen violence might have on behavior and beliefs of youths. An example is the deaths and injuries to young people who imitated a stunt from the football movie *The Program*. The strong public belief that too much screen violence desensitizes young people to actual violence suggests that concern over movies will not disappear. Moreover, the sexual content of movies worries conservative critics as well.

This book looks at sexuality in popular culture differently from how many conservative critics view it. Presentations of women's sexuality are most often what conservative critics oppose in the popular culture, and many respondents to the surveys did the same. Frequently female characters who utilize sexual power to get what they want in other competitive areas of life draw the most ire, especially among white men, because use of this tool threatens traditional patterns of male domination.

The internet worries conservatives too. With the relative ease of access to websites that contain violence and pornography, many believe that young people's values will be perverted by use of the internet. Some call for censorship, or at least the use of filtering software in public libraries to prevent young people from accessing this allegedly dangerous material. Conservative radio call-in host Dr. Laura Schlessinger has led this fight.

Does the culture war metaphor make sense for understanding public concerns over the content of popular culture in Anglophone Canada, Ireland and the U.K? Are there other concerns with the popular culture in these places?

Canada, Culture Conflict, and Anti-Americanism

Certainly something akin to the U.S. culture war exists in Canada, but as is always the case, the battle is more muted. For example, in 2008 Conservative Canadian Prime Minister Stephen Harper's government proposed a law which would have pulled financial assistance for film or television productions that the country's Heritage Minister defined as offensive or not in the public interest. Stephen Waddell, the national executive director of the Alliance of Canadian Cinema, Television, and Radio Artists (ACTRA) condemned the law and wondered if it was motivated by a "fundamentalist perspective" that had come to Canada from the United States ("Tories Plan").

Part of the motivation for the proposed law came from a controversial film called *Young People Fucking*, which did receive some government assistance for its production. Evidently the content of the film was less controversial than its title, as the film portrays the romantic misadventures of several young couples, and one threesome. *Toronto Star* film critic Peter Howell wrote, "Canadian filmmaker Martin Gero's very funny and insightful feature debut is far less shocking than its detractors—most of whom haven't even seen it—would have you believe . . . If you're looking for porn, you've come to the wrong place. There are a few bare breasts, a couple of bare asses, one naughty strap-on and that's about it. The nation's moral fibre remains intact" ("Young People F—ing"). Nevertheless, conservative supporters of ending government assistance for "offensive" productions, such as Diane Watts, remained firm. She wrote, "some filmmakers want *carte blanche* to use government grants any way they choose regardless of the consequences of the productions. Artists should be held responsible for their work, the same as plumbers, lawyers, physicians and carpenters" ("Diane Watts" 2009).

It is important to note that the artists' negative response to the proposed law included the issue of American influence over Canadian culture. Scholars have long noted the existence of Anti-Americanism in English-Canada's identity and nationalism (Brooks 2006, Millard, Riegel, and Wright 2002, Edwardson, 2002–2003, Mackey 2002, Granatstein 1996, Gibbins 1995, Wright 1988). Brooks (2006, 140) is very direct when he writes, "no serious discussion of a distinctive Canadian identity in English-speaking Canada . . . can ignore the crucial role that anti-Americanism has played in its construction and maintenance." This is not surprising, given Canada's counter-revolutionary tradition as well as its uncomfortable location next to a political and cultural hegemon.

But, while broad agreement exists among scholars that anti-Americanism has played a role in the origins and maintenance of the identity of English-speaking Canadians, the extent and significance of its existence in Canada remains an open question. Doran and Sewell (1988) argue that no latent anti-Americanism exists among Canadians, but their definition of the concept is quite strict and includes two dimensions. First, anti-Americanism includes, "perceptual distortion such that a caricature of some aspect of behavior is raised to the level of general belief. In addition, based on that perception, it involves hostility directed toward the government, society, or individuals of that society" (p. 106). So, disliking the policies of President George W. Bush would not constitute anti-Americanism per se, but believing all Americans are war-mongering fools, and therefore opposing Bush and hating Americans would. We will return to the issue of anti-Americanism in response to popular culture by young Canadians, as we must, due to the fact that the overwhelming majority of popular culture consumed by young Canadians is produced in the United States.

Ireland and Lifestyle Issues

Culture wars as a metaphor does not mean the same thing in Ireland as it does in the United States. The modernization of Ireland, especially since the 1990s, has created an uneven pattern of change that has produced a mixture of traditional and modern value orientations (Hardiman and Whelan, 1998). One overall trend is that Irish society has dramatically liberalized since 1960, with the legalization of divorce through constitutional referendum, the slight relaxing of abortion laws, and the removal of the "special position" clause of the constitution for the Catholic church (Schmitt 2000). Schmitt claims, however, that the availability of British and American TV programming has contributed significantly to the liberalization of Irish society, and concurs with Girvin (1997) in the assessment that conservative Irish see the liberalization as a major loss for the quality of life in Ireland, and the conflict between modern and traditional values is a central one in Irish political life. In that some of the sources of media that contribute to the liberalization are British and American, the struggle must in part be one of resistance to these influences, if not necessarily outright anti-Americanism.

Anti-Americanism in the U.K.

Anti-Americanism does not appear as significant in the U.K.'s identity and politics as is the case in Canada. However, Singh (2007) offers a history of British anti-Americanism that comes from both the left and right. Leftists rail against inequality and racism in the U.S., while conservatives dislike American individualism, race-mixing, and rejection of tradition. Based on survey evidence, Singh concludes, however, that, "in the main, the British remain markedly 'warm' towards Americans as a people" (p. 201).

Anti-Americanism does, however, flare up when there are great disagreements over international relations between large sections of the U.K. public and the United States government. For example, in February, 2003, between 750,000 and two million took to the streets of London to protest the imminent U.S.-led war against Iraq. It is difficult to say that this represents true anti-Americanism (several prominent

American activists spoke at the rally), or just opposition to specific policies. Playwright
Harold Pinter suggested the latter interpretation would be correct in his comments.
He said the U.S. was "a country run by a bunch of criminal lunatics with Tony Blair
as a hired Christian thug" ("Million March" 2009).

Values and Entertainment Culture

Lifestyle issues are important to young people generally, and especially among
the young who are deeply engaged the popular culture. Of course, the young are not
homogeneous, except for their age. Different elements of the popular culture suggest
to them competing sets of values by which to live their lives. We can frame these issues
in the old left/right, or liberal/conservative, framework when the popular culture
frames them this way. However, it seldom does. Usually, the conflicts presented in
the popular culture are between hedonism, on the one hand, and delayed gratification, on the other. Religion is presented as the source of problems, or the solution.
Sexual intercourse is either presented as a recreational activity to enjoy with many
partners, or monogamy, children, and long-term relationships are endorsed. Traditional
authority is ridiculed and institutions are mocked, or the authorities and institutions
are supported. The individual's needs and desires are paramount, or the community's
needs are lionized. The popular culture emphasizes individual rights, or responsibility trumps individualism. These are the distinctions that define the culture wars. The
popular culture presents messages that fit on each side of these continua. The question is whether these messages have any effect on young people.

A fundamental question this research asks is, do youths actually recognize and
believe the messages of the entertainment media? Does the sociopolitical content of
the entertainment media influence their values, or are presentations of violence, promiscuity, and so on in pop culture merely reflecting reality? Does pop culture preference and use influence the sociopolitical attitudes of youths, or do their sociopolitical
attitudes influence their cultural preferences and use levels? Shea (1999) presented a
plausible *interactive* model of the influence of popular culture. In this way, popular
culture both reflects political reality and in turn shapes it. He offers the example of
rap music's reflecting the violence of American cities and consequently encouraging
greater violence among rap fans. This model is especially plausible if we account for
the ideological upbringing of youths as well.

Importantly, the relationship between the U.S. federal government and Hollywood
movie and television program makers suggests that political events drive the content
of the entertainment media, which in turn influences political beliefs about those
events. By meeting with Hollywood executives to determine what kinds of cultural
products could be produced to aid the war effort in Afghanistan, the Bush administration showed that it believed that the popular culture influences the political beliefs
of Americans. It also became clear that some Hollywood movie and television powers agreed with the administration about this influence, and were eager to enlist in
the effort to fight terrorism by presenting the U.S. and Americans in the best light
possible in their programs and movies. However, some producers, directors, and actors

questioned the enlistment of the entertainment industry in what they perceived as a new propaganda war, while conservative critics doubted the sincerity and usefulness of "liberal" Hollywood's becoming involved in putting America's best image forward to the rest of the world.

Karl Rove, one of President Bush's top political advisors, met in early November, 2001 with a group of entertainment industry executives that included leaders of Viacom, Disney, MGM, Fox, and Warner Brothers. Jack Valenti, chairman of the Motion Industry Association of America and Melissa Gilbert, President-elect of the Screen Actors Guild, also enthusiastically attended the meeting. Ideas proposed included making first-run films more quickly available for front-line troops and production of documentaries and public service announcements on virtues like tolerance, volunteerism, and support for the U.S.O. (Calvo and Abramowitz 2001; Calvo 2001). Rove and Valenti in particular were quick to point out that decisions over "content"— the actual plots, themes and messages of programs—would remain the sole province of Hollywood. In other words, government would not dictate to television executives and movie-makers what subjects they should cover and how they cover them. However, Valenti cast some doubt on this after the meeting when he mentioned specific content, saying, "One of the big thrusts that we will try to do is . . . make it clear to the millions of Muslims in the world that this is not an attack on Muslims" (Calvo 2001). There were doubts in Hollywood about the allegedly benign nature of these discussions as well.

Chief among the critics were television director Larry Gelbart, most famous as the creator of long-running television series M*A*S*H; Oliver Stone, who directed such successful movies as *JFK, Nixon,* and *Platoon;* and well-known Hollywood liberal actor and director Robert Redford. The primary concern among these Hollywood players was that the federal government would try to influence the content of movies and television, and thus create serious first amendment freedom of expression quandaries as well as basic creative control problems. "If (Rove) is not out here to talk about content, why the trip?" Gelbart asked (Calvo and Abramowitz 2001). Redford echoed these concerns, saying, "To keep it simple, what was the purpose (of the meeting)? Who is the person designing it? What does Karl Rove stand for?" (Calvo and Abramowitz 2001). Stone, who is a Vietnam veteran and supported the war in Afghanistan, argued that it would be wrong for television programs and movies to be completely negative about U.S. Middle-East policy, "but national security must not smother reform or constructive dissent" (Calvo and Abramowitz 2001).

While actors, producers, and directors were worried about losing creative control and the right to criticize American policy, a number of conservative critics worried that Hollywood's participation in the war effort was at least confused, or actually hypocritical. Conservative author Michael Medved argued that the claims of Hollywood not to want to engage in propaganda rang hollow because they frequently propagandize in favor of liberal causes like homosexual rights, gun control, and political correctness in general (Medved 2001). "In the past 30 years, the popular culture has adopted new themes that suggest American nationalism is neither necessary nor

appropriate," Medved claimed, as well as arguing that Hollywood ought to feel com-
pelled by the national crisis created by the terrorist attacks of 11 September to put
past American transgressions such as the destruction of Native Americans and slav-
ery into proper global and historical context. He also argued that even a small shift
in Hollywood presentations, such as "portray(ing) obsessive anti-Americanism as poi-
sonous, irrational, and self-destructive," would greatly aid the war effort.

Columnist Don Feder (2001) was even less circumspect than Medved about the
potential value of Hollywood's contribution to the war effort, arguing that Hollywood
movies present a wildly inaccurate image of the U.S. military, history, intelligence
services, corporations, and middle class. "If Hollywood's view of America is correct,
who in his right mind would want to defend it?" asked Feder.

While not wanting to decide between these competing claims about the value of
enlisting Hollywood in the service of the U.S. government during wartime, one thing
is clear. After the 11 September, 2001 terrorist attacks on the World Trade Centers
and Pentagon, the Bush Administration and Hollywood not only put aside some of
their traditional political differences, but agreed that television and movies influence
the sociopolitical beliefs of Americans about world events. This book takes their beliefs
seriously in its investigation of how the process actually works.

Scholars agree that entertainment changed after 9/11, but there is much disagreement about exactly how it changed. Dixon (2004) suggests that for a brief period after
the attacks, Hollywood produced a number of escapist movies and television shows,
in part because, "the reality of destruction and physical violence (had) been made con-
crete and immediate," by the attack (24). However, Americans' appetites for film and
TV destruction soon returned, especially for conflicts presenting Americans as heroic,
or working hard to prevent new attacks. As discussed elsewhere, country and western
music responded most jingoistically to 9/11, as well as to the war in Iraq. While Toby
Keith's "Courtesy of the Red White and Blue" can be seen as the anthem for vengeance
after 9/11, Darryl Worley's "Have you Forgotten" blends 9/11 into a justification for
the Iraq War (Schmelz 2007). Bruce Springsteen offered a more nuanced approach
to 9/11 and the Afghanistan War, but could be seen as justifying vengeance as well
(Garman 2007). Thousands of popular and scholarly articles have been written about
this, but very few attempt what we do here: determining the effects of entertainment
content, rather than just describing and analyzing them.

Pointing the causal arrow in socialization research that examines influences other
than the family and family selected agents of socialization has always been very difficult. Even so, the present analysis offers a plausible argument that the entertainment
media influence the sociopolitical beliefs of young Americans. However, this argument does not exclude the opposite position. Because the interactive model makes the
most sense, I do not to assume that just because pop culture influences sociopolitical
attitudes that the causal arrow might not *also* point in the other direction sometimes.
However, the influence of the entertainment media on sociopolitical attitudes is a
more interesting and important question for political scientists to answer than the
other formulation.

Another basic argument needs to be considered in light of the interactive nature of the relationship between politics and popular culture. Increasingly, Americans use images, plots, and characters from the popular culture to help understand the political world around them. For example, since the 1970s it has been common for more enlightened Americans to refer to narrow-minded bigots as "Archie Bunkers" because their attitudes are similar to the television character played by Carroll O'Connor on the series *All in the Family* from 1971 until 1979. There are literally hundreds of other examples of this phenomenon. For a long time sensitive, liberal men were compared with the later version of "Hawkeye Pierce," Alan Alda's character on *M*A*S*H*. Stumbling, bumbling and generally annoying neighbors were "Kramers" from the *Seinfeld* character. Disaffected, lower-middle class white men became "Al Bundy," while good-hearted, but incompetent, fathers became "Homer Simpsons." "Mary Tyler Moore" represented liberated women in the 1970s and Bill Cosby represented the burgeoning black middle class in the 1980s.

Before the advent of television and the movies, people made sense of their world through reference to mythology. People overcame "Hurculean" tasks. Doubters were Cassandras, whereas difficult journeys became odysseys. Now we have the characters the pop culture creates. Whereas once we had the characters of Homer's telling of Greek mythology to help us make sense of lour lives, now we have the exploits of Homer Simpson.

Plots, of course, matter here too. Sometimes life in the movies or on television points to something better than the way we live now. Therefore, for example, homosexual Americans threw parties when Ellen Degeneres's character came out of the closet. Having won the U.S. presidency so infrequently, Democrats were at least able to enjoy the Democratic administration of Jed Bartlet on *The West Wing* (often derisively called "The Left Wing" by Republican and conservative critics) TV show from 1999 to 2006. Of course, there is a darker side too. Most Americans who saw the episode remember where they were when Radar O'Reilly announced on *M*A*S*H* that Colonel Henry Blake's plane had been, "shot down over the Sea of Japan. It spun in. There were no survivors." Of course, in some ways that fictional tragedy helped Americans come to grips with the finality of death and the insanity of war.

Americans' immediate response to the terrorist attacks of 11 September demonstrates the value of the popular culture too. Whereas Americans thought of movies when they saw the planes hit the World Trade Centers in part because they had never seen anything like it before, there is some comfort in the plots of movies where terrorists confront Americans because the Americans always win. Thus, not surprisingly, rentals from some New York City Blockbuster video stores for movies like *The Siege*, *Die Hard with a Vengeance*, and *Armageddon* increased by more than half (Bernardin, 2001, p. 2).

More deliberately, less than a month after the terrorist attacks on the U.S. of 11 September, 2001, the popular NBC political drama *The West Wing* confronted, in a hastily penned, yet powerful episode, key issues related to terrorism such as its origins in U.S. Middle East policy, Muslim and Arab stereotypes, and the proper U.S.

response. This shows the entertainment industry, immediately after one of this country's greatest political challenges, trying to influence the national debate. More than a few left-leaning Americans assert, tongue-in-cheek, that the president on *The West Wing*, Jed Bartlett (played by well-known liberal Martin Sheen) is their president—which is reminiscent of the National Rifle Association stickers during the Clinton administration asserting that "Charlton Heston Is My President." With this level of respect for the values represented by the characters on the show, it would be no surprise if they were actually able to influence some Americans' beliefs about how to respond to the terrorist attacks.

Learning Theory

In examining this linkage of the popular media to the culture wars, the three models of continuity and change presented by Jennings and Niemi (1974, 1981) as well Inglehart's (1990a) theory of the culture shift to post-materialism will be applied. At the individual level, learning theory helps explain the influence of entertainment media on young people's political values. Learning theory begins with Thorndike's law of effect (Skinner 1974). The law of effect describes operant learning, whereby behavior is shaped and maintained by its consequences. Behavior that is rewarded tends to increase in frequency, while that which is punished tends to decrease in frequency and may eventually disappear. Contingencies in the social environment determine whether a particular behavior is rewarded or punished.

Agents of socialization (parents, schools, churches, peers, news, and entertainment media) have some degree of control over the contingencies of reinforcement to which youths are subjected. Both commonality and conflicts of interest occur between agents of socialization and youths. A young person may experience either rewards or punishments through experience with the popular culture. One could witness a behavior in a movie, television program, or song that is the product of the existence (or lack) of an ethical/moral system. If the message contradicts the individual's preexisting ethical/moral beliefs, that is an unpleasant experience and thus constitutes negative reinforcement. The individual thereafter avoids repeating the unpleasant experience by avoiding contexts or the product(s) of the popular culture that led to the unpleasant experience. Conversely, should other components of the social environment (e.g., peers) provide positive reinforcement for initially unpleasant experiences, an individual's ethical and moral beliefs might change over time. If the message of the popular culture agrees with the young person's, this is pleasure, and thus positive reinforcement of the individual's beliefs. It is the pushing and pulling of these various experiences on a youth's initial values that result either in a hardening of those values or a change in values.

Edgar and Edgar (1971, 609) differentiated between two broad schools of socialization theory: passive and active. In passive socialization theory, the basic question is, "what do the media do to people?" while in the active model the question is, "what do people do with the media?" Arguing further that, "a basic mechanism by which people learn to accept values, attitudes, and forms of behavior is the imposition of sanctions, either rewards or punishments, usually by someone with superior power or someone who is respected," the authors set out the possibility that television programming may offer psychological rewards or punishments for behavior, and if empirical research were able to demonstrate this to be the case, then we would much more fully understand television's effects as an agent of socialization (p. 610). The same may be true for music and film. If songs and movies can be shown to reward or punish certain ideas then we will more adequately understand them as agents of socialization as well.

Recognition of the active role individuals may play in their own socialization is crucial. We should, therefore, consider not just socialization agents' impact on individuals, but the active role individuals play in the political learning process. This will account for both strands of socialization theory, as well as cultural imperialism. Many of the individuals we are studying in this work live in an entertainment media environment saturated with the cultural products of a foreign country. For example, Canadian respondents report that on average just 17.9% of their personal collections of music are from Canadian artists. Irish respondents report that just 15.7% of their collections are from Irish artists, while the U.K. respondents claim an average of only 41.1% .

In its original formulation, cultural imperialism theory might cause us to expect this saturation to overwhelm young people into an acceptance of American values (see Schiller 1976). As the theory developed, however, scholars came to recognize that "Western" culture was not monolithic, as well as the important and active role played by audiences in constructing their own meanings from the raw materials provided by foreign cultures. For example, in a study of how Israeli audiences received the 1980s U.S. TV series *Dallas*, Liebes and Katz (1990) found major differences in interpretations among, for example, recent Russian immigrants (who focused on the show's politics) and Moroccan immigrants (who tended to focus on the show's morality). Similarly, Gray (2007) analyzed the reactions of non-Americans to the cartoon series *The Simpsons*, and found that the overwhelming majority interpreted the show as a parody of traditional suburban American family values.[1] Recognition of the active model of socialization as well as the more sophisticated version of cultural imperialism theory will help us understand how non-Americans perceive American popular culture as well as their own culture.

The literature on political socialization has not drawn upon theory from the field of social biology. This theory, however, may be especially relevant to understanding potential limits to the influence of parents on children. Children are not blank slates. Under ordinary circumstances they can be expected to be partly susceptible but also partly resistant to parental efforts at shaping their beliefs and behavior. In general, a parent and child both share a common interest in the child's success and welfare. However, there may be conflicts of interest as well because the parent may have other

---

1   Gray's article is also noteworthy for its presentation of a brief history of the rise, fall, and rise again of cultural imperialism theory, especially pp. 129–134.

children or the ability to have and raise additional children, whereas the child has less interest than the parent in these efforts directed toward its siblings, and more interest in itself (Trivers 1974). Parental manipulation of children generally should be directed at getting them to cooperate more with their siblings than they are inclined to do. It should also be directed at encouraging children to engage in activities that will lead over time to the children becoming successful in having and raising children of their own.

Whether right or wrong, in contemporary American society it is easy to identify the basic principles that lead over time to children becoming successful in this sense (Essock-Vitale and McGuire 1988; Buss 1995). For women, the correlates are marriage, age at first marriage (younger is better), physical attractiveness, marriage to a man of high social standing, and no promiscuity. For men, the correlates are marriage, younger age of wife, number of wives, education and economic resources. Thus parents ought to reinforce "traditional" or "conservative" values. Girls ought not to be promiscuous, should marry when young to men with money, and should focus on their physical appearance. Men, however, ought to be encouraged to achieve financial success and to marry and provide for a young, attractive woman.

To what extent do parents actually instruct children on appropriate models of behavior? Lakoff (1996) has identified two polar models of parenting—the strict parent and the nurturing parent. The strict parent model is controlling and establishes clear-cut contingencies of reinforcement by making frequent and predictable use of rewards and punishments. As a strategy of socialization, it is designed to prepare children for entry into a world where success depends on individual achievement. Authority, hierarchy, and absolute values and standards characterize such a society. The nurturing parent model is less controlling, protects children from clear-cut dangers, but relies less on parentally created contingencies and more on reinforcement in the larger social world to shape children's behavior. As a strategy of socialization, it is designed to prepare children for entry into a world where success is defined by personal happiness and the nurturing relationships that are established with others.

The problems that parents experience today in raising children are different from preceding decades. What if contingencies of reinforcement in the larger social world work at cross-purposes to the goals of parents? That is, the entertainment media are driven by the profit motive. Hollywood makes money when it sells large numbers of tickets. Record companies make money when they sell CDs. Television studios make money when they produce hit programs that get high ratings and command top dollar for advertising. Quite often, however, the most effective way for the popular media to attract youths is to depict behaviors that at least initially are highly pleasurable— promiscuous sex, drugs, and general hedonism. The popular media, however, frequently depict these behaviors as without terribly negative consequences. In effect, the entertainment media tell youths that their parents and other agents of socialization have lied to them, or are wrong about the negative consequences of these behaviors. Thus, in many cases we expect a competition for influence of young people between parents, the church, the school, and other traditional agents of socialization on the one hand, and much of the popular media on the other.

Do youths actually recognize and believe the messages of the entertainment media? A youth successfully influenced by the strict-parent model (conservative youths), may disregard the messages out of hand because they have never been reinforced by parents (and the church and school which were likely selected for the child by the family) and are unlikely to be reinforced by them. This is the one group likely to find much to object to in the entertainment media. Youths raised in this fashion probably consider the contingencies depicted in movies, on television, or in music to be a fantasy, and will turn away from these entertainment media. Moreover, they might reject these messages and actively oppose them, and perhaps even find their conservatism hardened by limited exposure to them.

Conversely, such youths may change their own values after repeated exposure to these messages. This transformation is especially likely to occur if the youths lose connections to other traditional agents of socialization, as often happens when young people go away from home to college. If youths are removed from the influence of parentally arranged contingencies (especially the strict father) as well as the K-12 schools and the church, continued exposure by such youths to the entertainment media may result in rapid changes in their attitudes and behaviors because of changing contingencies of reinforcement. A youth can avoid unpleasant experiences with the values in the popular media by avoiding the popular media, or less likely, changing values. Thus, we expect the greatest change in youths' values in the years immediately after they move away from home for the first time.

Youths brought up under the nurturing parent model have probably learned by trial and error experience which messages in the entertainment media to accept and which to reject. They are better able to assign relative weights to parental messages and those of other agents of socialization, and to make informed choices. It is unclear in what direction the entertainment media should be expected to influence these youths. It is likely their preexisting values will be reinforced, but change is more likely for them than for conservatives raised by strict-parents.

Unfortunately, questionnaires do not offer a direct measure of home political environment. However, they do measure youths' perceptions of the political ideology of their parents, which is utilized as a surrogate for their perceptions of their parents' social conservatism. Parents' ideological dispositions as gauged by youths are a valid indicator of the degree to which they were raised by either the strict parent or the nurturing model, that is the degree to which they perceive their parents as socially liberal or conservative. When youths say that a parent is conservative they are likely to mean that they perceive that the parent has been conservative on social issues—a strict-parent. When they say that a parent was a liberal they mean that they perceive that the parent was liberal on social issues—a nurturing parent. Moreover, if youths err in their perceptions of parents, they are likely to project their own attitudes onto their parents (see Niemi 1974 and Tedin 1976). Because one of the key dependent variables this research explores is whether youths perceive themselves as more liberal than their parents, the bias interjected by using respondents' perceptions of parents will be a conservative one.

A troubling phenomenon in recent decades has been the growth in the numbers of single-parent families, commonly headed by women. There is ample scientific evidence that single parents on average do a worse job of raising children, using a variety of outcome measures. There are even some two-parent families where there is minimal parenting in the traditional sense. A youth raised with minimal parenting and not subjected to parentally arranged contingencies of reinforcement may not see through the fantasy of the messages, be reinforced by them, and think that they are valid.

Lakoff's basic argument is simple enough. Conservatives and liberals have adopted different perspectives with respect to the family and how children should be raised. Conservatives favor the strict parent model. Liberals favor the nurturing model. These family values are carried over by metaphor (nation as family) to politics. The bulk of the entertainment media supply little or no reinforcement for the strict-parent model of the family. Generally, the popular culture makes fun of it. Even a cursory scan of popular movies, television, or songs shows that the culture is replete with bumbling fathers, relativistic morals and ethics, and promiscuous sex from both genders. Moreover, the entertainment industry seems generally to support homosexuality and other forms of identity politics, or at least a tolerance for alternative lifestyles. Further, those who attempt to promote an absolutist or traditionally conservative ethic are maligned as either out of touch with the times, or just plain mean.

Therefore, some relationships exist between previous socialization and family model in which it occurred, and response to popular culture. The overwhelming majority of respondents to the surveys are between the ages of 17 and 22. Thus, they are in some ways at the end of the socialization process as youths. Our measures attempt to investigate the various influences that have influenced and continue to affect their choices about political values and issue positions. Because of the general opposition of the popular culture to the conservative strict-parent ethic, individuals successfully socialized under such a model (conservatives) will be the least influenced by popular culture and the more likely to reject the messages in it. Young liberals, those raised in the nurturing parent model especially, may in fact be more likely to be influenced by the popular culture and less likely to reject the messages of that culture out-of-hand.

There is a tacit assumption in this theory that must be discussed. This work is based on surveys of university students enrolled in introductory-level university courses. Thus, almost all of them are between the ages of 17 and 22 years. Their responses to the questions are a snapshot of people at a fairly late stage of the socialization process. It is difficult in such a context to witness all the influences that may have contributed to each individual's political values, or for that matter, the total effect of entertainment media. However, the present analysis investigates the entertainment media's influence by determining the respondents' perceptions of their parents' politics, by examining what kinds of schools they attended, their socioeconomic class, race, gender, religion, news media use habits, and of course use of the entertainment media.

Because this is not a longitudinal study, it cannot be established with certainty which influences are more important at earlier stages of development. Thus, the model of socialization assumes that young people's political values are relatively well founded by the time they begin using and thinking about large amounts of self-selected entertainment media. The young people approach the media with preexisting values formed by the traditional agents of socialization. However these values were likely "cultivated" by early use of entertainment media as well, especially television and theatrical movies viewed at home, the least restricted of the popular media.

This book does not directly account for the early influence of entertainment media, and this is not necessary to demonstrate that the media have an effect. However, it is clear that early exposure to the entertainment media has an effect on children. There are messages in the media younger children may not consciously absorb, but they still influence their political values. The Disney movie *The Lion King* endorses hierarchy, patriarchy, and monarchy. Would a six-year-old recognize this? In all likelihood not. However, the message may still influence the child. *Sesame Street* consciously attempts to teach children more than mathematics and the alphabet. It attempts to teach multiculturalism and tolerance. Do young children recognize this? Certainly not. Are they influenced by it? Almost certainly. *The Spice Girls* made a direct effort to teach young girls self-respect and self-confidence. Because a young girl chanting a chorus of "If you want to be my lover/first you have to be my friend" does not consciously know that she is increasing her self-esteem does not mean it is not occurring.

To make a long story short, when youths responded to the questionnaires their political values likely were well formed. Moreover, the encounters with the popular culture they remember are very recent and very conscious. Their values are sometimes simplified into two rough categories: conservatives formed by strict parenting and liberals formed by nurturing families. Much of this work seeks to determine what effect the relatively liberal content of the entertainment media has on these two distinctive groups of young people. However, because this culture wars framework is best suited to understanding the U.S., and to a lesser degree, the Canadian socialization situations, it is in those contexts in which we apply it most thoroughly. The cultural imperialism and Anti-American frameworks best informs Canadian, U.K., and Irish situations, so they are most vigorously applied there. From the perspective of culture wars and family socialization dynamics, one group that deserves some special attention is young people who rate themselves as more liberal than both of their parents.

Which Americans Are Becoming
More Liberal Than Their Parents?

Some youths are more liberal than their parents, whereas others are more conservative. Of course some hold the same ideology as their parents. The popular media present messages that are generally liberal, especially in terms of lifestyles issues. Therefore, young people who are more liberal than their parents are the most likely to have been positively influenced in this choice by the entertainment media. Ideology is measured on a seven-point scale.[2] Categories here are collapsed in the following manner: 1, 2, and 3 are liberal; 4 is moderate, while 5, 6, and 7 are conservative. Respondents are asked to identify each parent's ideology on the same scale. Those who are both liberal and more liberal than both parents are the focus of this investigation. These include youths who locate themselves on the liberal end of the scale and both parents at either the moderate position or at the conservative end of the scale, and youths who locate themselves at the moderate position and both parents at the conservative end of the scale. Parents' ideological dispositions as gauged by youths are a valid indicator of the degree to which they were raised by either the strict parent or the nurturing model, that is the degree to which they perceive their parents as socially liberal or conservative.

Most U.S. youths are not more liberal than parents. However a substantial proportion (15.1%) are, and there is a sufficient n (107) to look for differences between those who are more liberal than their parents and those who are not.

Are there differences related to sex, race, and age? There is no relationship between sex and being more liberal than both parents. Whites are significantly more likely than blacks to be more liberal than their parents. This relationship is demonstrated in Table 2.1. One might expect that those who are more liberal than both parents are older than those who are not because with age comes opportunity for other agents of socialization to influence young people. This expectation, though, does not materialize, as there is no relationship between age and being more liberal than one's parents.

---

2   Another, potentially superior, measure of ideology would be to create an index based on responses to the specific questions which have ideologically oriented answers, such as respondents' beliefs about abortion, the role of women, flag burning, homosexual rights, gun rights, and so on. We reject this option for two reasons. The first is practical. Respondents were asked only to rate their parents on the seven-point scale, not on the series of issue belief questions. So, use of the seven-point scale is the only means of comparing parents and respondents. Second, the seven-point ideology question is a valid measure of ideology because responses to it correlate in the right direction with the issue position questions we did ask. In other words, self described liberals/leftists give liberal/left answers on the issue questions and conservatives give conservative responses.

Table 2.1: Race and Being More Liberal Than Parents, U.S. Respondents

	Black	White	Hispanic	Other	Totals
Not More Liberal	90.0%	81.7%	87.0%	87.7%	84.6%
More Liberal	9.1%	18.3%	13.0%	12.3%	15.4%
Totals	100.0%	100.0%	100.0%	100.0%	100.0%

Chi-Square (3) = 8.088, Sig. (two-tailed) = .044

U.K., Ireland, and Canada

For the U.K. and Irish samples a slightly different question was asked. Rather than use the word "Liberal" we used the more culturally appropriate "left," but used the same seven point scale. In the Irish sample, about 16.5% of respondents were both left and more left than both parents. In the U.K. sample, the percentage was higher, at 18.5%. There is no relationship in either the U.K. or Irish samples between sex and likelihood of being more liberal than both parents.

Among the Canadian respondents, 16.2% define themselves as more liberal than both parents. There is no relationship between sex and being more liberal than both parents. We did not ask for respondents' race in the U.K., Irish, or Canadian surveys. The relationship between popular culture preferences and being more liberal/left than both parents will be investigated later in this book.

3

The Size and Scope
of the Entertainment Media
and What Young People
Think of Them

We spend incredible amounts of time and money amusing ourselves through movies, situation comedies, television dramas, spectator sports, and all forms of recorded music. Any activity on which so much time is spent is likely to affect the sociopolitical values of those spending the time and money.

The Size of the U.S., Canadian, Irish, and U.K. Entertainment Industries

The reach of the entertainment media may be measured in several ways; dollars spent in various markets and number of consumers are among the more common. In terms of movies, a popular film will be shown simultaneously on thousands of screens throughout a country, and a very popular film like *Spiderman 3* will gross more than $336,500,000 in the U.S. alone before going to video. U.S. domestic box office reached $9.63 billion in 2007, while worldwide box office for U.S. films reached $26.7 billion.

In terms of music, according to the Recording Industry Association of America, total U.S. music sales reached $15 billion in 1999, but have dropped to around $8 billion as of 2007 ("2007 Year-End"). Digital download sales have made up some of the difference, coming in at $1.3 billion in 2007. In 2005, digital formats made up just 9% of industry revenue, while in 2007 they accounted for 23%. The U.S. radio industry, which of course includes news and entertainment, generates revenues of $16.7 billion annually ("Radio Industry Revenues" 2009).

In terms of television viewing in the U.S., a typical episode of the popular television hospital drama *House* draws almost 16 million households, whereas the popular situation comedy *Two and a Half Men* draws almost 13 million households. Moreover, the networks believe these shows are worth astronomical amounts of money to produce and distribute. For example, in 1998 NBC signed a three-year contract with *E.R.* producers Warner Bothers television for $850 million, or approximately $13 million per episode (Carmody 1998).

The U.K. media industry generated $61 billion of revenue in 2008, with publishing accounting for 41.3%, broadcast and cable TV accounting for 36.9%, movies and entertainment for 15.1%, and advertising at 6.7% ("Media in the United Kingdom" 2009). In the U.K. in 2008, music revenues declined 13% to £1.02 billion (Sabbagh 2008). Revenues from CD sales dropped 16% to £871 million, while digital sales increased 28% to £132.2 million. A popular TV program on BBC1 will attract close to ten million viewers, while on BBC2 two to three million are common. Independent television network ITV's most popular broadcasts will also average around 10 million viewers.

Nielsen reports that in 2007 in Canada just under 42 million physical musical recordings were sold, while 25.8 million digital tracks were sold ("Nielsen Music 2007"). Millions of movie tickets are sold every year in Canada, but the overwhelming majority of them are sold to viewers to watch foreign—mainly U.S.—films. The majority of the most popular Canadian TV shows originate from the U.S. as well. To make the top 30 shows for a week a program needs to draw a minimum of about a million viewers, while the most popular shows will usually have just under three million viewers ("2008–09 National Top Program Reports Archive" 2009).

Listening to Music and Thinking about It

There are several reasons to believe that, among all of the various socializing influences of the popular culture, music has the greatest likelihood of influencing the politics of young people. Most important is the amount of exposure and commitment, that is the amount of time and money young people spend on music. Of the young Americans surveyed, 45.9% listen to the radio more than two hours per day. Also, 59.9% of respondents report listening to their own music collections for more than an hour per day. The average number of pieces of recorded music (including records, cassettes, and compact discs) owned is 78.

Among Anglophone Canadian youths, most (58.5%) listen to the radio less than an hour per day, but 25.9% listen between one and two hours. The average number of CDs owned is 88. Unfortunately, we did not ask about downloaded music.

Among Irish respondents, the plurality (27.8%) listen to the radio more than three hours, and the majority listen at least an hour per day. The plurality of respondents (42.3%) listen to their own collections between one and two hours per day. The plurality of U.K. respondents (49.3%) listen to the radio less than an hour per day, while the plurality (36%) listen to their own collections between one and two hours. The Irish respondents own a mean of 68 CDs. The average is a bit more complicated to compute for the U.K. respondents because of an outlier who claimed to own 10,000 CDs. The mean is 224, but the median, a better measure of central tendency when there are extreme values such as this, is 100 discs.

The diversity of popular music is also significant. Young people's tastes in music are varied. Rap is the most popular among U.S. youths, attracting 25.8% of responses to the question of one's favorite music. Alternative rock finished a close second, with 24.4%. Classic rock attracted 8.6%, and rhythm and blues attracted 7.8%. Country attracted 5.6%, whereas the remaining preferences were scattered among jazz, blues, no preference, and so on. This diversity creates the potential for socialization of competing values.

Not surprisingly, very few respondents in Ireland or the U.K. said country music was their favorite. In Ireland, alternative rock was the most popular (23.6%), followed closely by R and B (22.2%). Interestingly, "other" was the modal category in each country (30.6% and 33.4%), which indicates that we missed an important category when constructing our surveys for these countries. Alternative rock was the most popular type in the U.K., attracting 27.4% of respondents, followed by R and B and rap (14.1% and 10.1%, respectively).

Among Canadian respondents, alternative rock was by far the most popular, attracting 37.8%. Classic rock was second (19.3%), followed by rap (13.9%) and country and R and B (both at 5.1%).

The political content of popular music is relevant, too. Therefore, the lyrics of songs with some kind of sociopolitical message from the top four favorite genres need to be examined, as well as the political activities of important musicians with each genre.

Rap Music

Rap music has drawn ire from conservative cultural critics and much interest from academic researchers. Tupac received the most attention, with U.S. respondents listing 36 different titles of his as either preferred or favorite songs. Tupac's birth name was Lesane Parish Crooks, but he changed his name to Tupac Amaru in honor of an Inca revolutionary and Shakur for the Arabic for "thankful to God." (www.tupac.com) Perhaps the outpouring of support for Tupac among U.S. respondents can partly be based on the fact of his premature death in 1996. Nonetheless it is undeniable that his music attracted much interest from the young U.S. respondents to the survey. Tupac could have been the poster-child for what conservative critics disliked about rap's sociopolitical content. Late in his life he became active in mainstream politics as well, by joining the Brotherhood Crusade (along with rappers Snoop Doggy Dogg and Mc Hammer), to oppose the anti-affirmative action California Civil Rights initiative. The album *Me against the World* typifies these concerns.

The album was released while Tupac was serving time for a rape conviction and recovering from an in-studio gang-style shooting. The title track of the album concerns the problems of inner-city life, especially violence. In it Tupac argues that he is not making excuses for outlaw behavior, but he also points out that the power structure in the U.S. ignores young African American males unless they are shooting. Taking an individualistic stance, he frequently asserts at the end of stanzas that, "It's just me against the world baby." Despite the seeming nihilism of all this, he ends the song very optimistically, by stating that although life is difficult sometimes, better days are around the corner, and that the individual must stay strong and, "stick your chest out . . . and handle it."

More recently, during the 2004 election campaign, rapper P. Diddy (with support from other rap stars such as 50 Cent) created a group to encourage the youth vote called Citizen Change. The group was best known for its over the top slogan "Vote or Die," which earned the group a substantial amount of criticism from traditional news media, but also from *The Daily Show with Jon Stewart*, and on the cartoon series *South Park*.

Alternative Rock

Alternative rock finished second among young U.S. respondents' preferences, and first in Canada, the U.K., and Ireland. Unlike with rap there was not one artist who attracted overwhelming preference from the U.S. respondents. Two acts, however, did attract more than any others. These are *Pearl Jam* and *Rage Against the Machine*. Each of these acts has been engaged in political activities and have written songs with sociopolitical content in the lyrics.

Eddie Vedder, the lead singer of *Pearl Jam*, led a crusade against the monopolistic practices of Ticketmaster. He has also endorsed or donated money to a number of political candidates, including Green Party presidential nominee Ralph Nader in 2000, and John Kerry in 2004. One *Pearl Jam* song mentioned by the respondents is entitled "Jeremy." The song is about the violent outburst in school of an abused child. Vedder wrote of a youngster ignored by his mother and father and picked on by peers who unleashes his wrath on the playground. The frequently repeated line, "Jeremy spoke in class today," ironically implies that the only way the child was able to receive the attention he needed was to lash out violently. Clearly the song is about the social consequences of the individual actions of abusive parents, neglectful school personnel, and cruel children.

Rage Against the Machine too was active politically. In 2000, the video for their song "Testify" concluded with Ralph Nader intoning, "If you do not turn on to politics, politics will turn on you." In "Bulls on Parade," a song mentioned as a favorite by respondents, *Rage* writes that the U.S. provides countries that require our assistance weapons instead of food and other necessities. U.S. foreign policy is driven by the need to help the munitions industry prosper, rather than the humanitarian impulse to promote literacy and other democratic values. The American public is either duped or willingly goes along with these immoral policies. The lyrics simultaneously condemn the U.S. military industrial complex's domestic and international consequences, as well as the band's perceived hypocrisy of American conservatives.

Classic Rock and Country

Classic rock attracted the next most U.S. fans in the survey, and did well among the Irish and U.K. respondents too (6.9% and 8.4%, respectively). Classic rock certainly began the modern era of political songwriting, with the likes of Phil Ochs, John Lennon, Crosby, Stills, Nash and Young, and many others. A natural question arises as to what salience songs against the War in Vietnam or other 1960s and 1970s specific events could hold for American youth today. However, the issues of civil rights, feminism, peace, and personal freedom, especially in terms of sexuality, probably do resonate with a generation of Americans who view politics in a very personalistic way.

Finally, country music has traditionally been a home for conservatives, patriots, and lionizers of rural and small-town America, especially its past. A new brand of country, "Young Country," tried somewhat to stay apolitical, but country remains conservative with more of its stars endorsing Republican candidates. Not many country songs were mentioned as favorites but a typical song with sociopolitical content is Aaron Tippin's "Working Man's Ph.D." In this song he writes, "There ain't no shame in a job well done / in driving a nail or driving a truck," and that too few Americans are doing the real work necessary to keep the country on the right track. He also endorses the quality of American made products. Interestingly, he ignores traditional means workers have used to "set things straight," such as government's protection of collective bargaining, and that is why it is fair to characterize the song as conservative—cathartic for workers to hear over beers after work—but conservative nonetheless.

Country and Western music retained its connection with conservatism and the Republican Party in the post 9–11 environment, as well as in the 2004 and 2008 elections. Country superstar Toby Keith recorded one of the most controversial reactions to the terrorist attacks of 9–11. Entitled "Courtesy of the Red, White and Blue / The Angry American," the song includes such lyrics as:

> Now this nation that I love / Has fallen under attack / A mighty sucker punch came flying in / From somewhere in the back

and, most famously:

> And you'll be sorry that you messed with / The U.S. of A. / 'Cause we'll put a boot in your ass / It's the American way

Keith has performed the song (and others, of course) at USO-sponsored events for U.S. soldiers in Iraq and other countries. Interestingly, Keith is a registered Democrat, but has compared himself with Connecticut Senator Joe Lieberman, whom he described as "a conservative Democrat who is sometimes embarrassed for his party." Keith also said, "People don't realize that I'm a registered Democrat. They automatically assume that I'm a chest-banging, war-drum-pounding Republican with my military stance" (Morse 2004).

Interestingly, some of Keith's supporters in the music industry include such leftists as Willie Nelson and Kris Kristofferson. They do not, however, include the *Dixie Chicks*, who generated controversy when singer Natalie Maines said in London that she was embarrassed to be from the same state as President Bush. Maines also said of "Courtesy . . . ," "I hate it. It's ignorant, and it makes country music sound ignorant. It targets an entire culture—and not just the bad people who did bad things. You've got to have some tact. Anybody can write, 'We'll put a boot in your ass'" ("Natalie Maines"). Keith called Maines a "big mouth" and had an altered photo of her snuggling with Saddam Hussein projected at his concerts (Henson 2007). Maines responded by wearing a t-shirt emblazoned with the letters "FUTK" at a country music awards broadcast. Initially claiming the letters stood for Freedom, Understanding, Truth and Knowledge, she later admitted they were an insult aimed at Keith.

After the London comments the *Dixie Chicks* faced a backlash from more than just Keith. Radio stations stopped playing their songs, some even crushed their CDs with a bulldozer. They received death threats and their sales plummeted. Even President Bush got in the act, saying, "'the *Dixie Chicks* are free to speak their mind . . . they shouldn't have their feelings hurt just because some people don't want to buy their records when they speak out. You know, freedom is a two-way street." While country and western has always produced some diversity in terms of the ideological orientations of its stars, it's clear from the Keith/*Dixie Chicks* feud and backlash against the *Chicks* that it's never been easy to be a liberal in Nashville.

In the 2004 and 2008 presidential elections, country music played a role as well. In 2004, President Bush was played onto stage by a song from country stars Brooks and Dunn, while Senator John Kerry took the stage to a Bruce Springsteen song. In 2008, Hank Williams re-wrote his country classic "Family Tradition" as "McCain-Palin Tradition." It included lyrics such as:

John is a maverick/And Sarah fixed Alaska's broken condition/They're gonna go just fine/We're headed for better times/It's a McCain—Palin tradition

Williams performed the song at several campaign events for the ticket as well. Also in 2008, country music star Aaron Tippin recorded "Drill here, Drill now," calling for increased oil exploration in the U.S. He performed the song at several campaign events with McCain and Palin.

Young People's Response to Music

More than any other element of popular culture, music elicits the strongest responses from young people to its political messages. For example, 78.5% of young Americans surveyed have disagreed with the message of a song. Interestingly, white youths are significantly more likely than blacks to have disagreed (83.3% compared with 68.7%). Men are more likely than women to have disagreed as well, although the difference is smaller (81.1% compared with 76.9%). Conservatives are slightly more likely than liberals to have disagreed with the message of a song (85.7% compared with 81.3%).

Canadian, U.K., and Irish respondents were asked not just if they had ever disagreed with the message of a song, but also if they have ever agreed. 79.1% of young Canadians have ever disagreed with the political message of a song, while an overwhelming 91.6% have ever agreed. There are no significant differences when controlling for sex, and respondents' race was not included in the Canadian survey. Only 63.3% of Irish respondents have ever disagreed with the message of a song, while 79.1% have ever agreed. 72.9% of U.K. respondents have ever disagreed, while 83.5% have ever agreed. Male Irish respondents are much more likely to have disagreed than are women (81.3% to 57.9%). Among the Irish there are no significant differences in likelihood of having agreed when controlling for sex. Among U.K. respondents there are no significant differences in likelihood of having agreed or disagreed with regard to sex.

When asked what specific political messages of songs they disagreed with, the results were extremely varied. About 26% of those Americans who disagreed with a message did so because of the musician's endorsement of violence, while 15.3% disagreed with what they perceived as a performer's stance against religion. As to violence, one respondent wrote, "Some rap (not all) glorifies violence against women, children and just society in general." In terms of religion, much of the criticism related to rocker Marilyn Manson who is well known for his lyrical attacks on organized religion. For example, a respondent wrote that he/she disagrees with "anything by Marilyn Manson. It disgusts me when I hear his music. He does not think there is a god." Another concern, attracting 14.4% of respondents was with songs that degrade women. Typical in this vein is the respondent who wrote, "A lot of rap talks too much about rape and male control." Another category of concern that received nearly 10% of responses was related to songs that promoted promiscuity and premarital sex. A good example of this is the respondent who wrote that he or she opposes, "I Want Your Sex" by George Michael." I believe he is corrupting the youth with his lyrics about premarital sex and promiscuity."

Agreeing and Disagreeing with Music: Canada

In terms of song messages agreed with, there were 157 total mentions of a specific band or performer. Mentioned more often than anyone else was former Beatle John Lennon, with 10% of the total mentions. Next most frequently mentioned was *Rage*

Against the Machine, with just over four percent, and U2 and *Black Eyed Peas*, with just under four percent each. In terms of nationalities, 65% of the mentions went to U.S. bands or singers, 15% to British acts, 13%t to Canadian artists, and five percent to the Irish. When they are thinking about the political content of pop music with which they agree, the young Canadians in this sample are predominantly thinking of U.S. music, but are more likely to think of Canadian content than is the case with other genres, notably films.

In terms of messages agreed with in songs, by far the most frequently mentioned theme agreed with is "anti-war." Young Canadians in the sample responded favorably to songs they perceived as being anti-war (with 24.8% selecting this as the theme with which they agreed)—both in general and as against the war in Iraq. Typical of a general anti-war belief is the respondent who reported agreeing with the song "What's Going On?" by Motown legend Marvin Gaye because it, "emphasizes the uselessness of war." This song choice is also important because it was almost certainly released before the respondent was born (the average age of respondents is 20.24 years, while "What's Going On?" was released in 1971, about 34 years before the surveys were administered). This indicates that while popular music is an important generational marker, music from generations past may still be relevant for contemporary young people, especially if they perceive older music to have something important to say about situations similar to the ones in which they are living. Thus an anti-war song from the Vietnam era may still resonate with young people thinking about the war in Iraq.

The second most frequently mentioned theme agreed with in songs, but attracting only 5.1% of respondents, include "anti-U.S." messages. An example of a song with an anti-American message with which a student agreed is "No News Is Good News" by the group *Newfound Glory*, which the respondent describes as, "about American politics and Bush and how he's ruining everything." The category of "general tolerance" also attracted 5.1 percent of respondents and included such comments as a respondent who approved of *Jewel's* song "Pieces of You," because, "we are all alike in some way, so why would we hate and abuse those around us?" Young Canadians are observed agreeing with large amounts of U.S. produced popular culture, but not necessarily having pro-U.S. beliefs reinforced.

In terms of messages disagreed with in songs, there were 79 discrete mentions of bands. Eminem received the highest number of mentions at 20%, while Britney Spears, *Green Day* and Toby Keith received eight percent each. Just over 86% of the artists mentioned as having been disagreed with are U.S. musicians, while eight percent are British and just four percent are Canadian. Young Canadians are more likely to disagree with a U.S. song and more likely to agree with a Canadian one.

Both messages against women's rights or that degrade women, and those that are pro-violence attracted 11.2% of disagreers. A comment that clearly indicates what respondents mean when they disagree with a song based on its opposition to or degradation of women comes from the respondent who opposed rapper Eminem, because, "he sings of men against women and children. This angers me—often the message is about spousal abuse."

In songs, too, respondents saw a pro-U.S. bias (8.6%). Many respondents, for example, mentioned disagreeing with what they perceived to be the excessive and violent patriotism of country and western star Toby Keith's post-9–11 song "Courtesy of the Red, White and Blue."

Canadian conservatives are more likely ever to have disagreed with the message of a song; liberals are more likely to have ever agreed with one. There are no differences with regard to gender in terms of young Canadians ever having agreed or disagreed with the political message of a song.

Agreeing and Disagreeing with Music: U.K. and Ireland

Only nine codeable messages in songs were disagreed with by Irish respondents, which is an insufficient number from which to discern a meaningful pattern. Also, only 14 themes agreed with could be coded, which again is an insufficient number to discover a pattern.

The situation with U.K. respondents is a little better. There were 46 codeable messages disagreed with. However, 18 different themes were mentioned, with anti-authority statements taking the plurality of responses, followed closely by concerns over pro-white racism and oversimplification of social issues. In terms of themes agreed with, there were 43 codeable responses, with anti-war being the most popular, followed by anti-American themes and anti-racist messages.

For Irish and U.K. respondents there is no statistically significant relationship between ideology and ever having agreed or disagreed with the message of a song, although in both countries those on the left are more likely to have ever agreed—the differences are substantial, but the sample sizes too small to produce statistical significance. Irish men are more likely than women to have ever disagreed with the message of a song.

Watching and Thinking about Television

A necessary condition for influence by television programming is that young people watch it. Almost 24% of U.S. respondents watch entertainment television more than three hours per day. About 50% watch television more than two hours per day. Only 23.5% watch for less than an hour per day.

For Canadian respondents, the plurality (37%) watch between one and two hours per day of entertainment programming, although 34% report watching less than an hour per day. The Irish respondents as well mainly watch between one and two hours of entertainment TV per day (32.9%), but a significant amount (31.6%) report watching between one and two hours. Among U.K. respondents 32.9% watch between one and two hours, but 32% report watching less than an hour per day.

To shed more light on the influence of television, it is useful to see whether youths detected political messages in entertainment television with which they disagreed because it is a measure of level of engagement with television programming. Those who have disagreed must at least have paid attention to the programming in order to form an opinion.

When asked if they have ever disagreed with the political message of a television program, 60.6% of the U.S. respondents answered in the affirmative. The overwhelming concern was television's promotion of homosexual rights. Nearly every one of these 30 responses came from the respondents' opposition to the episode of the television program *Ellen* wherein the main character revealed her homosexuality. An example of a negative response to this broadcast is the individual who wrote, "I don't believe homosexuality is morally right." A close second was concern over the lack of sexual morals in television programs. An example of one of these responses is the respondent who wrote, "(I disagree with) most soap operas (because) marriage is a joke." Combined, these concerns accounted for almost 40% of the responses. These data indicate once again that young people discern political content of television in the form of lifestyle or culture wars issues.

Interestingly, young U.S. conservatives are more likely than liberals to have disagreed with the message of a television program (69.1% compared with 58.8%). White youths are more likely to have disagreed than African Americans as well (63% compared with 54.1%). Finally, men are more likely than women to have disagreed (61.8% compared with 59.4%).

Agreeing and Disagreeing with TV: English-Speaking Canada

In terms of messages agreed with in a TV program, Canadian respondents offered 83 total mentions of a specific show, including news and entertainment programs (most of the references were to entertainment programs). Just under 16% of these mentions went to the hybrid *The Daily Show with Jon Stewart*, while just over seven percent went to *The West Wing*, just over six percent went to *Oprah* and five percent went to *The Simpsons*. Just over 18% of mentions went to Canadian productions, while 80% went to U.S.-made programming (French and Norwegian programs received a single mention each).

The distribution of themes agreed with in a television program by young Canadians covered a wide range of concerns, and therefore no category stood far above the others in terms of popularity. Both "general tolerance" and "anti-U.S." messages received strong support, as did beliefs best categorized as supportive of "general morality." A good example of the belief in tolerance is the respondent who liked the message of *Buffy the Vampire Slayer*, because it, "dealt with a lot of teenage issues and always promoted tolerance and acceptance." A good example of agreement with the theme of general morality is the respondent who wrote he/she agrees with the, "usually good messages about family values and moral values," in programs such as *The Simpsons, Smallville,* and *CSI.* It is interesting to note that respondents saw *The Simpsons* as promoting family values and morality, since when the show first began airing in 1989, conservatives decried it for lacking family values. However, more recent commentary on the show has argued that it does promote traditional values (Cantor 1999).

In terms of messages disagreed with in television, 61 total mentions of a program name resulted. Three shows attracted just over eight percent of the mentions: *Law and Order, The Swan,* and *Will and Grace. Oprah* and *The Bachelor/Bachelorette* attracted just under seven percent each. Just under seven percent of the mentions went to Canadian programs, the rest to U.S. productions.

The plurality category again was "pro-U.S." bias, attracting 14.7% of disagreers. No other category attracted as many responses, but programs that degraded women raised the ire of 7.4% of respondents, while concerns with programs' "general immorality" and pro-homosexuality or gay rights attracted 6.3% each. Most of the concerns over homosexuality centered around the television programs *Will and Grace* and *Queer Eye for the Straight Guy.* These concerns reflect the increased prevalence of shows with gay characters, or a focus on gay issues.

Canadian conservatives are more likely to have ever disagreed with the message of a TV program; interestingly, they are also more likely ever to have agreed with one. There are no differences with regard to gender in terms of young Canadians ever having agreed or disagreed with the political message of a TV show.

Agreeing and Disagreeing with TV: The U.K. and Ireland

There is insufficient data from the Irish surveys to say anything systematic about the pattern of political ideas agreed with and disagreed with in the entertainment media. Unfortunately, the U.K. data does not allow for analysis either, for there were too few responses that could actually be coded so as to detect any patterns. There are no relationships between ideology and ever having agreed or disagreed with the message of a TV show among Irish and U.K. respondents. Irish men are more likely than women to have ever disagreed with the political message of a TV show, and U.K. women are more likely than men ever to have agreed.

Going to and Thinking about the Movies

An agent of socialization cannot have influence unless individuals are exposed to it. Do young people watch movies? If they do not, then the political content of movies does not matter. Based on available data there can be little doubt that young people watch many movies. When U.S. respondents were asked to mention their favorite movie and those they have seen recently and liked, 502 movies were mentioned. When asked to name their favorite movie, there were 588 responses; only 121 (21%) either could not remember or did not have a favorite. Of movies mentioned as favorites, no film attracted more than 3.2% support; that movie was *Titanic*, at the time of the data collection a very recent release.

Young Americans obviously see many films. Do they perceive any political messages in the movies they see? The capacity of young people to discern a political message in a movie and agree or disagree with it suggests the extent to which they are conscious of, influenced by, or resistant to attempts by Hollywood to shape their political views. Moreover, disagreeing with the message of a movie indicates a greater level of involvement with the cinema. When the respondents were asked if they have ever disagreed with the political message of a movie, 59.4% answered yes. The most frequently mentioned concerns are violence, racism, and sexuality. An example of a respondent's concern over violence is the individual who wrote that he or she disagreed with the message of the film *Natural Born Killers* because, "the portrayal of serial killers was not satirical enough and could be construed as glorification." In terms of racism, a U.S. respondent disagreed with the message of *Waiting to Exhale* because it, "seemed to stereotype African-American males as liars and cheats." An example of a concern with sexuality is the respondent who wrote, "I can't name a specific movie but I oppose films that promote sex before marriage." Based on these responses it is clear that young Americans not only watch many movies, but actually are aware of their political content and frequently disagree with it. Moreover, they are concerned with the lifestyle, culture wars issues mentioned earlier.

Conservatives are more likely than liberals to have disagreed with the message of a movie (67.1% compared with 62.2%). Whereas 65.9% of male U.S. respondents have disagreed with the message of a film, only 58.4% of women have. Finally, 64% of white respondents have disagreed with a movie, only 52% of blacks have.

Agreeing and Disagreeing with Movies: English-Speaking Canada

In terms of movies agreed with, there were a total of 184 mentions of specific films. Among those mentioned most often are Michael Moore's *Fahrenheit 9–11* (27% of mentions) and *Bowling for Columbine* (20%), and *The Corporation* (three percent). Almost all of the films mentioned are U.S.-made blockbusters and only two are Canadian: *The Corporation*, which was mentioned six times; and *Jesus of Montreal*, a Quebec film which was mentioned just once. When the young Canadians in this sample think about the political content of movies, they are thinking about U.S.-made films, and predominantly the films of one controversial U.S. filmmaker.

In terms of movie messages agreed with, anti-U.S. messages were most popular, being offered by about 11.7% of respondents who offered an answer. A typical response that fits the category of anti-U.S. messages shows both the depth of the sentiment, as well as the complexity of responses to these questions. A respondent wrote he/she agreed with Michael Moore's movie *Fahrenheit 9–11* because, "he illustrates how the

Bush Administration wanted to distract the American public from their interest in money, and lack of concern for both troops and Iraqi civilians." This is coded as anti-U.S. because included in that category are both general anti-U.S. sentiments, as well as specific disagreements with particular contemporary or historical administration policies. An example of a more general anti-U.S. sentiment from a movie with which a respondent agreed is the respondent who concurred with Michael Moore's films *Bowling for Columbine* and *Fahrenheit 9–11* because they are, "anti-Bush, anti-American and anti-war."

What is most fascinating here is the evidence that some Canadian anti-Americanism is being fuelled by the contents of films made by a U.S. filmmaker. Canadian youths are watching U.S. films almost exclusively, yet the content of these films is not necessarily positive for the United States. This supports Gray's 2007 conclusions about the interpretation of the *The Simpsons* by non-Americans, who see in the show a severe critique of suburban U.S. life.

The second most common message agreed with in a movie involved pictures the respondents perceived of as, "anti-violence." An example of this is the respondent who agreed with the message of *Bowling for Columbine* because, "there is too much violence, Americans live in fear and therefore consume, keeping the economy going." The preference for the message of this film also demonstrates another important point about how young people utilize movies in the formation or maintenance of their beliefs. Popular films from controversial film-makers immediately come to respondents' minds when filling out surveys, but may fade in relevance as time passes. In other words, respondents utilize the entertainment most available to them.

The third most frequently mentioned category, attracting 5.8% of responses were "anti-capitalist" messages. Again, this often revolved around Michael Moore's films, this time referring to Moore's first film *Roger and Me*, a documentary about General Motors' abandonment of Flint, Michigan.

Despite the fact that *Fahrenheit 9–11* was the film most often mentioned as having been disagreed with, "pro-U.S." bias is the most frequently mentioned theme, at 12.9%. A clear example of this is the Canadian respondent who wrote about a movie that fictionalized the American Revolution, "I disagreed with the movie *The Patriot* because it was a false indication of what actually happened and was a piece of American propaganda." The second most frequently mentioned theme respondents disagreed with was "pro-violence," at 7.9%. A comment which demonstrates the complexity of young people's relationship with the entertainment media comes from a respondent who disagreed with the violence in the *Kill Bill* movies. The respondent wrote, "I disagree with the message of vigilantism, the notion of violence solving problems. However, I still liked watching the movie for the cinematic experimentation by (director Quentin) Tarantino." These kinds of comments demonstrate young people may find much both to agree with and disagree with in the same popular culture production. Young people are not empty vessels into which the entertainment media pour their ideas, and they do attempt to balance the positive and negative aspects of the media they experience in forming their reaction to it.

Canadian conservatives are more likely to have ever disagreed with the message of a movie, and they are slightly more likely to have ever agreed with one too. There are no differences with regard to gender in terms of young Canadians ever having agreed or disagreed with the political message of a movie.

Agreeing and Disagreeing with Movies: Ireland and Great Britain

In the British and Irish surveys respondents were asked both whether they had ever agreed or disagreed with the political message of a movie. Among Irish respondents, 48.5% had ever disagreed with the message of a movie, while 67.7% had ever agreed with the message of a film. Among U.K. respondents, 65.6% have ever disagreed with the message of a film, while 80.1% have ever agreed. There are no statistically significant differences in ideology between disageers and non-disagreers in either Ireland or the U.K. The same is true for ever having agreed with a movie's political message. Irish men, however, are significantly more likely to have ever disagreed with the message of a film.

While there is an insufficient sample size to perform a meaningful analysis of the themes agreed with and disagreed with by Irish respondents, there is sufficient data to perform such an analysis for U.K. respondents. The most frequently disagreed with theme in movies is perception that the film has a pro-U.S. bias. An example of this concern comes from the respondent who wrote of disagreeing with the film *Air Force One*, and described it as "an American pride film that has the antagonists, archetypically, as Russian terrorists." Some respondents described Mel Gibson's epic *Passion of the Christ* as anti-Semitic. *Pearl Harbor* was one of the films accused of oversimplification.

There are no relationships between ideology and ever having agreed or disagreed with the message of a movie among Irish and U.K. respondents. Irish men are more likely than women to have ever disagreed with a movie's message. U.K. males are too, but the difference is not statistically significant.

It is interesting to note that the bulk of interpretable messages agreed with were sentiments in favor of "negative" themes—in other words they were perceived of as being against something bad, instead of for something good: anti-racist; anti-U.S.; anti-violence; anti-war (in that order). For example, *Fahrenheit 9/11* was agreed with "because it exposed the lies of American politics," and not for any of the positive messages it contained.

Popular Politics

Young people today think about politics in a very personalistic way. They see as political the personal choices they make about living arrangements, sexuality, tolerance, and so on. They appear to be living proof of the old feminist mantra, "the personal is political." Thus it makes sense that they shun traditional kinds of political participation (voting in particular) in favor of more direct, volunteer activity because they can see directly the results of their activity (Clymer 2000). This is one of the reasons why the environmental movement has exerted such pull on this generation. One need not join a group or participate in a protest to become an environmentalist. All one needs to do is recycle one's trash—certainly an individual activity with direct results.

It should also not surprise us that there is a cadre of very young Americans who hold strong conservative moral opposition to what they see as the immoral messages of popular television, music, and movies. As Wade Clark Roof has pointed out, there is a renewed interest in religious and spiritual matters among Generation-X (in Halstead, 7) Certainly most mainstream Christian denominations also present a morality at odds with the one presented by the entertainment media. Moreover, the generation to follow Generation-X, sometimes called the Millennial Generation, represented in the Canadian, U.K. and Irish samples, have been described as conventional in their morals and happily subservient to traditional authorities. Not surprisingly, such youths would find much to disagree with in the entertainment media.

Most young people have ever agreed or disagreed with the messages of music, television, or movies at one time or another. Conservative Americans are more likely than liberals to have disagreed. In general, white American men are the most likely to have disagreed with the political messages of music, television, and movies. Part of the explanation for this may be that white men are more likely to be conservative than are women or minorities. Perhaps though, some white males feel threatened by the increasing frequency of strong women and minority characters, as well as actors and performers. Perhaps white males feel their traditional dominance threatened and object to messages that promote empowerment of women and minorities—especially if the power of women is promoted through promiscuity and minority males through violence.

4

The Political Influence of Movies

For a number of reasons it makes sense to believe that movies are the least influential aspect of the popular culture in terms of political socialization. First, with the exception of major blockbusters, most movies are seen only once. Thus, there is not repeated exposure, which is generally believed to increase the influence of an agent of socialization. Repeated exposure is one key reason why parents, peers, schools, and churches have so much influence over the development of political attitudes in children.

Also, movies are a complicated genre. There may be more than one message in any film, and viewers may fail to identify and interpret multiple meanings. This is not to suggest that it is unreasonable to believe movies may influence young adults' political beliefs; it is just that the influence of movies is more problematic in terms of research than television or music.

Regarding the influence of movies it is important to think again about the socialization process, which involves learning that is both conscious and unconscious. It is not necessary that young people are aware of the sociopolitical themes in movies in order for socialization and learning to occur. It is unreasonable to expect young people to tell researchers everything they have learned from a movie because it is unlikely that they are conscious of everything they have learned. Some things they will remember and talk about, while other things they will not.

Let us think about this issue with some examples. The most popular film with the U.S. respondents to the survey was *Titanic*. This film focuses on the delights of romantic love and how the memories of it transcend time and tragedy. The movie suggests that while money may motivate many marriages, women should marry for love instead. The rich passengers on the ship are caricatures of arrogance and upperclass snobbery, while the poor are just as caricatured as genuine and fun-loving, even in the squalor of the bowels of the ship. How much of this would a young person actually take away from this film? That is hard to say. Of course, in the case of this particular film it may be more likely that young viewers will detect nuanced political messages because it was one of the blockbusters, and hence merited repeated viewing. Moreover, it helps that the hero was from the lionized lower classes, whereas his antagonist hailed from the upper echelons of society (and of the ship as well). It is reasonable to argue in fact that any class or group from which the sympathetic heroes of a movie come are more likely to be well remembered and supported by young viewers. For example, Tom Cruise played a fighter pilot in *Top Gun*, another very popular film among the survey respondents. Certainly it is not unreasonable to expect that fans of this film will hold more favorable attitudes toward fighter pilots than those who are not fans of the movie.

What young children learn about politics from movies depends on what movies they watch and at what age they view them. The movies young children view often do not contain overt and obvious political content (e.g., *Home Alone*), or, if they do, the content emphasizes timeless themes of good versus evil, the need for hierarchy and authority, and monarchy (e.g., *The Lion King*). Do these movies influence the prepolitical ideologies of children? Perhaps they do. It may be unreasonable to believe that *The Lion King* could influence young American children to believe in the need for a restoration of the monarchy. However, it is not unreasonable to believe that another Disney production, *The Hunchback of Notre Dame*, may teach cultural and ethnic tolerance by creating a sympathetic gypsy character as the heroine of the film.

When children are old enough to take an interest in and to watch movies in theaters that have obvious sociopolitical content, some of these may be R-rated and youths may not attend them before they reach the age of 18 without being accompanied by a parent or guardian. Many theaters enforce this rule rigorously. Thus, when youths do finally get exposure to movies with political content, they are often old enough already to have a base of political knowledge, ideology, values and issue positions derived from not only traditional agents of socialization, but exposure to other entertainment media as well.

Youths comprise a large percentage of moviegoers, and major studios cater to the youth market. Major studios routinely produce and release movies that appeal to this market because their profits depend heavily on getting young people to attend movies. A cursory examination of one weekend's top grossing films shows the extent to which movies are aimed at the young. For the weekend ending 4 February 2001, the number one movie was *The Wedding Planner*, starring Jennifer Lopez and Matthew McConaughey, then two twenty-something actors who are very popular with young Americans. Second on the list was *Valentine*, wherein four college girls make fun of one of their nerdy classmates, who exacts his violent revenge years later. Other films in the top ten clearly aimed at young viewers included *Snatch*, Director Guy Ritchie's incredibly fast paced and violent look at the London underground. *Save the Last Dance* is the tale of the interracial love affair of two college aged young people. These four films' popularity demonstrates the legitimacy of Hollywood's concern with attracting the young audience.

What general themes in movies are likely to attract youths? While they are not always mature enough to handle such themes, young people can be expected to display a strong interest in movies with adult themes. They are particularly interested in the pleasures of life that seem to be readily available to adults but are denied to them because of their age, lack of financial resources, and immaturity. Thus, at least in American culture, there is a ready audience among youths for movies with themes and characters that are linked to socially taboo and mostly adult behaviors: sex outside the confines of marriage; illegal drug use; violence; vulgar language; and general hedonism. Youths routinely try to acquire and view X-rated and pornographic videos. This behavior is so common in fact that it is a commonly discussed aspect of young people's everyday lives. Young people prefer R-rated and PG-13 movies, and they avoid G-rated films as too childish for them.

Most importantly, movies sometimes depict the behaviors mentioned above as if they did not have negative consequences, or as if the consequences were just a normal part of growing up. Movies indirectly tell youths that their parents and other agents of socialization have lied to them about the negative consequences of these behaviors. Thus, movies may compete directly with parents, the church, the school, and other parentally selected agents of socialization for the attention of youths and, ultimately, influence over youths' sociopolitical values.

In chapter 3 we learned that young white conservative males are the most likely of U.S. respondents to have disagreed with the sociopolitical message of a movie. This is the case because young white conservative males have the most to lose in the sociopolitical hierarchy by an increase in power among women and nonwhites—power which is often gained in movies through promiscuity and violence among these groups, respectively. This chapter explores the influence of movie exposure, young people's perceptions of the ideologies of actors, and the influence of movies on young people's becoming more liberal than their parents.

Movie Exposure

Returning now to the issue of young people's disagreeing with the political message or theme of a movie, the specific messages with which young people disagreed can be categorized by their ideological perspectives. A liberal would disagree with depictions of violence, racism, traditional roles for women, and so on. A conservative would disagree with antireligion themes, prohomosexuality positions, and support for premarital sex, promiscuity, and nudity. Of course, some youths have never disagreed with the sociopolitical themes of a movie. A good test of the theory of socialization and political learning that informs this work is to examine the ideological perspective of the messages of movies disagreed with by youths. Table 4.1 represents the distribution of ideological perspectives taken by U.S. respondents against movies.

Table 4.1: Ideological Orientation of Objection to Movies, U.S. Respondents Only

Perspective	Percent	n
Liberal	7.8	53
Neutral	0.4	3
Conservative	5.0	34
Have not Disagreed	38.7	264
Disagreed/Did not Say Why	44.7	305
Disagreed/Unclear Reason	3.5	24
Totals	100.0	683

Clearly, disagreers who would not say why they disagreed are the plurality, with those who have not disagreed at all coming in second. In terms of disagreement with an ideological perspective which can be characterized, liberal perspectives were the most frequently mentioned, with conservative a fairly close second. However, the interesting test is the relationship between youths' self-reported ideologies and the ideological perspective of disagreement. Liberals are those who rate themselves 1, 2, or 3 on the 7-point scale; moderates are those who rate themselves 4; and conservatives are those who rate themselves 5, 6, or 7. The hypothesis is that conservatives will be more likely to voice conservative objections than liberals will be to raise liberal objections; furthermore liberals will be more likely than conservatives never to have disagreed. The notion here is that conservatives have been taught by conservative, strict parents to reject the allegedly indecent messages of the popular culture, whereas liberals are likely to have been taught the value of tolerance and openness by nurturing parents. Limited exposure of conservatives to the entertainment media is expected to render more durable their preexisting conservatism, whereas liberals are taught to take in as many influences as possible and sort them out using their own standards. Table 4.2 shows the relationship between self-reported ideology and the ideological perspective of disagreement with movies among U.S. respondents.

Table 4.2: Ideology and Orientation of Disagreement with Movies, U.S. Respondents Only

Perspective	Liberal	Moderate	Conservative	Totals
Liberal	10.7%	5.5%	6.6%	7.6%
Conservative	3.0%	2.6%	12.5%	5.0%

table continued on next page

Never Disagreed	27.8%	42.3%	33.6%	38.7%
Disagreed/Did not Say Why or Un-definable	47.6%	49.6%	46.7%	48.2%
Totals	100.0%	100.0%	100.0%	100.0%

Chi-square (6) = 29.034, sig. (two-tailed = .000)

Conservatives are slightly more likely to disagree with the movies from the conservative perspective than liberals are to disagree from the liberal perspective. This result is as expected. Furthermore, liberals are a bit more likely than conservatives never to have disagreed with the message of a movie, which is also as expected. Moreover, moderates are the most likely never to have disagreed, and this is as expected as well because moderates may be more likely than others not to have very well-founded political beliefs, and thus they find little to disagree with anywhere.

These data indicate the existence of a disaffected group of conservative youths who disagree with the sociopolitical themes in movies and may become hardened in their conservatism by exposure to messages with which they disagree, and a group of liberals who are more selective and can take or leave the messages of movies. Perhaps most interestingly and troublingly, there is a group of youths who describe themselves as moderate and in fact may not have any well-formed sociopolitical beliefs and so find little to object to in the popular culture, or the remainder of the political culture in general. Certainly future research ought to focus on the development of political attitudes in these young people who have theoretically experienced the socialization impact of parents, churches, schools, peers, news, and entertainment media and come away with very little in terms of coherent ideology to show for it.

Political Knowledge

What is the relationship between movie viewing and political knowledge? Political knowledge has been measured here by asking U.S. respondents to identify the office or political position held by a number of political figures in the U.S. system. The easiest to name is then-Vice-President Al Gore, whom 91.4% correctly identified. On the other extreme was Stephen Yokich, whom only 2.3% were able to identify correctly as the president of the United Auto Workers union. Summing the number of correct responses creates a rough and admittedly imprecise additive index of political knowledge where 0 indicates none correctly identified, and 11 indicates all correctly identified. The mean number correct for all respondents was 4.30 with a standard deviation of 1.99.

Are movies a source of information concerning the key figures of the U.S. political system? Alternatively, are they a source of misinformation? Those who spend relatively more time with movies ought to have a higher level of political knowledge than others. This indeed appears to be the case. The only measure of movie use is indirect. Does the respondent have a favorite movie? If so, then it is expected that the respondent is a more frequent viewer than if not. Because in order to develop a favorite movie, it is assumed one must view more movies. This assumption may not be true, but it is the only measure available. Those who remember a favorite movie have a mean political knowledge score of 4.35, whereas those who do not identify a favorite film have a score of 4.09. The difference, however, is not significant at traditional levels (one-tailed significance = .116).

Are U.S. respondents who have disagreed with the message of a movie more knowledgeable about politics? The hypothesis is that they are because disagreeing with the message indicates not only having seen movies but actually paying attention to their sociopolitical content. This appears to be the case. Those who have disagreed with the message of a film have a mean political knowledge score of 4.41, whereas those who have never disagreed have a mean score of 4.23. The difference is not significant at the .10 level (one-tailed significance = .135)

Finally, how about those U.S. respondents who BOTH remember a favorite movie and have disagreed with the message of one? The hypothesis is that their level of engagement with the films is the greatest and that they ought to have a higher level of political knowledge than those who either cannot remember a favorite film or who have never disagreed or both. In fact, those who both remember a favorite film and have disagreed with the message have a political knowledge level of 4.44, while the others have a score of 4.18. Furthermore, the difference is significant at the .05 level (one-tailed significance = .038).

The Influence of Actors[1]

Movie actors often take political stands outside their artistic works. Do these actions influence voters? Evidently Eddie Murphy, an actor not known as much of an activist, believes so. In 1992 he indicated that he did not like the nominees for president, and thus refused to vote. "If I were to vote for someone and publicly support them, it could sway how somebody else votes," he said ("Boycotting the booth," USA Today, 3 November 1992, D-2). In terms of actors who do take political stands, Bruce Willis is a well-known Republican, as is Arnold Schwarzenegger. Well-known Democrats and liberals include many of the acting Baldwin family, Kim Basinger, Whoopi Goldberg, Robert Redford and so on. Do stars influence their young fans to take ideological positions similar to their own? This is a very difficult matter to examine scientifically. For one thing, the data show only young people's perceptions of the ideology

---

1   This analysis is performed for U.S. respondents only because Canadian, Irish and U.K. respondents were not asked to rate the ideology of any actors.

and issue positions of actors, not necessarily their actual positions. To the extent that there is a degree of consensus among young people about an actor's ideology, we can take that consensus as an actor's actual position. The best approach may be the simplest, in that it results in the smallest error. The actors' true positions will be presumed to be the mean value of young Americans' perceptions of that actor.

In the survey, U.S. respondents were asked to rate several actors and musicians on the seven-point ideology scale. Table 4.3 indicates the mean perception of the ideologies for several famous movie actors. Arnold Schwarzenegger is the star of many action films and a Republican. Jim Carrey is one of the most popular comedic actors in the U.S. today, but he does not advertise his ideology or partisanship. Bruce Willis is an action movie star and a Republican. Will Smith is an African American comedic and dramatic actor who also does not advertise his politics. As the table shows, young people's perceptions generally correspond well to reality. Schwarzenegger is considered the most conservative, with Bruce Willis a close second. Jim Carrey is perceived as liberal, which may reflect either projection of respondents' ideology onto the actor or a general perception of the liberalness, especially in terms of life-style, of Hollywood in general. Finally Will Smith is perceived as liberal. This may be more a measure of white respondents' perceptions of the politics of African Americans than Smith's actual ideology.

Table 4.3: Perception of Ideologies of Actors, U.S. Respondents Only

Actor	Mean	n	Std. Dev.
Schwarzenegger	4.43	488	1.46
Willis	3.37	464	1.56
Smith	2.93	491	1.31
Carrrey	2.85	468	1.49

The most interesting relationship to think about here is the relative influence of parents and movie actors. Correlation analyses showed small but significant relationships between U.S. respondents' ideology and their perceptions of the ideologies of each actor, with the exception of Schwarzenegger. The correlations with both mothers and fathers were larger though. The best way to sort out these influences is to compare respondents' self-placement on the seven-point scale with each parent and with several actors, and to control for race. Then absolute distances between respondents and parents can be measured, and from respondents and actors. An interesting and relevant finding would be if there were any U.S. respondents who placed themselves closer to the actors than their mother, because in all cases and races the relationships between respondent and mother were the strongest. If so, it is possible for some youths that actors are a greater influence over their ideology than parents. Table 4.4 indicates the results of this analysis.

Table 4.4: Youths' Ideological Positioning Relative to Mother and Various Actors, U.S. Respondents Only

	Caucasians	African Americans
Youths Closer to Arnold Schwarzenegger Than Mother	20.9%	13.0%
Youths Closer to Jim Carrey Than Mother	23.2%	21.6%
Youths Closer to Will Smith Than Mother	24.0%	21.1%
Youths Closer to Bruce Willis Than Mother	28.5%	18.1%

As the table indicates, 20.9% of Caucasian youths and 13.0% of African Americans place themselves closer to Schwarzenegger than their own mothers. About 23.2% of whites place themselves closer to Jim Carrey than mom, while 21.6% of blacks do so. Interestingly, 24% of white youths place themselves closer to Will Smith than their mothers, while only 21.2% of black youths do the same thing. Finally, a whopping 28.5% of whites place themselves closer to Bruce Willis, while only 18.1% of blacks do so. Some interesting trends are evident here. First, the actor who has the most white youths close to him is Bruce Willis, whereas Jim Carrey takes top honors for African Americans, although Will Smith is a close second. The lack of political statements by Carrey and Smith suggests projection. Interesting though is that more whites place themselves closer to Will Smith, an African American, than do black youths. Perhaps this is part of the phenomenon of white youths' finding a certain cache in associating themselves with African American and urban culture in general.

Movies and Politics in the U.S.

There are some interesting findings with regard to the political influence of movies. Moreover, the data and conclusions inspire some informed speculation as well. First, young people do watch movies. The movies they watch are Hollywood blockbusters. There are many young people who have disagreed with the message of a film who see a clash between the values portrayed on the screen and their own values. Movies, it appears, reinforce preexisting values of youths raised in liberal home environments, generating greater tolerance among those already inclined to support the message; however, among youths raised in conservative home environments, the movies probably harden conservative views among those already inclined to support such positions. Furthermore, commitment to movie-watching also seems to correlate with slightly increased political knowledge.

Youths who are social conservatives are often repelled by the messages they witness in films, and they either oppose or disregard them. Although they watch movies and detect political messages, they reject them. They have well-founded political opinions on life-style, culture wars issues. When those beliefs are challenged by movies, they recoil against the film and harden their attitudes. Thus their pre-existing attitudes are actually made more durable by messages contradictory to their values. Perhaps these youths will change their minds after more repeated exposure and exposure to the same message from other agents of popular culture, combined with distancing from parents and the church.

Youths raised in liberal homes are probably more likely to have experienced conflicting values in their contacts with various agents of political socialization. They may be less influenced by the messages of movies. For example, young women have had the opportunity to observe adult women in all kinds of social roles (e.g., homemaker, career woman) both in real life and fictitiously and so may be less disturbed than men at women's nontraditional portrayal in movies. It is young men, after all, who are the most threatened by these portrayals because they see autonomous nontraditional females as a threat.

That a number of youths, both black and white, are willing to place themselves ideologically closer to some actors than their mothers might tell us a number of things. First, it might mean that they are projecting their ideology onto the actors. Undoubtedly in some cases this is true. However, it might mean that many parents realize their children will confront a myriad of ethical and political choices and that it is important that they be able to make their own informed choices. Some might call this weak parenting. At a younger age youths more closely identify with their parents, but as they move away from home and K-12 schools and perhaps even the church, other agents of socialization (like the movies) step in to replace traditional ones. Of course, a longitudinal study is needed to determine the changes in relative influence of different agents of socialization as youths grow older. It is clear that parental influence wanes, but it is much less clear what influences replace that of parents.

Also, although the survey does not allow us to quantify the phenomenon in the same way as with many important relationships in this book, movies increasingly provide the metaphors that help us understand political events. Never was that fact made more clear than when Americans first began discussing the 11 September 2001 terrorist attacks on the Pentagon and World Trade Centers. Many Americans' initial reaction to the attacks was to say that they looked "just like a movie." It is not surprising, given the horror and unprecedented nature of the attacks, that Americans' frame of reference was blockbuster, Hollywood fiction. Certainly the terrorists understood this, too. As Neal Gabler put it, "this was the terrorists' own real-life disaster movie— bigger than 'Independence Day' or 'Godzilla'or 'Armageddon'" (*New York Times*, 16 September 2001, section 4, p. 2).

According to Gabler, the terrorists intended the delay between the first and second plane's crashing into the twin towers to allow news cameras to get in place and capture the awful images. Only with wide dissemination would the terror the attackers intended successfully spread across the country. As Gabler argues, once Americans saw the planes crash, they would imagine the events leading up to the crash in technicolor terror through a reservoir of images implanted in their minds by Hollywood. Because of our steady diet of Hollywood horror, the terrorists could count on Americans' imagining the terrorists, "packing the knives in their bags, driving to the airports, boarding planes and, finally, jumping from their seats, killing the flight attendants and commandeering the planes." Of course, in the movies the terrorists ultimately fail to destroy America, and that fact may provide some comfort to Americans as they interpret the events of 11 September through the lens of Hollywood.

Moreover, in thinking about the plane that failed to reach the terrorists' intended target and crashed in Pennsylvania, Americans' self-image and confidence was improved by reliance on movie metaphors as well. While the public wondered why that plane crashed and U.S. military officials denied that it had been shot down by the U.S. Air Force (even though President Bush had given the order to shoot down threatening civilian airplanes) another, more comforting story developed that several passengers on the plane struggled with the hijackers and that eventually caused the plane to crash far away from its intended target. Of course Hollywood movies are full of images of rugged Americans taking matters into their own hands. From John Wayne westerns to Rambo, American minds have a wealth of images of tough Americans doing the right thing when outlaws attack the innocent. While we will never know with certainty the exact circumstances surrounding why that plane crashed in rural Pennsylvania, and there is no evidence that the Air Force brought it down, the belief that heroic Americans fought back against the terrorists and sacrificed their own lives so that others might live is a comfort made possible in no small part by the images provided by American cinema.

Movies and Politics: U.K., Ireland and Canada

The most interesting thing to think about with regard to how British and Irish youths might be influenced by movies is to examine the relationship between the nationality of the production (as supplied by the Internet Movie Data Base or IMDB) and youths' having agreed or disagreed with something in the film. If our belief in the existence of a more subtle theory of cultural imperialism is correct, the likelihood of a U.S. film being disagreed with ought to be greater than the probability of a U.S. production being agreed with. For the purposes of this analysis, Irish and U.K. respondents are combined. In total, U.K. and Irish respondents mentioned 147 films with which they agreed. Naturally, many individual films were mentioned more than once. Of movie titles agreed with, an amazing 89.1% are U.S. productions. There were 54 mentions of film titles with a theme the respondents disagreed with, including, again, many films mentioned more than once. Of these, 94.4% were U.S. productions. While this difference is not huge, it does support our hypothesis that Irish and U.K. respondents would be more likely to disagree with an American production than agree with one. Perhaps more importantly, the figures demonstrate the extent to which Hollywood movies permeate other English-speaking cultures.[2]

---

2   Almost all of the popular movies in Canada are foreign—mainly U.S.—productions, so seeking differences in the nationality of the movies agreed with or disagreed with is unlikely to yield any significant results.

5

The Political Influence of Entertainment Television

It is not unreasonable to expect entertainment television to influence the sociopolitical beliefs of young people. The review of previous research indicates that both entertainment and news television have the power to influence young people's attitudes in a number of important political and moral spheres. Besides this evidence, another reason to expect entertainment television to influence young people's political values is the fact that young people watch more entertainment programming than they watch the news. U.S. respondents to the questionnaire on which this research is based report watching the news on television an average of only 3.8 days per week (and because higher amounts of news-watching is a socially acceptable answer to the question, this is probably an overestimate), whereas 49.8 percent report watching more than two hours per day of entertainment television (for a good analysis of American youths' nonnews watching habits see Stephen Earl Bennett 1998). This means at a minimum the American respondents to the survey watch 14 hours per week of entertainment programming. This level of commitment and contact with any potential agent of socialization is certain to increase the potential for that agent to exert influence.

The plurality of Irish respondents (32.9%) report watching between one and two hours per day of entertainment television; 31.6% admit to watching between two and three hours. Among U.K. youths, 32.9% report watching between one and two hours, but 32% report watching less than an hour per day. Among Canadian respondents, 37% report watching between an hour and two of entertainment TV per day, while 34.1% report less than an hour per day. Still, among respondents from all of the countries in our samples, sufficiently large quantities of TV are being watched to justify inquiry into the impact of its sociopolitical messages on young people.

Because the theory of cultural imperialism informs our inquiry into Canadian, U.K. and Irish responses to the popular culture's political content, participants in the surveys from those countries were asked how often they watched their national stations. Very small numbers of respondents answered that they watched the national stations either all or none of the time, but there is sufficient diversity in the responses to use this variable later in the analysis of TV's effects on their political beliefs.

Next, both television news and entertainment programming often present compellingly realistic political and moral situations to viewers. In this way they both act at least as catalysts for thinking about important political issues. Both kinds of programming often choose one side over another in political controversies, and try to influence their viewers to choose that side. Moreover, if news commentators have as much influence as previous research indicates they do, then it is not unreasonable to suspect that television actors, either in their personal statements or performances, sometimes try to influence the public's beliefs and are at least occasionally successful. Moreover, because of their fame, entertainers are often courted by political parties to run for office, and there have been some notable political successes among television actors. Fred Grandy, who played "Gopher" on *The Love Boat* served in the U.S. House of Representatives from his home state of Iowa. Ben Jones, who played Cooter on *The Dukes of Hazzard* also served in the House. Fred Thompson, who acted in TV's *Law and Order* among other projects, represented Tennessee in the Senate from 1994 to 2003, and made a short-lived bid for the Presidency during the 2007–2008 Republican primary season. Rob Reiner, who played Mike Stivic ("The Meathead") on *All in the Family* has not run for office himself, but has been very active in many liberal causes and campaigns. Of course B-movie actor and television pitchman Ronald Reagan parlayed his stardom into terms as California Governor and U.S. President.

In contrast to most movies, television programs (sometimes even specific episodes) are viewed repeatedly. Viewers come to know the characters and the actors who perform on their favorite programs. When television programs are at the height of their popularity viewers frequently discuss twists and turns of the plots over coffee at work. Gatherings of friends often devolve into discussions of what this television character did to that one on last night's episode. The characters become important parts of viewers' lives. It is not as if the characters are perceived as real by viewers, but they are not seen as purely fictional either. Moreover networks now frequently sell myriad products that relate to popular programs. They market clothing, books about families and relationships by the shows' stars, computer games, posters, home appliances, and so on. A cookbook based on the phenomenally popular show *Friends* was published, and it sold very well. It is instructive that a cookbook was published because cooking and entertaining are activities shared with actual friends and family. The producers of the show saw a golden opportunity to profit from the melding of the virtual friends of the television series with the real friends of the fans of the show.

Frequency of contact is traditionally thought to improve the chances of a socialization agent's having an impact, therefore parents and schools are the most significant, primary agents of socialization. From the simplest propaganda models to more sophisticated theories of influence and learning, scholars agree that repetition of even flagrantly false or controversial messages can cause individuals to believe in them. Certainly entertainment television programming's structure lends itself to this possibility. Since entertainment programming is fiction, viewers are relaxed and inclined to suspend their suspicions, lending greater credibility to political messages than the same message would possess if presented on the news, where viewers retain their skepticism.

The final reason why entertainment television is likely to influence the political beliefs of young people is because television entertainment programming often has contained both overt and less obvious political messages. Famously, the writers of *Murphy Brown* had their main character decide to have a child out of wedlock, leading to criticism from then Vice-President Dan Quayle. The characters on the program then responded to Quayle's criticism. The police drama *N.Y.P.D. Blue* frequently explored issues of police behavior, criminal justice, and racism. The CBS drama *Family Law* presented an episode with a strong anti-death penalty message. The episode also criticized the modern Democratic Party for excessive conservatism. These examples (and there are hundreds of others) show that current entertainment television is not in its entirety devoid of political messages. Politics, especially politics as contemporary youths define the term, frequently occur on entertainment television, for example when conflicts regarding the social consequences of personal choices are featured. The question remains, however, whether or not youths are influenced by the political content of entertainment television.

Political Influence of Entertainment Television: Culture Wars Again

Since the inception of television, scholars have debated whether or not this medium can perform any socially valuable function. Perhaps the most interesting recent perspective on this issue comes from Neil Postman in his work *Amusing Ourselves to Death* (1985). Postman argues that television cannot educate people, but that it can still perform a socially useful function by doing what it does best: presenting eye-candy and fluff entertainment. He argues that because television is a visual medium it is foolish to expect it to present logical arguments, for which the linear written form of language is best suited. Postman does not mean this assessment cynically. In limited doses he believes there is nothing wrong with accepting that television can only entertain, not educate. He believes we ought to enjoy programming and not expect so much of the medium.

Now, of course, this is not the prevailing belief of government or entertainment executives, especially regarding cable programming. The History Channel, Arts and Entertainment, and C-Span are just a few of the public and for-profit networks whose creators believe that television can educate, inform, and perhaps persuade. If Postman is right then these channels cannot perform these functions, even if people view them regularly. The present data indicate that with respect to youths not even that is occurring.

Postman's theory, and the non-viewing of news and public affairs channels by young Americans, does not necessarily preclude the possibility of political influence by entertainment programming, however. Postman merely argues that sustained, intelligent argument is impossible through television. This does not mean that individuals' attitudes, beliefs, and actions cannot be shaped by television, in fact it makes it seem more likely because television images operate on the emotional level. For example, there is the well-known story of reporter Lesley Stahl's attempt to criticize Reagan administration policies in a piece where the narration was critical but the images positive. After the report was aired, an administration official thanked Stahl for the piece because the positive nature of the images more than outweighed the negative connotation of the words.

Moreover, if the public is not motivated by emotional or sexual appeals then why would companies spend tens of billions of dollars per year on Madison Avenue, trying to influence what products Americans think they need? Because intelligent argument is not possible does not mean that less rational or conscious processes of influence are not at work.

Entertainment television's presentation of political events certainly may play agenda-setting, framing, and priming roles in the political worlds of its young viewers. Because they watch so much television, it is not unreasonable to suspect that the issues entertainment television selects to present may become the issues viewed as significant by young viewers. Moreover, the obvious positions taken in certain programs and by popular actors may influence young people to take similar views, and to construct their opinions through reference to political reality as mediated by entertainment television. Young people may be encouraged to look at political issues through the frameworks presented by entertainment television, with regard to lifestyle politics issues. For example, if network programs consistently present gay characters in a positive light, the conservative and equally tenable position that homosexuality is an unnatural and immoral aberration will instead appear controversial and aberrant.

Young people today think about politics in ways different from the traditional political science conceptualization. They define liberalism and conservatism more in terms of lifestyle and personal freedom than in terms of the budget, federalism, foreign policy, and so on (see Inglehart, 1990a, 1990b, and 1997) As myriad scholars, politicians and demagogues have argued, there is a culture war occurring in the U.S. (e.g., Bork, 1997; Gitlin 1995; Medved 1993; 1998). Mainly, it is a battle to shape the values of American youths and their positions on a wide variety of social issues including abortion, homosexuality, violence, women's role, drug use, promiscuity, single parenting, and other related issues. Will those values be traditional conservative ones or will those values be more contemporary, liberal ones?

The Political Influence of Exposure to Entertainment Television

There are two good ways to determine the political influence of entertainment television. The first relates to overall levels of use. Researchers can read about and watch the programs rated as favorites (or the programs that consistently score the highest in the ratings) and think about and rank their political content on standard scales. Then we can correlate overall amounts of entertainment television viewing with different ideological and issue positions of young people.

Furthermore, we can attempt to isolate the influence of some of the more popular programs by first reading about then watching them with an eye for their sociopolitical messages. Then we can draw correlations and inferences concerning the relationships between the messages of the shows and the holding of similar views by young fans. Both methods are utilized in this chapter.

As demonstrated by the discussion of recent and popular entertainment television above, there is a tolerant, accepting liberalism prevalent in the moral, ethical, and political content of the genre. Therefore, those who spend relatively more time with television ought to be more tolerant on lifestyle liberalism issues. Table 5.1 shows the correlations between hours per day spent watching entertainment television and various political attitudes.

Table 5.1: Kendall's Tau-c Correlations between TV Use and Selected Variables, U.S. Respondents*

Variable	Tau-c	Sig. (one-tailed)
Abortion	.034	.133
Women's Equality	.016	.297
Newer Lifestyles	.041	.099
Moral Relativism	.012	.352
Homosexuality as Acceptable	-.059	.029
Ideology	-.011	.366
Number of Corrupt Officials	.034	.138

*See appendix for wording of questions

The correlations generally were small and statistically insignificant. There is, however, a small negative and statistically significant relationship between the number of hours per day of entertainment television watched and support for the morality of homosexuality (more television watching means less support for the morality of homosexuality). Moreover, greater television watching indicates slightly more agreement with the belief that newer lifestyles contribute to the breakdown of society. These findings are at best mixed, but suggest a slight tendency of more conservative lifestyle views. This is a puzzle.

Does watching more entertainment television make U.S. youths more conservative? If so, why? One possible explanation is that some young Americans are disgusted with what they see as lax moral standards on television and consequently become more conservative in reaction against it. The political learning works in the following way. Young people already have political attitudes when they watch television. For the argument, let us assume that these are relatively conservative views concerning lifestyle issues—the views of a youth raised in a strict parent household. The opposite of their position is presented in the programming. Rather than change their minds, increased exposure hardens already conservative views. Liberals likely become more liberal or are not influenced at all.

In terms of homosexuality, this may be part of the explanation. Among those U.S. respondents who define themselves as liberal, there is a tau-c correlation between entertainment television use and support for the morality of homosexuality of -.136 (one-tailed sig. = .027). For conservatives the correlation is .061 (one-tailed sig. = .171). Thus, it appears that repeated exposure to entertainment television among self-identified liberals actually influences them to become less tolerant of homosexual lifestyles, whereas for conservatives it has no influence. The conservative finding makes sense. The liberal result does not.

The tau-c correlation between beliefs about women's roles and entertainment television use among self-identified U.S. liberals is .077 (one-tailed sig. = .050). This means increased television use correlates with an increased belief that women's place is in the home. Again there is no relationship among U.S. conservatives. The conservative finding makes more theoretical sense than the liberal finding.

In terms of newer lifestyles contributing to the breakdown of society, the relationships are again problematic. Among self-identified American liberals, the tau-c correlation between the belief that newer lifestyles contribute to the breakdown of society and entertainment television use is .105 (one-tailed sig. = .026). Thus, increased entertainment television use correlates with an increasingly strong belief that newer lifestyles contribute to the breakdown of society. Among conservatives the relationship is -.092 (one-tailed sig. = .084). Thus, it appears that entertainment television use influences young conservatives to become more tolerant of newer lifestyles and young liberals to become less tolerant. Neither of these relationships makes much theoretical sense. However, perhaps among liberals there is a saturation effect with the tolerant messages of television. Enough may be enough after a while, and liberals recoil against that with which they formerly agreed. Among conservatives, it may be that enough repeated exposure to entertainment television may in some cases weaken their conservatism. There may be a reason for conservatives to fear the liberalizing effects of television.

Interestingly, in terms of abortion, U.S. conservatives' views become more liberal with increased entertainment television use (tau-c = .144, one tailed sig. = .007), whereas for self-identified liberals there is no impact.

Among the Canadian respondents there was not a single statistically significant correlation between increased exposure to entertainment television and any of a myriad of political belief questions that were asked. The same was true for Irish and U.K. respondents.

However, just measuring relationships between entertainment television use and belief components of ideology might not tell the entire story. For example, there is a possibility that despite all the contrary evidence and analysis, entertainment television by and large actually presents conservative instead of liberal messages. In terms of one of the programs most associated with progressivism, *The Simpsons*, Cantor (1999) makes the claim that the show actually presents a conservative message. His is one of very few articles to make this sort of claim, however. More recently, Brian Anderson argued in a book entitled *South Park Conservatives* (2005) that the cartoon from the title is part of the new conservative media including talk radio, Fox News, and right wing blogs that have counterbalanced what he believes to have been a vast left wing conspiracy in the mainstream media. *South Park* follows the (mis)adventures of several foul-mouthed fourth graders and has savaged such liberal icons as Bono, Al Gore, and Barbara Streisand, as well as criticizing environmentalists, anti-smoking crusaders and voter registration drives.

More likely, though, using entertainment television might be a necessary but not sufficient condition for political influence to occur. Many young people may have the television on when performing other tasks like homework or household chores. This type of exposure is unlikely to exert much influence on their political beliefs because there is little emotional investment along with the time spent. Perhaps young people must actively engage with the program, its characters, and plots for them to have an effect. The next thing to look at is the relationship between preference for particular programs and beliefs.

Let's think again about the importance of disagreement with the sociopolitical content of entertainment television. In chapter 3 we saw which young U.S. respondents were more likely to disagree with television's messages. To investigate this issue in more depth the messages young people have disagreed with in television can be categorized by their ideological perspective. A liberal would disagree with depictions of violence, racism, and traditional roles for women. A conservative would disagree with anti-religion, pro-homosexuality, and the glorification of premarital sex, promiscuity, and nudity. Of course, some youths have never disagreed with a television program. A good test of the theory of socialization that informs this work is to look at the ideological perspective of the messages of television programs disagreed with by U.S. youths. The following table represents the distribution of ideological perspectives taken against television.

Table 5.2 : Ideological Perspective of Themes Disagreed with in TV Programs, U.S. Respondents

Perspective	Percent	n
Liberal	5.8	39
Conservative	9.1	61
Have Not Disagreed	39.4	265
Disagreed/Did Not Say Why	41.8	281
Disagreed/Undefinable	4.0	27
Totals	100.0	673

Clearly most youths did not supply ideologically grounded reasons for their disagreement with a television program. Nevertheless, among those who did, conservative perspectives outnumber liberal ones by nearly a two-to-one margin. This is as expected. Conservatives ought to have more to disagree with in entertainment television than others. Is there a relationship between youths' self-reported ideologies and the ideological perspective of disagreement? It is likely that there is. Conservatives are more likely to disagree from a conservative perspective than liberals are to disagree along liberal lines, and liberals will be more likely than conservatives never to have disagreed. This tests the strict versus nurturing parent model because conservatives are taught by strict parents to reject the indecent messages of the popular culture, whereas liberals are taught the value of tolerance. Limited exposure of conservatives to the entertainment media likely hardens their preexisting conservatism, whereas liberals are taught to take in many influences and sort them using their own standards. Table 5.3 shows the relationship between respondent ideology and the ideological perspective of their disagreement with entertainment television.

Table 5.3: Ideology and Orientation of Disagreement with Television, U.S. Respondents

Perspective	Liberal	Moderate	Conservative	Totals
Liberal	9.2%	4.1%	3.9%	5.9%
Conservative	35.7%	5.6%	19.7%	9.0%
Never Disagreed	41.2%	41.9%	30.9%	39.1%
Disagreed/Did Not Say Why or Undefinable	43.8%	48.3%	45.4%	46.1%
Totals	100.0%	100.0%	100.0%	100.0%

Chi-square (6) = 36.367, sig. (two-tailed = .000)

As table 5.3 demonstrates, 41.2% of self-described liberals in the U.S. sample have never disagreed with the message of a TV show, whereas only 30.9% of conservatives report this. These data confirm the hypothesis that liberals are more tolerant of the popular media and thus treat them like any other influence. Moreover, conservatives are about five times more likely to disagree with a TV show from the conservative perspective, whereas liberals are only slightly more likely to disagree from the liberal perspective. Hence, there is a cadre of conservative youths who react negatively to the sociopolitical messages of entertainment television.

The Political Influence of Television Preferences

Based on television preference, it might be expected that there would be ideological or issue position differences between fans of the program and nonfans, especially if the programs are perceived by young viewers as having something to say about morality and politics. In other words, the audience in general could be expected to be turned off by attitudes with which they disagree, and supportive of presentations of attitudes with which they agree. It is expected that fans of the programs to have their attitudes strengthened when the show agrees with their positions, and to be more likely to change attitudes when they are continuously exposed to a show that contradicts their values. As indicated in chapter three, the top six U.S. programs among the respondents are *Seinfeld, E.R., Party of Five, Beverly Hills 90210, The Simpsons,* and *Sportscenter.*

The Simpsons, *Conformism, and Gay Rights*

One of the most political shows to make the favorites list is *The Simpsons.* Interpreting the overall political ideology of *The Simpsons* is very difficult (see Cantor, 1999 for an analysis of the show as conservative; for an overall view of the show through the lens of George Meyer, one of its major writers, see Owen, 2000; for a fascinating look at the show from the European perspective, see Ingle, 2000, who says, "The series' subtext is to subvert all traditional American images" (9) The program certainly takes on political, moral, and social issues frequently. The problem is the relatively fragmented and scattered nature of the positions taken on the issues. The reason for this is that the program is a satire, which means that multiple interpretations are not only possible, but probably encouraged by the writers. Liberals certainly would be justified in believing that the writers of the program are kindred spirits. However, the opposite interpretation is possible, too. For example, in the 1997 season, *The Simpsons* introduced a homosexual character for one episode. Most viewers would recognize in fairly short order that the episode is a parable about tolerance and support for homosexuals' rights because only after the gay character saves Homer Simpson's life does Homer become tolerant. However, not all viewers who watch the program might get the message. Viewers not attuned to subtlety might think that the program's writers in the episode were attacking the gay lifestyle and making fun of homosexual men.

There is a relationship between preference for *The Simpsons* and attitudes toward homosexual rights, but the relationship is not in the direction one would expect based on an interpretation of the show's writers intentions. Whereas 71.4% of *Simpsons* fans disagree with the claim that homosexual lifestyles are morally acceptable, only 45% of nonfans hold this position (Chi-square(2) = 7.577, sig. (two-tailed) = .023).

The potential for audience confusion that comes from show's scattered approach to satire is a reasonable explanation for the "wrong" direction of this significant difference. Just as some people did not correctly interpret Bruce Springsteen's song "Born in the U.S.A.," a phenomenally popular song in 1984 (the eponymous album on which it appears has sold 15 million copies) that was seemingly blindly patriotic but in reality spoke to patriotism's irrelevance and danger to everyday working people's lives, not everyone understands the messages of tolerance toward gays from the writers of *The Simpsons*. From classics such as Thomas More's *Utopia* through contemporary works, it has been fairly standard for writers to use subtlety and satire to hide their messages from authorities and censors. Thomas More created a fictional island to criticize life in England during the 1500s and simultaneously keep his head on his shoulders. Springsteen wrote a song whose chorus appeared blindly patriotic, but whose verses told the story of despair of an unemployed Vietnam veteran. Perhaps *The Simpsons* writers, both from the interest of writing funny material and not hitting viewers over the head with obvious political messages, bury their true opinions under a mound of satire.

Another politically significant message of *The Simpsons* is defiance of all authority. When the show was at the peak of its popularity, the main character Bart Simpson was the reason. He is an extremely mouthy, defiant, and free-spirited ten-year-old. He has been far and away the most frequently appearing character on *Simpsons* merchandise, and has clearly been the most popular character (he still endorses more products in television commercials than the other characters). It is expected that young fans of the program will be influenced by the defiance of this character and therefore to be more likely to oppose fitting in with others, and instead to believe that it is better to do what one thinks is right. This expectation is confirmed by the data.

Simpsons fans are more likely than nonfans of the program to believe it is better to conduct one's life according to one's own standards, rather than fitting in. Whereas 85.1% of nonfans hold this position, a whopping 96.3% of fans do (Chi-Square(1) = 2.628, sig. (two-tailed) = .105). Obviously there are numerous other factors that might influence the selection of this position on individualism. In other words, perhaps fans of the program are more defiant and individualistic before they watch the show. If this attribute indeed applies, then watching *The Simpsons* might reinforce these attitudes of individualism. *Simpsons* fans are more individualistic than others. It appears that in some cases the media may at least confirm more liberal attitudes in those who already have them, or may in fact help create these attitudes in those without them. Moreover, there are political consequences of conformism. When asked if they planned to vote in the 1998 elections, 88.2% of those who believed in being true to one's self asserted they planned to vote, whereas only 83.7% of conformists said they planned to vote. Whereas the difference was not statistically significant (chi-square (2) = 1.552, sig. (one-tailed) = .107), the relationship may still be meaningful.

E.R., *Homosexuality, and Cynicism*

The second most popular program might have political influence as well. As suggested earlier, *E.R.* is a very political program (for an analysis of the show from both the perspective of social relevance and contribution to progress in entertainment programming see Meisler 1995). First, their position on homosexual rights is clearly supportive because of the positive light in which they present gay and lesbian characters. It is expected that fans of the program will be more supportive of the morality of homosexual lifestyles. This is in fact the case. Whereas 43.1% of *E.R.* fans agree that homosexuality is morally acceptable, only 34.1% of nonfans hold this position. However, the relationship is not statistically significant (chi-square = 2.644, sig. (one-tailed) = .134). Another way to measure the difference is to compare the means on the five-point scale (where five represents strong agreement with the belief that homosexual lifestyles are morally acceptable and one represents strong disagreement). For *E.R.* fans the mean is 3.03, whereas for nonfans the mean is 2.69. This .34 point difference is significant at the .043 (one-tailed) level.

Importantly, the hospital where the characters of *E.R.* work is a county hospital. Thus the characters are public employees and represent a public service to the show's viewers. Few of the characters are completely unsympathetic. By and large, the major protagonists are hard-working, committed doctors and nurses who put their often poor and oppressed patients' interests above their own. Even the most unsympathetic character is still a terrific surgeon who saves his patients with his skills as a surgeon whereas antagonizing the more sympathetic characters with acerbic personal manner and budget-consciousness. Moreover, this is the tradition in entertainment media. George Gerbner pointed out that good business characters on prime-time outnumbered bad ones by a rate of two to one, whereas for police the ratio was 12 to one, and for physicians it was 16 to one (in Gitlin 1983, 268). All professionals have been presented in a positive light, but physicians receive especially favorable coverage.

Fans of the program are expected to be less cynical about the motives of public official and are more likely to believe that the government is run for the interests of all rather than a few big interests. The data indicate that this is in fact the case. Whereas 38.3% of *E.R.* fans believe the government is run for the benefit of all, only 22.7% of nonfans hold this hopeful position (Chi-square (1) = 5.768, Sig. (one-tailed) = .008). *E.R.* fans are significantly more likely than nonfans to believe that the government is run for the benefit of all. This is at least in part due to the influence of the benevolent public servants presented on the program. Also, whereas significantly more women report *E.R.* as their favorite program, it is not gender that predicts position on the question of cynicism because there is no statistically significant relationship between gender and belief about in whose interest the government is run.

Sexy television, Women, and Morality

Several programs such as *Party Of Five*, *Beverly Hills 90210*, and *Days of Our Lives* have been criticized for their excessive and promiscuous sexuality. Differences of opinions on matters of sexuality and women's equality are expected between fans of these shows and nonfans. On placement on the seven-point scale of women's equality (where one represents support for complete equality) fans of these three programs are almost .50 of a point lower than nonfans (1.42 for fans, 1.91 for non fans) and the difference is significant at the .002 level. Fans of these sexy programs are more supportive of women's equality than nonfans. However, interpretation of this result ought to be tempered by the fact that of the 81 respondents who rate one of these shows as their favorite, 71 are women. The real test of the influence of these programs is the difference of opinion between women fans of these programs, and women nonfans. Results for these calculations are presented in Table 5.4. It is apparent that women who rate sexy daytime and prime-time soap operas as their favorite are more supportive of women's equality.

Table 5.4: Preference for "Sexy" Television Programs and Attitudes toward Women's Equal Roles*

Variable	Mean for Women Who Rate Sexy Programs as Favorite	Mean for Women Who Don't Rate Sexy Programs as Favorite	Sig. (one-tailed)
Women's Equality	1.30	1.50	.095

*Question: Recently there has been a lot of talk about women's rights. Some People feel that women should have an equal role with men in running business, industry, and government. Suppose these people are at one end of a scale at point 1. Others feel that a woman's place is in the home. Suppose these people are at the other end, at point 7. And, of course, some people have opinions somewhere between at points 2, 3, 4, 5, and 6. Where would you place yourself on this scale?

Watching such shows may also influence views about newer lifestyles and whether or not they are contributing to the breakdown of society. Table 5.5 shows the relationship. The fans of these shows, perhaps surprisingly, are more likely to agree that newer lifestyles are contributing to the breakdown of society. This apparent contradiction needs explanation.

Television often presents subtle and contradictory messages with regard to women (Douglas 1994). The female characters on the sexy programs mentioned above are usually very strong figures; they are also frequently promiscuous, sexually scheming, and likely to lie to get what they want. This dichotomy influences women's reaction to these shows. It appears that women who prefer these programs are positively moved by the strength of the women characters, but simultaneously offended by the lack of moral standards strong female characters demonstrate in doing whatever it seems to take in order to get what they want. This may indicate a relatively high level of sophistication among young women television viewers in that they are able to prefer some aspects of complicated characters whereas opposing others. Moreover, it is interesting that the characters are in fact complex, rather than merely one-sided caricatures. This may indicate that television writers are more willing now than in the past to create realistic female characters.

Table 5.5 : Sexy Television Preference and Support for the Claim That Newer Lifestyles Contribute to the Breakdown of Society* (Women Only)

	Nonfans	Fans	Totals
Disagree	29.9%	15.5%	27.4%
Neutral	21.6%	29.6%	22.9%
Agree	48.6%	54.9%	49.6%
Totals	100.0%	100.0%	100.0%

Chi-Square(2) = 6.590, sig. (two-tailed) = .037

*Question: The newer lifestyles are contributing to the breakdown of society.

Seinfeld and Conformism

Certain kinds of entertainment programming may promote a relativistic sociopolitical belief system as well. For example, Seinfeld has often been described as a program "about nothing." More precisely, however, there is almost no development of characters throughout the series. Moreover, the characters in general are self-serving, greedy, and unlikely to show concern for others. The only ethical standards prevailing among the characters on the show are the values developed by the small circle of friends who serve as the center of the show's rather limited universe. Seinfeld is expected to promote conformism—that is, the belief that it is better to fit in with those around you rather than following your own perceptions of right and wrong. The data indicate, this in fact appears to be the case. Whereas 19.7% of Seinfeld fans believe it is better to fit in, only 13.9% of nonfans hold the conformist position (Chi-Square (1) = 1.476, sig. (one-tailed) = .112). Clearly there are myriad influences on so important a belief as conformism; however these results are clear. Seinfeld fans choose to go along with the group when presented with a conflict between the group's values and the individual's. Clearly the relationship is reciprocal. The program provides support for those who would refuse to abide by objective sociopolitical standards. Thus, for conservatives especially, this program must seem cynical, vapid, and mean-spirited—certainly not funny.

Sports Programming

Preference for sports programming might influence young people's sociopolitical beliefs as well. As Chomsky argues, sports programming promotes irrational attitudes of submission to authority (*Manufacturing Consent* 1993). Prisuta (1979) observes that high-school aged sports fans are more authoritarian, nationalistic, and conservative than other young Americans. Conversely, proponents of participation by young people in sports argue that it helps young people resist drug use and other forms of peer pressure as well as making them more religious, rule-abiding, patriotic Americans (for a comprehensive analysis of the arguments for and against the sociopolitical benefits of sports see Nimmo and Combs, 1990, chapter 6). Which position is correct? To test the influence of sports programming, respondents who listed Fox's *N.F.L. Sunday, American Gladiators, Golf's Greatest 18, Hockey Night in Canada, Monday Night Football, N.F.L. Countdown, N.F.L. Primetime, The Olympics, The Practical Sportsman, Sports Final Edition, Sportscenter, WCW Nitro,* or *WWF Raw* as their favorite television program have been defined here as fans of sports television. It appears that being a fan of sports programming predicts lower levels of conformity and a greater belief in following one's own sociopolitical standards. Table 5.6 demonstrates the results.

Table 5.6: Sports TV and Conformism*

	Sports Fans	Non-Sports Fans	Totals
Better to Fit In	6.7%	14.8%	14.5%
Use Own Standards	93.3%	85.2%	85.5%
Totals	100.0%	100.0%	100.0%

Chi-Square(1) = 1.540, sig. (one-tailed) = .108

*Question: Which of the following statements comes closer to your own views? You might agree to some extent with both, but we want to know which is CLOSER to your views. ONE, it is better to fit in with people around you; or TWO, it is better to conduct yourself according to your own standards even if it makes you stand out.

Again, these findings must be interpreted with some care, but it appears that sports programming encourages individualism rather than conformism. However, there is no significant relationship between being a fan of sports television and beliefs about flag burning, how many government officials are corrupt, or holding political beliefs that are more liberal than both parents. Conversely, sports fans are much more likely than nonsports fans to rate themselves as conservative (34.5% compared with 22.3%), but the relationship is not significant at traditional levels (chi-square (2) = 2.408, sig. (one-tailed) = .150). In addition, sports television fans are more prone to believe that women's place is in the home. On the seven-point scale mentioned above (where one represents gender equality) sports television fans score a mean of 2.35, whereas non-sports fans score 1.84. This .51 point difference is significant at the .018 (one-tailed) level.

In the Irish and U.K. surveys respondents were not asked to identify their favorite television program, so analysis such as that presented above is impossible. Moreover, the disparate findings suggest that another approach to the influence of television might yield more interesting findings for U.K., Irish, and Canadian respondents. This involves looking at entertainment TV use through the lens of cultural imperialism.

Canadian respondents were asked how often they viewed Canadian stations, as well as to rate various countries/provinces on the standard 100 degree temperature scale (where higher temperature ratings mean the individual feels more warmly about the place). There is a .232 Kendall's tau-b (sig (two-tailed) = .000) correlation between increased watching of Canadian stations and temperature rating of Quebec. Anglophone Canadians temperature rating increases from 33.1 degrees for those who never watch Canadian stations up to 61.4 degrees for those who watch Canadian stations most of the time. This is a very significant finding, because one of the missions of the Canadian Broadcasting Corporation is to promote unity by telling Canadian stories, and this is evidence they are succeeding at this.

While there was not a significant correlation between Canadian station dependence and ratings of Canada, the few who watch the least Canadian television, who say they watch Canadian stations none of the time, rate Canada at 76 degrees; those who watch Canadian stations most of the time give Canada 86.6 degrees. There was a Kendall's tau-b correlation of -.151 (sig. = .002) between Canadian station watching and U.S. temperature rating. Those who watch Canadian stations the least rate the U.S. at 51.7 degrees, while those who watch Canadian stations most of the time rate the U.S. at only 36.2 degrees.

Similar results obtain for the Irish and U.K. samples. Among Irish respondents, watching Irish stations more frequently leads to higher temperature ratings of Northern Ireland. Among U.K. respondents, increased viewing of U.K. stations correlates with higher temperature ratings of both the U.K. and Ireland. Watching local stations has no effect on Irish or U.K. respondents' ratings of the U.S.

Television Use, Other Media Use, and Political Activity

What influence ought entertainment television be expected to have on other political and social activities? It is not unreasonable to believe that the mere act of spending many hours per week in front of the television might influence one's political and social behaviors (Medved 1999). Watching entertainment television ought to correlate with decreased talking to others about politics. This reality is both a factor of time, as well as the passive nature of the medium. In other words, the more time one spends with entertainment television, the less one has to spend with other humans talking about politics. However, whereas people do not necessarily believe the people they see in television programs are real, they may in some ways replace time spent with other real humans with time spent with virtual friends on television. Finally, one gets good at activities one practices. If one practices throwing a baseball fast and accurately, one might become a good pitcher. If one practices speaking one's mind on the sociopolitical issues of the day one might become a good thinker and orator. Conversely, if one sits on one's couch for long periods of time staring at the antics of one's virtual friends on the idiot box, one gets good at that and therefore not good at baseball, oratory, or much else that requires action.

It is unclear what relationships to expect between entertainment television use and other media use, although one might expect negative relationships with newspaper reading and news television watching. Again this is in part a factor of time and a factor of practice. Table 5.7 shows the relationships between entertainment television use and three measures of spectator and participant politics.

Table 5.7: Kendall's Tau Correlations between Entertainment Television Use and Selected Variables, U.S. Respondents*

	Tau-c	Sig. (one-tailed)
Talking About Politics	-.070	.008
Reading the Newspaper	.004	.224
Watching TV News	.283	.000

See appendix for wording.

First, there is a significant and negative relationship between hours spent watching entertainment television and talking to family and friends about politics among U.S. respondents. Apparently, watching entertainment television detracts from conversation. Second, and unexpectedly, there is no relationship between entertainment television use and reading a newspaper. Third, as the number of hours of entertainment television watched increases, one watches more news programming as well. Apparently, some who watch entertainment television are also induced to watch news television, even though only the latter is correlated with political knowledge, which is measured on a fairly crude 11-point scale where a 0 indicates the inability to identify correctly any political leaders and 11 is the ability to identity each one. See appendix for list of leaders.

Perhaps the most interesting finding is the negative relationship between entertainment television use and talking to others about politics. It has long been suggested that television isolates viewers because people often watch television alone. Watching entertainment television makes it less likely that a person has both the motivation and the ability to talk to others. It is a passive activity. Although viewers watch and listen to other people, they do not interact with them, and they may even become less skilled in conversation, be it about politics or any other subject.

Similar relationships exist in the Canadian data. There is a significant and negative correlation between time spent with entertainment TV and time spent talking with family and friends about politics. There is a positive and significant relationship between news and entertainment TV use. Canadians were also asked about time spent looking at news sites on the internet, but there is no correlation between that variable and entertainment TV use. There are however, small and statistically significant correlations between time spent at news sites on the internet and time spent talking to others about politics, watching news on TV, and reading a newspaper. Evidently, some young people are just "news junkies" and utilize multiple sources for information.

Among Irish respondents, only watching news TV and entertainment TV were statistically significantly correlated. The same was the case for U.K. respondents. However, among U.K. respondents, time spent looking at news sites on the internet is positively and statistically significantly correlated with talking about politics with friends and family, reading a daily newspaper, and watching news on TV, again indicating the existence of a cadre of highly news-interested young people.

Race and the Influence of Television in the U.S.

Are there significant differences between Caucasian and African American youths in the amount of entertainment television used? Are there any effects from these differences? African Americans are members of a partly distinctive subculture in American society with respect to the popular media. Entertainment television use is measured in a four-point scale where 1 is less than one hour per day and 4 is more than 3 hours per day. African Americans average 2.95 on the scale, whereas Caucasians average 2.35. The difference is statistically significant at the .000+ level. Moreover, 36.6% of African Americans watch more than three hours of television per day, whereas only 19.5% of whites report watching this much television. Does this difference in quantity of entertainment television watched mean anything? Perhaps the influence of entertainment television on political knowledge depends on a threshold. That is, differing levels of use only become significant above a certain cutoff. Furthermore, perhaps blacks are more open to influence by television. Table 5.8 presents some interesting relationships.

Table 5.8: Tau Correlations between Entertainment Television Use and Selected Variables*

Variable	Blacks		Whites	
	Tau-c	Sig. (one-tailed)	Tau-c	Sig. (one-tailed)
Knowledge	.118	.031	-.012	.384

table continued on next page

Talking Politics	-.111	.045	-.078	.028
TV News	.223	.000	.262	.000
Newspaper	-.019	.388	.036	.192
	(n=153)		(n=432)	

See appendix for wording of questions.

These results indicate that among African Americans there is a positive and sig-nificant relationship between entertainment television use and political knowledge and watching news on television. Among African Americans, there is a stronger nega-tive relationship between entertainment television use and talking to others about politics. For whites, the most interesting relationships are the negative one between entertainment television use and talking about politics, and the positive but insignifi-cant one between TV use and reading a newspaper.

There are three possible explanations for these differences. African Americans may be more easily influenced by entertainment television. There is no obvious rea-son why this should be the case, however. Second, perhaps entertainment television use must first reach a certain minimal level by individuals before it becomes influen-tial (which may be similar to the dynamic with regard to conservative youths' seem-ing to become more liberal with increased exposure). Interestingly, blacks watch more news television than whites. African Americans averaged 4.69 days per week watch-ing the news on television, whereas whites watched the news on average 3.51 days. The difference is significant at the .000+ level as well. Blacks watch more entertain-ment television as well. On the 4-point scale where 1 represents less than an hour per day and 4 means more than 3 hours, whites averaged 2.35 whereas blacks averaged 2.95 hours. Again this difference is significant at the .000+ level. Not surprisingly therefore, both kinds of television watching are more strongly correlated with blacks' political knowledge than is the case for whites.

Finally, perhaps African Americans watch significantly different kinds of enter-tainment programming than whites, and they may therefore learn more from it and become less likely to engage in political conversations. It may be more important what is viewed, rather than just how much of it is seen. For example, 12.9% of whites report that *E.R.* is their favorite program, making it the favorite show among whites; 12.6% of whites report that *Seinfeld* is their favorite program, making it the second most popular program. The most popular show among blacks is *Martin*, attracting 12.1 % of respondents. *New York Undercover* attracted 6.5% of black viewers, making it the second most popular program. The differential socializing impact of these programs is difficult to determine. Apparently *E.R.* and *Seinfeld* have political influence over their viewers. It is unclear what impact, if any, *Martin* and *New York Undercover* can be expected to have. Moreover, small sample sizes (only 15 blacks report *New York Undercover* as their favorite, yet it still ranks second) make a statistical analysis impos-sible. Perhaps these programs are popular among blacks because they have predominantly African American casts (*Martin*), or because they feature strong black characters (*New York Undercover*) and have plot-lines whose themes resonate more in the African American community than the content of *The Simpsons* or *Seinfeld*.

Politics and Television

Television appears to influence young people's sociopolitical values. Some general conclusions are in order first. Does the apparent lack of coherence in their views indicate simple confusion? Apparently not, for limited television use results in a hardening or increased durability of the conservative values of U.S. youths who are already conservative. Their disproportionate negative reactions to entertainment television simply mean the unpleasantness of the experience with television leads to more variable patterns of reinforcement, similar to gamblers who lose most of the time but win every now and then. Nevertheless, it is expected that increased distance from parents will lead to television's having a greater influence—especially if there are massive amounts of television use coupled with peer support.

Conversely, the liberal values of liberal American youths appear to be reinforced by the liberal messages of much of the content of entertainment television—although there may be a backlash due to saturation of liberal messages. The few conservative messages liberals are exposed to appear to have little or no influence over their political attitudes and beliefs.

Preference for certain programming among U.S. respondents appears to correlate with the holding of the political beliefs endorsed by the program. Fans of *The Simpsons* are less conformist than nonfans, and they are also less tolerant of homosexuality. Fans of television programs that present promiscuous sexual relations as the norm are more favorable toward women's equality than nonfans. The differences remain large and significant when only women fans are examined. Fans of *Seinfeld* are more conformist than nonfans, whereas fans of sports programming are less so. Fans of *E.R.* are more tolerant of homosexuality and more likely to view government officials as working for the benefit of all.

Entertainment television watching not only influences political attitudes and beliefs but participation in other activities as well. Entertainment television use positively correlates with watching the news among respondents from all four countries. Most interestingly, entertainment television use negatively correlates with talking to others about politics, especially among African Americans. Thus, one of the most frequent worries about watching too much entertainment television—isolation from the community—appears to be well-founded. This finding is the most worrisome for the future of democracy, which requires active citizens communicating frequently about their troubles. If entertainment television use causes people not to talk to one another, then for that reason alone its increasing prevalence is problematic.

Finally, race matters. African Americans watch more and different television than whites and appear in some cases to be more strongly influenced by it. In fact, as other studies have shown entertainment television is one of the more segregated places in

America today. The programs, networks, and schedule are segregated. African Americans appear primarily in situation comedies, series broadcasts on minor networks, and on shows that air on Monday and Friday nights (Braxton 2000). Also, studies show blacks and whites prefer different programs, although there has been a slight overlap in recent years with both blacks and whites preferring shows like *E.R.*, *Monday Night Football, The Practice* and a few others (De Moreas 2000). This segregation and differential impact are certainly subjects worthy of further inquiry.

6

The Influence of Music on Political Socialization

Among all of the various socializing influences of the popular culture, music has the greatest likelihood of influencing the politics of young people. Since Plato's time, political philosophers have speculated about the ability of music—in its entirety, not just its lyrics—to influence the character of youths (see Holloway 2001). The reasons to believe that pop music may influence the politics of young people must begin with how much time and money they spend on it. As indicated in chapter 3, among the young Americans surveyed, 45.9% listen to the radio more than two hours per day. In addition, 59.9% report listening to their own music collections for more than an hour per day. This means that nearly 20% of the average American young person's waking hours are spent listening to music exclusively. Moreover, this amount of time does not include listening to the popular music which is now pervasive in movies, television programs, and commercials. There is a financial commitment as well. The average number of pieces of recorded music owned by the young people surveyed is 78 (which at the low price estimate of $15.00 each means the average youth's collection cost $1,170 to acquire). Moreover, 65% of the U.S. youths surveyed were able to identify the name and artist of the first piece of recorded music they ever purchased, which demonstrates the importance of this action and product in emotional terms, self-identity, and individuation. Young people not only spend time and money on music, but they are emotionally committed to it as well.

Recall as well that Canadian, Irish, and U.K. youths indicated similar commitments to music. Among Anglophone Canadian youths, 25.9% listen to the radio between one and two hours per day, and 22.7% listen to their own collections for more than three hours per day, while 28.7% listen for at least an hour. The average number of CDs owned is 88, which at $15.00 per disc represents a $1,320 commitment.

About 27.8% of Irish respondents listen to the radio more than three hours, and the majority listen at least an hour per day. The plurality (42.3%) listen to their own collections between one and two hours per day. The plurality of U.K. respondents (49.3%) listen to the radio less than an hour per day, but 36% listen to their own collections between one and two hours. As discussed in chapter three, the Irish respondents own a mean of 68 CDs, while the typical U.K. respondent owns 100 discs.

Music is not only important to young people in terms of how much money and time they spend on it, but also for how it helps them form and understand their communities and interpersonal relationships, that is, how it helps them "imagine" their community. Benedict Anderson (1983, page 1) argues in his book *Imagined Communities* that a nation is "imagined" because, "the members of even the smallest nations will never know most of their fellow members, meet them, or even hear of them, yet in the minds of each lives an image of their community." At the dawn of the age of mechanical reproduction, the colonial nations of the Americas imagined their community through the census, the map, and the museum, but the dawn of nationalism also involved imagining through administrative organizations, language, religion, novels, newspapers, and mythology. Any community, not just nations, may be imagined by its members. Moreover, if we truly wish to understand the influence of music on young people's politics, we ought to think this way about youth subcultures founded around musical preferences, which are the topics of the three chapters that follow on the influence of rap music, alternative rock, country and western, and classic rock.

In terms of the possibility of music's serving as a realm in which the community is imagined, Mattern's (1998) work is particularly useful. Mattern (1998: 33–37) described three models of political action in popular music: *confrontational; deliberative;* and *pragmatic.* In the *confrontational* model musicians who represent an oppressed group advance the cause of the group by exposing the exploitation in song, and thus seeking sympathy and support. In the *deliberative* model, "members of a group use musical practices to debate their identity and commitments, or when members of different groups negotiate mutual relations" (p. 35). In *pragmatic* political action, a shared political interest is assumed, and political action, "involves efforts by members of a single group to identify and address shared concerns collaboratively, or it may involve attempts to tie together the concerns of different groups in order to build a collaborative effort spanning different groups" (p. 36–37). The research here focuses on how young people are influenced by the political themes of popular music and positions taken by musicians.[1] Because

---

1   Not everyone agrees that lyrics in and of themselves are effective carriers of meaning, and should therefore be considered as potential persuaders. Simon Frith argues that we should not interpret lyrics in the same way we might interpret poems: disconnected from their vocal and musical context. He even asserts, "song words are not about ideas ('content') but about their expression." Simon Frith, *Performing rites: On the Value of Popular Music* (Cambridge: Harvard University Press, 1996), p. 164. Even more directly, he suggests, "(love) songs don't cause people to fall in love, but provide people with the means to articulate the feelings associated with being in love." So how the singer stresses words, for example, is crucial to understanding their intent, and we must not assume our interpretation of lyrics is the same as everyone else's. As

young people think about politics in such personalistic ways, the deliberative/pragmatic approach to understanding music's influence is most applicable. In other words, just because there may not be as many topical and protest songs now as there once were does not mean that music is not just as influential or even more so than it was in the 1960s heyday of singers' singing songs of social significance.

Music Exposure and Political Orientations

Does listening to one's own music collection have any influence on young people's overall political ideology and specific beliefs? There is good reason to believe that there is a liberal, progressive bias in pop music, especially in terms of lifestyle issues. First, the analysis in chapter 3 shows that American conservatives are more likely than liberals to find messages in pop music with which to disagree. It is unlikely they would do this because the messages are conservative.

Let's think again about importance of disagreement with the sociopolitical content of pop music. In chapter 3 we saw which young U.S. respondents were more likely to disagree with messages in music. To investigate this issue in more depth, the messages young people have disagreed with in popular music can be categorized by their ideological perspective. A liberal would disagree with depictions of violence, racism and traditional roles for women. A conservative would disagree with antireligion, prohomosexuality, and the glorification of premarital sex, promiscuity, and so on. Of course, some youths have never disagreed with a song's lyrics. A good test of the theory of socialization that informs this work is to look at the ideological perspective of the messages of music disagreed with by youths. The following table represents the distribution of ideological perspectives taken against pop music.

Table 6.1: Ideological Perspective of Themes Disagreed with in Songs, U.S. Respondents

Perspective	Percent	n
Liberal	13.7	95
Conservative	13.5	94

table continued on next page

an example of the peril of lyrical interpretation, he offers the frequent misinterpretation of protest songs, in particular Bruce Springsteen's "Born in the U.S.A.," which is a sad tale of the eventual incarceration of an unemployed Vietnam veteran. Nonetheless, the Republican Party wanted to use the song for President Reagan's hyper-patriotic re-election campaign in 1984. I take Frith's admonitions seriously, yet I hold to the belief that the misinterpretation of lyrics by some should make scholars more careful in how they interpret the content of lyrics, not abandon the project.

Have not Disagreed	21.9	152
Disagreed/Did Not Say Why	46.5	323
Disagreed/Undefinable	4.3	30
Totals	100.0	694

Young Americans' disagreement with songs is just about evenly split between conservative and liberal opposition (although the plurality disagreed and did not say why). What about the relationship between ideology and perspective taken against songs? Conservatives are expected to mention conservative objections to songs more frequently than liberals mention liberal objections. Liberals are probably more likely than conservatives never to have disagreed with a song. Youths who are conservative have been taught to reject the indecent messages of what early agents of socialization such as parents and churches have defined that way. Conversely, liberals are likely taught by nurturing parents the value of tolerance. Limited exposure by conservatives to the indecent messages of pop music probably find their conservatism strengthened, whereas liberals may not be influenced at all. Table 6.2 shows the relationship between self-reported ideology and the ideological perspective of disagreement with a song.

Table 6.2: Ideology and Orientation of Disagreement with Pop Music, U.S. Respondents

Perspective	Liberal	Moderate	Conservative	Totals
Liberal	16.6%	13.2%	10.6%	13.8%
Conservative	15.7%	7.5%	23.2%	13.9%
Never Disagreed	17.0%	28.8%	15.9%	21.7%
Disagreed/Didn't Say Why or Un-definable	50.7%	40.5%	50.3%	50.5%
Totals	100.0%	100.0%	100.0%	100.0%

Chi-square (6) = 32.030, sig. (two-tailed = .000)

U.S. liberals are pretty evenly split in terms of the orientation of their objections to a song's message, whereas the orientations of conservatives are more than twice as likely to be conservative. Moreover, liberals are slightly more likely never to have disagreed with the message of a song. Again the data demonstrate that conservatives, many perhaps raised in the strict parent model, are disaffected by the popular culture, disagree with it, and thus have their pre-existing conservative values hardened by exposure to music they find indecent or otherwise morally repugnant. Moreover, it shows that there are liberal, permissive messages in music, which may not influence conservatives but may have a profound impact on moderates and liberals.

Does increased listening to music on the radio or from one's collection in and of itself therefore influence the sociopolitical attitudes of young Americans? Tables 6.3 and 6.4 show the relationships between listening to music and various political beliefs.

Table 6.3: Kendall's Tau-c Correlations between Listening to Music Collection and Selected Variables, U.S. Respondents*

Variable	Tau-c	Sig. (two-tailed)
Moral Relativism	.086	.007
Oppose Newer Lifestyles	-.074	.014
Ideology (1=liberal)	-.056	.069
Homosexuality Acceptable	.047	.147
Support Abortion	.030	.290
Women's Equality	-.022	.432

*See appendix for wording of questions

Table 6.4: Kendall's Tau-c Correlations between Radio Use and Selected Variables*

Variable	Tau-c	Sig. (two-tailed)
Ideology (1=liberal)	-.086	.007
Women's Equality	-.055	.058
Oppose Newer Lifestyles	-.056	.080
Moral Relativism	.044	.175
Support Abortion	.041	.180
Homosexuality Acceptable	.034	.301

*See appendix for wording of questions

Clearly these correlations indicate that listening to the radio and to one's own music collection influences young Americans' political values. Listening to one's own music collection correlates with greater acceptance of newer lifestyles, increased moral relativism, increased support for homosexuality, and greater liberalism on the ideology scale. Moreover, because this activity involves listening to one's own self-selected collection (which a young person chose for him- or herself), the influence is more of a reinforcing one than a potentially changing one.

Increased listening to music on the radio correlates with increased support for women's equality, greater acceptance of newer lifestyles, and increased liberalism. Beliefs influenced by listening to music on the radio are different from those influenced by listening to one's own collection. While one chooses the stations to which one listens, one cannot change the songs played by the station. Unless one is constantly changing the station each time a song is played that is unfamiliar, the likelihood is high when listening to the radio that one will hear new songs—songs that potentially contain new sociopolitical messages.

Among Canadian respondents, there is a small but statistically significant relationship between hours listening to music on the radio and ideology: more hours correlates with increased conservatism. There were negative correlations between hours listening to the radio and support for gay marriage and marijuana legalization. More in the expected direction, increased listening to one's own collection correlates with greater support for moral relativism, support for gay marriage, and the legalization of marijuana.

Among Irish respondents, there are no significant correlations between listening to music on the radio and the various political beliefs. Among U.K. respondents, increased listening correlates with less support for the legalization of marijuana and less support for using British troops in U.N. peacekeeping operations. Among Irish respondents, the more frequently they listen to their own collections the more supportive they are of marijuana legalization, gay marriage, and moral relativism. Among U.K. respondents, increased listening to one's own collection correlates with less support for the idea that women should stay home, increased support for gay marriage, and with increased leftism on the seven point ideology scale.

Each of the effects discussed above is small, but statistically significant. What do they mean? Does the listening to music cause the attitudes, or does the arrow of causality point the other way? The relationship is probably interactive—liberals' attitudes are reinforced and strengthened, conservatives are either uninfluenced or find their attitudes hardened, whereas those unclear of their attitudes may find the choice easier with support from music and musicians. Moreover, increased time spent listening to one's own collection should be more likely to reinforce existing beliefs because respondents purchased the collection. Listening to the radio could lead to persuasion, because listeners are more likely to hear unexpected messages there.

The Politics of Pop Stars

Now let us examine U.S. youths' perceptions of the political ideology of various popular music performers. This may be a necessary first step for influence to occur. After all, if the pop stars have no sociopolitical beliefs, they probably are not trying to influence their fans. The hypothesis is that youths do discern differences in political ideology among performers based not only on the content of their music and their political activities, but also the general lifestyle image portrayed by the artist. Table 6.5 indicates the responses.

Table 6.5: Respondents' Perceptions of the Ideologies of Popular Musicians, U.S. Respondents

Artist	Mean Ideology	n	Std. Dev.
Garth Brooks	4.43	450	1.35
De La Soul	2.96	291	1.60
Will Smith	2.93	491	1.31
Eddie Vedder	2.63	360	1.48
Zack De La Rocha	2.63	253	1.60
Madonna	1.91	541	1.37

The means tell us much about young people's perceptions of the politics of popular musicians. First, five of the six musicians are at scale values of three or less, which means youths view them as liberal. Next, Garth Brooks is considered the most conservative. This is plainly because he is a white country and western performer. He carries the conservative image even though in 1992 he released the song "We Shall Be Free," which called for the freedom to "love anyone we choose," and clearly was meant to defend homosexual rights. *De La Soul* is a rap band that is Afro-centric in their world-view, but whose songs are not only Afro-centric, but often just plain funny as well. It is not surprising they are considered to be liberal by the respondents. Will Smith is also considered to be liberal and it is not clear that this is accurate. Perhaps his rating is due more to his being an African American than his avowed political positions, although his starring role in the movie *Enemy of the State* (where he plays an innocent lawyer caught in a web of government surveillance) may have influenced this perception as well. Eddie Vedder and Zack De La Rocha are both liberal, even radical left-wing activists and performers. The students' perceptions in these cases are accurate. Finally, Madonna is rated the most liberal, and more respondents ventured a guess as to her ideology than any other performer. She is not well known as a political activist; however, she has portrayed a life of pure hedonism, especially in terms of sexuality. The respondents' ranking of her as the most liberal among these musicians indicates how deeply young people embrace a definition of liberalism in terms of lifestyle issues, and not the traditional terms of the budget, federalism, and so on.

What relationship exists between the ideologies of these musicians and the respondents' self-reported ideologies? What kinds of comparisons would help put these relationships in perspective and help us understand the ability of musicians to influence the beliefs of young fans? Because parents are the most important agents of socialization, comparing correlations between the musicians and parents would yield the most insightful results.

Fans of the kind of music a particular musician performs would be ideologically similar to that performer. Because they have already invested themselves emotionally in the music, they have opened themselves to influence by the genre's performers. Certainly, for example, fans of rap music would be more open to influence by Tupac, Snoop Doggy Dogg, and *De La Soul* than fans of country and western music would be. Similarly, fans of country music would be more susceptible to influence by Garth Brooks, Tim McGraw, and Merle Haggard than would rap or alternative rock fans.

When looking at fans of the kind of music performed by the artists in question, the relationships between self-reported ideologies and perception of the ideologies of the performer are large and significant. It is important to put these relationships into perspective. The best way to do this is to compare them with the relationships between respondents and parents because all the previous research points to the importance of parents in the socialization process. If the relationships between respondents and musicians approaches or exceeds that of parents, then that is clear evidence for the importance of musicians' influence on young Americans' sociopolitical beliefs.

Interestingly, the relationship for each parent is larger for rap and country fans than for alternative fans. Alternative fans, however, appear to be more influenced by the ideology of popular musicians. For alternative fans, the relationship with Zack de la Rocha is greater than for either parent. Whereas there is a .373 correlation between respondents and Mr. De La Rocha, there is a .306 with mother and .221 for father. Apparently, many fans of alternative are closer ideologically to alternative musicians than to their own parents. This phenomenon is important and requires additional discussion.

Table 6.6: Correlations between Self-Reported Ideology and Ideology of Musicians for Only Fans of Music in Question, U.S. Respondents

Rap Fans Only:	Tau-b	Sig. (two-tailed)
Mom Ideology	.574	.000
Dad Ideology	.500	.000
De La Soul	.227	.006
Will Smith	.144	.053
Alternative Fans Only:		
Zack De La Rocha	.373	.000

table continued on next page

Mom Ideology	.306	.000
Dad Ideology	.221	.001
Eddie Vedder	.209	.006
Country Fans Only:		
Mom Ideology	.611	.000
Dad Ideology	.443	.003
Garth Brooks	.273	.066

The bulk of fans of *Rage Against the Machine* and *Pearl Jam*, the bands of Zack de la Rocha and Eddie Vedder, respectively, are young, white, suburban males. Whereas violence in schools is neither a new phenomenon nor one contained to white suburban schools, there has been a spate of school shootings in the past few years that has attracted the attention of the media. In most cases the shooters were young, white, suburban males. That these youths are demonstrably more strongly influenced by the politics of certain pop stars ought to get the attention of parents, teachers, and the press. Now, neither artist in the survey endorses violence as a solution to social or personal problems, but one wonders what influence they (and others) could have if they did.

Canadian respondents were asked to rate the ideology of a number of Canadian musicians as well. Gord Downie of the band *Tragically Hip*, Sarah McClachlan, and Avril Lavigne were each rated slightly left of center, with Lavigne and McLachlan being perceived as more liberal than Downie, who is considered something of a Canadian nationalist. With regard to each musician and mother and father, Canadian respondents' ideology statistically significantly correlated with each parent, but not with any of the musicians, except Gord Downie. U.K. and Irish respondents were not asked to identify the ideology of any performers.

Youths Who Are More Liberal Than Their Parents Revisited

What influence ought one to expect musical preferences to have on this phenomenon? It is reasonable to hypothesize that U.S. alternative rock and classic rock fans should be the most likely to be more liberal than their parents, whereas country fans should be the least likely. This is because alternative rock musicians are the most likely to engage in left-wing political campaigns and to promote progressive causes. Classic rock means, primarily, music from the 1960s and 1970s. This time period was the heyday of liberal political content in popular music. It is not unrealistic to expect that the peace and freedom messages of the music may influence its young fans today. Country and western music has traditionally and accurately been portrayed as the most conservative genre. Thus, its fans are unlikely to be more liberal than their parents.

As expected, U.S. country fans are the least likely to be more liberal than parents, whereas classic rock and alternative rock fans are the most likely. Also, however, when controlling for race, it turns out white rap fans are statistically significantly more likely to be more liberal than both parents.

Table 6.7: Relationship Between Music Preference and Being More Liberal Than Parents, U.S. Respondents Only*

	Country	Classic Rock	Alternative Rock	Rap	Other	Totals
More Liberal	5.0%	23%	20.2%	12.0%	13.5%	15.1%
Not More Liberal	95.0%	77.0%	79.8%	88.0%	86.5%	84.9%
Totals	100.0%	100.0%	100.0%	100.0%	100.0%	100.0%

Chi-square(8) = 11.535, sig. (two-tailed) = .021

Question: What kind of music is your favorite? Choices included Country, Jazz, Classic Rock, Alternative Rock, Rap/Hip-Hop, and Other (which the respondent was asked to specify).

Interestingly, the same analysis of favorite music preference and being more liberal than both parents yielded no significant results among Canadian, Irish, or British respondents. Given that country and western music is not very popular in Ireland or the U.K., those results are not much of a surprise. Also, the differences between alternative fans and others discusses in chapter 8 certainly indicate that musical preference and political beliefs are related in those countries.

Musicians often try to influence their fans through non-lyrical methods. For example, many artists allow interest groups to set up information tables at their concerts, and most of these interest groups are liberal. U.S. respondents mentioned The National Organization for the Reform of Marijuana Laws, which endorses the legalization of marijuana, Greenpeace, and Amnesty International most frequently when asked to name which groups had been present at concerts they had attended. Because of the liberal perspective of these groups, those who have attended such performances are more likely to be more liberal than both parents.

Clearly, attending concerts where interest groups have set up information tables correlates with U.S. respondents' holding political views more liberal than parents. Whereas among those who had been to such concerts, 27.3% are more liberal than both parents, only 12.9% of those who had not been to such concerts are more liberal than their parents, and the difference is statistically significant. Attempts by pop stars to influence young Americans' sociopolitical beliefs in a liberal direction appear to work.

Having attended concerts where interest groups had set up information tables did not correlate with being more liberal than both parents within the Irish sample. However, there was a significant relationship in the U.K. sample, with 25.6% who had been to such concerts being more liberal than both parents and only 17.4% of non-attendees holding such beliefs. A larger difference exists in the Canadian data and is statistically significant. Whereas 27.4% of concert attendees are more liberal than both parents, only 13.9% of non-attendees are.

Music Preferences and Political Socialization

To what kinds of music do young Americans listen? As shown in chapter 3, rap music is the most popular, attracting 25.8% of responses to the question of one's favorite music. Alternative rock finished a close second with 24.4%. Classic rock attracted 8.6% of responses, and rhythm and blues attracted 7.8%. Country attracted 5.6%, and the remaining preferences were scattered among jazz, blues, no preference, and so on. When U.S. youths are asked to identify their favorite song ever, there is a great diversity of responses. Among 406 valid responses, no single song attracted the support of more than five respondents. The "most popular" song, Garth Brooks's "The Dance," was hardly overwhelmingly popular in that it attracted only 1.2% of responses. Thus, it is not particularly useful to identify the political content of the most "popular" songs. Instead, the political content of the top six kinds of music preferred by respondents needs to be analyzed by looking at both the political content of some songs from the genre and also what scholars and critics have said about the music.

Rap music's political significance falls into three broad categories. First, there is Afro-centric rap, which broadly speaking, presents to young listeners a relatively positive message about self-respect, racial pride, and dignity. There is not a great deal of Afro-centric rap. It is also true that much of rap includes socially negative messages. A good deal of rap music endorses drinking, killing, misogyny, and other socially deviant or illegal actions. This rap is generally referred to as "gangsta" rap. There is more of this than Afro-centric rap, but it is not the majority either. Justifications for such lyrics run the gamut from legitimacy arguments about rap's representing street-life to claims that the artists are merely trying to grab listeners' attention. Finally, most rap appears to be concerned with the same issues with which most popular music is concerned: male-female relationships. It is probably the majority, but its political significance is probably the least, except for the construction of gender roles.

A final word on rap is necessary in this chapter (the next chapter covers rap in much more detail). The questionnaire from which the data are generated did not permit respondents to differentiate what kind of rap they prefer. Therefore, this kind of analysis is impossible in this book.

Alternative rock at first appears bereft of obvious political significance; however, there are some notable exceptions. Those bands or performers that are exceptions are liberal/progressive in their politics. Some bands have allowed Amnesty International and Greenpeace to set up information tables at their concerts (e.g., *The Indigo Girls, U2, REM,* and many other popular alternative bands). Some acts have recorded and performed at benefits for Native American rights activist Leonard Peltier, the Tibetan freedom movement, and other progressive causes. The politics of alternative rock are liberal, especially in terms of lifestyle issues like women's equality, homosexual rights and antiracism.

Classic rock came in third in popularity among U.S. respondents. There is a great deal of politics in this genre, but it may not be likely to influence young listeners. This is because the politics of protest from the 1960s prevalent in this music may not be very relevant to the lives of young people at the beginning of the twenty-first century. What reason is there to believe that songs of protest against Vietnam or in favor of "Flower Power" will resonate with the children of the parents who made this music popular in the first place? Perhaps, however, the lifestyle liberalism prevalent in much of the music (the "do your own thing" spirit of the sixties in terms of sex, drugs, and rock and roll) does mean something to young people today and correlates with greater liberalism in fans of classic rock.

The modern variant of rhythm and blues is completely devoid of obvious sociopolitical messages, and therefore its influence will not be examined. Generally country and western music is considered the most conservative of popular music, and not without some justification. Country lyrics are more likely to endorse traditional moral values than are other kinds of music. C&W performers are more likely than other performers to endorse Republican candidates. Support for traditional American values is further indicated by support for family farms. Farm-Aid involved Country musicians and helped raise money and consciousness for the plight of American family farms. Jazz was preferred by 2.7% of U.S. youths, which means 19 respondents preferred this relatively nonpolitical form of music. Therefore its political significance will not be examined.

Seventeen other styles of music attracted a combined 11.1% of U.S. responses. The most popular of these was dance, followed by Gospel, and rock 'n' roll. None of these attracted more than 13 responses and thus do not permit much analysis. Another 13.8% of respondents did not answer the question or wrote an inappropriate response.

There is a relationship between race and music preference. In terms of country music 89.7% of its fans are white, whereas 86.7% of classic rock fans are white and 93.6% of alternative rock fans are white. Because of this lack of variation, race will not be used as a control in examining political differences between fans of these kinds of music and nonfans. Rap is the only kind of music attracting both large numbers of fans and a racially diverse fan base. Whereas 41.5% of rap fans are black, 36.4% are white; 15.9% are other and 6.3% are Hispanic. Therefore race must be accounted for when examining the political impact of this style of music.

It is expected that country fans, based on the frequently conservative, patriotic and conformist political content of their musical preference, to be the most conservative. It is reasonable to hypothesize that rap, alternative and classic rock fans would be the more liberal, but it is difficult to speculate in which order they ought to occur. Rap and alternative fans ought to be the most liberal, with classic rock coming next. Table 6.8 shows the relationship.

Table 6.8: Music Preference and Ideology, U.S. Respondents

	Country	Classic	Alternative	Rap	Other/ None	Totals
Liberal	28.9%	33.0%	37.6%	35.3%	34.9%	35.3%
Moderate	55.3%	30.5%	36.5%	50.9%	39.9%	41.9%
Conservative	15.8%	35.6%	25.9%	13.9%	25.2%	22.9%
Totals	100.0%	100.0%	100.0%	100.0%	100.0%	100.0%

Chi-square (8) = 21.316, sig. (two-tailed) = .006

Alternative fans are the most likely to define themselves as liberal, whereas country fans are the least likely. This is as expected. Classic rock fans are the most likely to define themselves as conservative, whereas rap fans are the least likely. Country fans are the most likely to define themselves as moderate, whereas classic and alternative rock fans are the least likely. This information indicates that fans of these kinds of rock tend toward extremes, whereas country fans do not.

When looking at whites only, music preference remains significant. White rap fans are twice as likely to be liberal rather than conservative (30.0% to 15.0%), and white alternative fans are much more likely to be liberal than conservative as well (37.3% compared to 25.9%). Music preference becomes insignificant at predicting ideology when examining African Americans only. Undoubtedly this is because of the small ideological variation among African Americans: only 14.2% of blacks consider themselves conservatives.

Similar, and statistically significant, results were found in the Canadian sample. While 46.7% of country and western fans defined themselves as conservative, only 12.2% or rap fans and 15% of alternative rock fans did. Only 21.8% of classic rock fans defined themselves as conservative. Irish alternative rock fans were more likely than fans of any other music to define themselves as left (50%), while rap fans were the least likely (100% of them defined themselves as moderate). In a more expected result, U.K. alternative rock and rap fans were the most likely to be left (59.8% and 48.6%, respectively).

What relationship is there between music preference and partisanship? The hypothesis is that rap and alternative fans are the most likely to be Democrats, with classic rock next and country last. Table 6.9 demonstrates the results.

Table 6.9: Music Preference and Party Choice, U.S. Respondents

	Country	Classic	Alternative	Rap	Other/ None	Totals
Democrat	43.3%	25.5%	28.8%	59.9%	45.1%	41.5%
No. Pref.	13.3%	21.8%	26.7%	12.2%	21.0%	19.3%
Independent	23.3%	16.4%	16.4%	11.6%	11.7%	15.1%
Republican	20.0%	36.4%	28.1%	16.3%	22.0%	24.1%
Totals	100.0%	100.0%	100.0%	100.0%	100.0%	100.0%

Chi-square (9) = 42.476, sig. (two-tailed) = .000+

Rap fans are the most likely to be Democrats with country fans coming in second. Country fans are nearly all white, so race does not account for this difference. It remains unclear why classic rock and alternative rock fans are the least likely to be Democrats.

When examining whites only, music preference becomes insignificant at predicting partisanship. When examining blacks only, music preference remains significant, but the numbers of African American classic rock, country and alternative fans are so low that meaningful analysis is impossible.

Among Canadians a similar and potentially more meaningful relationship exists. Alternative rock and rap fans are much more likely than country fans to prefer the Liberal Party or the social democratic New Democratic Party. Country and Western fans are more likely than these others to prefer the Conservative Party. There were no statistically significant relationships between music preference and political party in the Irish or U.K. samples, although alternative rock and rap fans were more likely to prefer the Labour Party than were others.

Influence of Music on Political Knowledge[2]

Listening to music from one's own collection on the radio could influence political knowledge in two ways. First, because some musicians try to inform and entertain, music listening may directly increase one's political knowledge. This is not the case however. There are no relationships between listening to one's own music or the radio and political knowledge.

---

2   Political knowledge was not measured in the Canadian, U.K., or Irish surveys, so the material here refers exclusively to U.S. respondents.

Second, music listening may influence other activities such as newspaper reading and television watching that may increase political knowledge. The more one listens to music the less time one presumably has for reading a paper or watching the news on television, two activities that contribute to greater political knowledge. Interestingly, listening to one's own music collection is positively related to listening to music on the radio (tau-b = .371, sig. two-tailed .000) and watching entertainment television (tau-b = .075, sig. two-tailed = .020). There is, however, no relationship between listening to one's own music and watching the news or reading the newspaper. Listening to music on the radio is also related to watching entertainment television (tau-b = .093, sig. two-tailed = .003). Listening to music on the radio, however, is not correlated with reading the paper or watching the news on television. Thus, listening to music is not associated with reading a paper or watching news on the television and has little impact upon these activities that would increase political knowledge.

Does musical preference influence political knowledge? This appears to be the case. It is expected that fans of the more politicized music to be more politically knowledgeable than nonfans. More specifically, fans of rap, alternative rock, and country ought to know a little more than others. The results are a bit surprising. Rap fans have a mean political knowledge score of 4.02, whereas nonfans score a mean of 4.40. The difference of .38 is significant (prob. = .030, one-tailed). Afro-centric rap includes political themes, but it comprises only a small proportion of the total output of rap musicians. The overwhelming majority of rap does not set out to educate its listeners politically.

What about the political knowledge of alternative rock fans? Fans of this music have a mean political knowledge score of 4.50, whereas nonfans score 4.24. Whereas this is a small difference, it is significant (sig. = .065, one-tailed). Fans of this music are slightly more knowledgeable than non-fans because of the overt attempts of so many musicians in this genre to educate their fans by making public statements, performing at benefit concerts, or allowing groups to set up information tables at their concerts. This is especially true with respect to information tables at concerts. About 24.4% of alternative fans report having attended a performance where information tables were set up, whereas only 15.1% of fans of other styles of music report this. Clearly alternative musicians are more likely to try to inform their fans about politics, and this effort may be yielding at least some minimal results.

What about classic rock? It is expected to have little impact on knowledge of contemporary political leaders because most of the politicians mentioned in the music no longer hold office. This is not the case however. Classic rock fans score a mean on the political knowledge index of 4.84, whereas nonfans score 4.25, and the difference is significant at the .028 (one-tailed) level. Perhaps the historical political content of classic rock primes fans of classic rock to pay attention to contemporary politics. Finally, despite the high prevalence of political messages in country music, its fans are no more knowledgeable than fans of other music. Perhaps the following statement is very generally true: Musicians who try to inform only through their music (country) may not be as successful as musicians who inform through music, concerts, and information booths at shows (alternative rock). Fans of the kinds of music where almost no attempt is made to educate or convince are less knowledgeable than fans of other music (rap).

Music and Politics

Music matters. Naturally, the relationships are complicated. Young people spend vast amounts of time and money on music, and music helps serve as a place where young people imagine their communities. It appears that music matters as a place of individuation and in fact influences young people's beliefs about what sociopolitical values ought to prevail in their communities. American liberals though find less to disapprove of in music, whereas conservatives find more. This is all as expected. Broadly speaking, listening to the radio affords more of an opportunity for young people to be influenced by music with messages that contradict their own beliefs, whereas listening to one's own music collection probably reinforces pre-existing beliefs.

There are several significant relationships between music use and beliefs among U.S. respondents. Some young people's overall ideology is more closely and strongly correlated with the ideologies of pop stars than with their parents. This reality especially applies among U.S. fans of alternative rock. Moreover, the more one listens to one's own collection, the more likely one is to be more liberal than one's parents. Moreover, if one has attended concerts where performers had allowed interest groups to set up information tables, one is much more likely to be more liberal than parents. Music preference matters in this, too. Classic rock and alternative fans are more likely than others to be more liberal than their parents.

Finally, there are some overall relationships between music preference and the politics of American youths. Alternative rock fans are the most likely to be liberal, whereas country fans are the least likely. Country and rap fans are the most likely to be Democrats, whereas classic rock fans are the most likely to be Republicans. In terms of political knowledge, overall music levels predict little. Rap fans are less knowledgeable, alternative and classic rock fans are more knowledgeable, and country fans know neither more nor less.

Canadian respondents are every bit as avid consumers of popular music as U.S. youths. Radio listening appeared to correlate with increased conservatism, while increased listening to their own collections seemed to reinforce greater liberalism. Canadian respondents' ideology correlated with only one rock star: the Canadian nationalist Gord Downie. Canadian youths may find in his iconic Canadian nationalism support for their pride in country, which has normally been considered more muted than American nationalism. Just like American youths who have attended such concerts, Canadian youths who have attended concerts with interest groups set up are more likely than other youths to be more liberal than their parents. Music preference matters in terms of ideology and partisanship as well: country fans are more conservative and prefer the party of the same name, while rap and alternative fans are more liberal and social democratic.

Significant findings in the U.K. and Irish samples followed a similar pattern. U.K. youths who have attended the political rock concerts are more likely than others to be more liberal than both parents, and U.K. alternative and rap fans are more likely to define themselves as left than are others.

The research in this chapter demonstrates both the possibility and extent of the influence of music on young people's sociopolitical beliefs. Because music is a medium of community imagining for youths, music preference likely matters a great deal. In other words, rap fans, alternative adherents, country mavens, and classic rock fans are different from others and each other. They are more likely to be influenced by their preferred music's lyrics and performers.

7

The Influence
of Rap Music on Young Adults'
Sociopolitical Beliefs

Rap History and Theory

Since its creation, rap music has been among the most controversial popular musical forms. Its potential sociopolitical influence has drawn the attention of social science scholars, as indicated in chapter 1. However, rap and hip-hop music have various meanings within the community of fans, and the meanings as interpreted within the context of community are likely to influence fans. Lusane (1993) calls these various elements educational, mass cultural, subversive, and farcical. More specifically, for some, rap music has become a vital form of political communication (Rose 1991; Decker 1993). This was certainly the purpose of a number of early rappers, such as De La Soul and Public Enemy. For many other fans, rap and hip-hop have become a space to work out basic community relationships, especially sex-roles. Rap and hip-hop have also been described as a reflection—and therefore not a cause—of the violence, drug, and sexual problems plaguing some American youths, especially black urban youths.

The political aspects of rap are often identified and celebrated by white writers and scholars. The New Republic's Michael Lewis asserted rap is, "the nearest thing to a political voice of the poor" (in Steyn 1996). What he means with this statement is not entirely clear, but there is an argument that the economic good times of the 1980s and 1990s left behind a large number of Americans—especially women, minorities, and residents of central cities. In the absence of a mainstream political party voice, rap and hip-hop artists seek to speak for these disaffected and disfranchised people (Ribadeneira 1992). Rappers themselves also recognize their role this way. Sister Souljah said during the 1992 residential campaign, "The reason why rap is under attack is because it exposes all the contradictions of American culture. What started out as an underground art form has become a vehicle to expose a lot of critical issues that are not usually discussed in American politics. (The current) political system... never intends to deal with inner city urban chaos" (Philips 1992, 6).

Support for the major U.S. political parties can be understood by looking at the demographic and political groups who usually support them in national elections. Traditionally, the Republican Party has relied on the support of conservatives (especially religious conservatives), those who live in small towns and rural areas, the business elite, and so on. The Democrats rely on labor (especially union members), blacks, women (especially single women), and urban residents for support. However, neither party has enough core support to win Presidential elections and control of Congress consistently (Ginsberg and Shefter 2000). Suburban and exurban swing voters, variously identified as "soccer moms," "NASCAR dads," and after 9–11 "security moms," thus become extremely important in deciding the outcome of elections, and both parties have been accused by groups in their core constituency of selling-out basic beliefs to attract these more independent voters. For example, when Ronald Reagan was president he proposed eliminating the federal Department of Education. Realizing the importance of the education issue to "soccer-moms," President George W. Bush dramatically expanded the federal role in education (while arguing for maintaining local control) through the No Child Left Behind Act.

Similarly, Democrats have been accused of abandoning core constituencies to influence swing voters. President Clinton pushed the North American Free Trade Agreement through Congress despite labor unions' vigorous opposition. Moreover, he eliminated the federal welfare entitlement and made it more difficult for death row inmates to challenge their sentences. While taking large contributions from entertainment industry executives, he also criticized the industry. During the 1992 campaign he was vociferous in his attacks on the statements of obscure rapper Sister Souljah, who suggested once that blacks ought to consider killing whites instead of each other (Edsall 1992). Just before the election, Sister Souljah said, "I believe if Clinton becomes president, the same things will happen that will happen if Bush stays as president" ("Boycotting the booth," USA Today, 3 November 1992, D-2). With no political party speaking about urban issues, rap and hip-hop artists stepped in to fill the void.

In terms of rap's serving as a reflection of the difficulties of life in the ghetto, one rap song that really attracted the ire of politicians was Ice-T's "Cop-Killer." In the song, the protagonist indicates he is both mentally and physically prepared to murder police officers. While not attacking the rapper directly or by name, then-President Bush said of the recording, "It's wrong for any company . . . to issue records that approve of killing a law enforcement officer" (Philips 1992). Ice-T defended himself by comparing his song with the Star Spangled Banner, "don't these politicians realize the country was founded on the kind of revolutionary political thought expressed in my song? . . . Anybody knows that the 'Star-Spangled Banner' is really just a song about a shoot-out between us and the police. Have they forgotten that Paul Revere became a Revolutionary War hero for warning everybody, 'The police are coming, the police are coming?'" (Philips 1992). Moreover, as Bono—lead singer of the Irish Rock band U2 put it, Johnny Cash sang about shooting a man in Reno just to watch him die and nobody ever suggested he be silenced or be sent to prison. Of course, nobody shot a man in Reno because Johnny Cash told him to, and the protagonist of Cash's song is in prison for his evil deeds, but the fact remains that American songs have always represented the violence that has been part of American life—whether on the frontier or in the big city (see Hershey-Webb 1999).

Certainly rap music, like other ethnic music, plays the role of providing a space in which members of a community work out their relationships. This may help explain some of the misogyny of modern rap, although as Johnson (1996) argues, we ought to recognize that the anti-female nature of much rap ought to be understood in the tradition of misogyny in both black and white culture. Misogyny aside, male and female rap artists speak about relationships with the opposite sex, and often they respond to each other. In fact there has been an increase in the past several years of female rap artists demanding respect or power over sexual situations(Queen Latifah, Salt 'n' Pepa, L'il Kim, to name but a few). In many ways male and female hip-hop artists speak on behalf of their listeners, and as anyone who has spent any time around young rap fans can attest, the listeners often parrot lines from songs in response to overtures from a member of the opposite sex (overtures which are often rap based too). Of course there's nothing new about this—the girl groups of the 1950s and 1960s did the same thing for women of the time (Rohlfing 1996), but the role of rap music in the creation, maintenance, and destruction of male-female relationships ought to be taken seriously.

A final note on sexuality and rap regards the extent to which much rap is aggressively homophobic. While Eminem is currently the poster-boy for homophobic rap, he is certainly not the first rapper to promote such views. In fact, social critic and rap expert Michael Eric Dyson calls rap, "notoriously homophobic" (in Jamison 1998; see also Dyson 1996). Of course, the important question is whether or not rap influences young listeners to become more homophobic.

What does this in-depth analysis of rap and hip-hop in terms of musicians, audiences, and messages tell us? With this background information about the history and interpretation of the genre, there are many plausible hypotheses about the influence of rap on young people's sociopolitical beliefs. Subsequently, the validity of these hypotheses will be examined to place our understanding of rap in a broader theoretical framework.

Rap and Equal Opportunity

First, rap fans are expected to be more supportive of equal opportunity for minorities, especially those influenced by Afro-centric rap. But also solely because rap is dominated by African American performers, fans of rap in general should recognize this rare prominence of blacks and thus support racial equality more strongly. Rap fans are expected to hold more morally relativistic beliefs than their counterparts, especially fans of violent rap. However, the solipsistic hedonism of much nonviolent rap might influence fans in a more relativistic position as well.

The data indicate that most of the U.S. respondents support equal opportunity regardless of whether they prefer rap or not. Whereas 88.5% of non rap fans agree with the claim that our society should do whatever is necessary to make sure everyone has an equal opportunity to succeed, only 81.4% of rap fans agree (Chi-square (2) = 1.749, sig. (two-tailed) = .209). Thus, rap is insignificant at predicting difference of position on equal opportunity whether examining youths of all races. Moreover, it is also irrelevant when predicting position on equal opportunity among only African Americans, or whites only. Evidently the belief in equal opportunity is so widespread among American youths that there is no reason to try to explain the sources of variation of the belief. In other words, social science cannot and does not need to explain constants. Questions about support for equal opportunity were not asked on the Canadian, Irish, or U.K. surveys.

Rap and Morality

What about the relationship between rap music and morality? As has already been discussed, because young people think of politics in terms of the social consequences of personal choices, it makes sense to examine the influence of rap and hip-hop on these choices. Unfortunately, the questionnaire upon which this research is based does not contain any questions about beliefs in the efficacy of violence or drug use. However, there are questions about newer lifestyles, moral relativism, and women's roles that are instructive. It is reasonable to expect rap fans to be less likely to believe that newer lifestyles contribute to the breakdown of society for two reasons. The first concerns the definition of "newer lifestyles." Whereas many may think that "newer lifestyles" is merely a euphemism for homosexuality (toward which, as indicated above, rap lyrics are generally very unfavorable), this is not necessarily or literally the case. Other "newer lifestyles" concerning sexuality, drug use, making a living outside the mainstream (read drug dealing) of society and so on are frequently endorsed in rap lyrics. Furthermore, if sufficiently cynical, rap fans might not care that rap contributes to the breakdown of a society, they find unacceptable anyway. Thus, their indifference or opposition to current society may influence them to answer the question in the negative, when what they really mean is they do not care if society is broken down.

Regarding newer lifestyles, those U.S. respondents who prefer rap music are somewhat less likely to disagree with the claim that newer lifestyles are contributing to the breakdown of society, and the difference is statistically significant. Whereas 23.5% of rap fans hold the more tolerant position and disagree with the statement that newer lifestyles do contribute to the breakdown of society, 28.6% of non-rap fans hold this tolerant position (Chi-square (2) = 3.174, sig. (one-tailed) = .103). Rap is, perhaps, a cynical statement that society is broken down but not a statement of support for the breakdown. This is evidence for the belief that rap is reflective of the miserable aspects of urban life but not an endorsement of them.

Moreover, when examining blacks only, this difference completely disappears and becomes statistically insignificant. When looking at whites only, the difference between nonfans and rap fans changes direction, grows dramatically, and remains significant (30% of white non-rap fans hold the tolerant position and disagree that newer lifestyles contribute to the breakdown of society, whereas only 18.8% of white rap fans hold the tolerant position and disagree). Perhaps for a number of white youths the most vivid (or perhaps only) experience with the violence, drugs, and sexuality of ghetto life is through rap. Thus, those white kids who have experienced through rap the problems of ghetto life are less likely to feel comfortable with rap's portrayals or potential endorsements of it and thus are less likely to hold the more tolerant position and disagree that "newer lifestyles" contribute to the breakdown of society.

Canadian respondents were asked directly if they agreed with the statement that gays should be allowed to marry, but there were no significant differences with level of agreement and being a fan of rap. The same is true for the Irish and U.K. samples: no differences between rap fans and all others on the question of gay marriage.

When examining the question of moral relativism (support for the claim that morality ought to change with the times), rap preference has an effect on black U.S. respondents, as shown in Table 7.1, but not on whites, as shown in Table 7.2.

Table 7.1: Rap Preference and Moral Relativism (Blacks Only)*

Morality Ought to Change with the Times:	Non Rap Fans	Rap Fans	Totals
Disagree	58.8%	38.4%	87.7%
Neutral	6.2%	4.1%	5.2%
Agree	35.8%	57.5%	46.1%
Totals	100.0%	100.0%	100.0%

Chi-square (2) = 7.298, sig. (one-tailed) = .013

*Question: The world is always changing and we should adjust our view of moral behavior to those changes.

Table 7.2: Rap Preference and Moral Relativism (Whites Only)*

Morality Ought to Change with the Times:	Non Rap Fans	Rap Fans	Totals
Disagree	38.6%	37.5%	38.4%
Neutral	9.9%	15.6%	10.0%
Agree	51.5%	46.9%	50.8%
Totals	100.0%	100.0%	100.0%

Chi-square (2) = 7.298, sig. (one-tailed) = .013

*Question: The world is always changing and we should adjust our view of moral behavior to those changes.

As the tables indicate, when controlling for race, rap preference influences youths' positions on moral relativism. The apparent reason why there is no effect on the races when mixed is because they seem to cancel each other out. Whereas rap preference appears to correlate significantly with greater moral relativism among African Americans, this is not the case with Caucasians. Among whites, rap preference appears to correlate with only slightly reduced moral relativism, and the relationship is not significant at standard levels.

Perhaps white U.S. rap fans enjoy the socially pathological messages of some rap music voyeuristically, but when asked in a serious setting, such as that produced by survey research, they assert that they oppose moral relativism. So, the findings on the possibility that newer lifestyles contribute to the breakdown of society and moral relativism are consistent. White rap fans are less tolerant and relativistic than other white youths.

Another explanation for this is the tradition of white men's feeling threatened by the power of black men, especially if they perceive the power as gained at their expense, through violence, or leading to sexual relations with white women. As Andrew Hacker put it, "white men regard black men as being better sexual performers. And that really drives us up the wall. Therefore all our efforts to de-man black men" (in Dreyfuss 1992, 66). As indicated in chapter three, white U.S. men are more likely than others to have disagreed with the message of a song. It is not unreasonable to believe that a great deal of this disagreement stems from this pathological fear of black men and manifests itself in disagreement with the messages of rap. This perception in turn, with limited exposure, little or no peer support, and a residual influence by parents and parentally selected agents of socialization, leads to a renewed conservatism.

Canadian, U.K., and Irish rap fans are no different than other respondents in terms of agreement with moral relativism. These respondents were asked a number of other questions which were not asked of Americans that could be influenced by being a rap fan, including support for marijuana legalization, strict gun control laws, and so on. Canadian rap fans are more likely to strongly agree with marijuana legalization, but the difference was not statistically significant. They were less likely to strongly agree that only police and the military should be allowed to have guns, but again the difference was not statistically significant. Rap preference explains nothing among Irish or U.K. respondents in terms of belief about the legalization of marijuana or gun laws.

Rap, Women, and Homosexuality

As demonstrated in chapter 3, rap music is the most likely to be perceived by the U.S. survey respondents as containing negative messages about women. Moreover, as demonstrated above, this issue has concerned scholars of rap and hip-hop. Therefore, rap preference would correlate with reduced support for an equal role for women in society, and more support for the claim that a woman's proper place is in the home. This appears to be the case, although the differences are not large and only approach statistical significance. Although rap appears to predict lower support for women's equality in the overall sample, the more interesting relationship occurs when race is controlled for. Black rap fans are less supportive of women's equality than black nonfans, whereas for whites there is little difference.

Table 7.3: Rap Preference and Views on Women's Role*

	Rap Fans	Non Rap Fans	Difference	Sig. (one-tailed)
All Respondents	1.95	1.83	.12	.142
Blacks Only	1.74	1.51	.23	.141
Whites Only	1.92	1.86	.06	.361

Again, it is interesting that the greatest impact is among African-Americans. European American voyeurism is again probably a large part of the explanation for the difference between blacks and whites. For a large number of European Americans, the only experience they have with black people or the way of life in the inner city is through the lens of rap. Whereas African Americans may use rap as a place to work out sexual relationships and much rap endorses misogyny, young blacks' opinions about the place of women may be influenced by the public positions taken by rap artists in their songs. Whites may be less likely to take the messages seriously as a recommendation about how to live, and instead take voyeuristic delight in witnessing pathological behavior. Among Canadian, Irish and U.K. respondents, rap fans are no different from others on the question of women's place in society.

As suggested earlier, rap lyrics are frequently not only misogynistic but also homophobic. Does this influence listeners' beliefs? Table 7.4 shows the relationship between rap preference and beliefs about homosexuality for white American youths, while table 7.5 shows the relationship for blacks.

Table 7.4: Rap Preference and Morality of Homosexuality, U.S. Respondents* (Whites Only)

Homosexual Lifestyles Are Morally Acceptable:	Non-Rap Fans	Rap Fans	Totals
Disagree	38.7%	50.0%	40.4%
Neutral	18.3%	18.8%	18.3%
Agree	43.0%	31.3%	41.3%
Totals	100.0%	100.0%	100.0%

Chi-square(2) = 3.560, sig. (one-tailed) = .085

*Question: Homosexual lifestyles are morally acceptable

Table 7.5: Rap Preference and Morality of Homosexuality, U.S. Respondents* (Blacks Only)

Homosexual Lifestyles Are Morally Acceptable:	Non-Rap Fans	Rap Fans	Totals
Disagree	61.7%	54.2%	58.2%
Neutral	22.2%	15.3%	19.0%
Agree	16.0%	30.6%	22.9%
Totals	100.0%	100.0%	100.0%

Chi-square(2) = 4.851, sig. (one-tailed) = .044

*Question: Homosexual lifestyles are morally acceptable

The first point is that African-Americans are much less likely than whites to agree that homosexual lifestyles are morally acceptable. Whereas 22.9% of blacks hold this position, 41.3% of whites do. However, among whites, rap fans are much less tolerant toward homosexuality than non fans. For blacks the relationship is the opposite. Black rap fans are much more tolerant of gay lifestyles than nonfans. What gives? Perhaps in some cases African Americans are less likely to take seriously the messages of rap artists and European Americans more likely.

Among blacks, rap preference has a small and statistically insignificant influence on how many officials respondents believe are corrupt, and whether the government is run for the benefit of all, or just for the benefit of some.[1] Among whites, rap has no relationship with how many officials respondents believe are corrupt, but a large relationship with belief about in whose interest the government is run. Among white rap fans, 82.7% believe the government is run for a few interests, whereas among white nonrap fans the belief is held by 69.5% of respondents. The difference is significant (chi-square (2) = 3.772, sig. (one-tailed) = .026). Again, rap seems to influence the beliefs of white fans more than others. Irish, U.K., and Canadian respondents were asked if they support gay marriage. Rap preference explains nothing in terms of beliefs about gay marriage for Irish, U.K., and Canadian respondents.

Influence of Rap Musicians

Musicians often take political positions outside of their performances and recordings. For example, the members of popular white rap band *The Beastie Boys* organize and perform at annual concerts calling on the West to do more to end Chinese military occupation of Tibet. Do such endorsements have any effect on the young fans of the performers? On some of the surveys, there was an indication that the position or quote was endorsed by *The Beastie Boys*, whereas on others the quotation or position was merely mentioned. In both cases, students were asked to agree or disagree with the position using a five-point scale where one means strongly disagree and five means strongly agree. The different questionnaire versions were randomly distributed to each of the classes. Respondents were instructed not to talk to one another about the questionnaire, nor to look at one another's answers. The hypothesis is that *The Beasties'* endorsement would lead to greater support for the celebrity's position, but it had no impact on the overall sample. Therefore white rap fans would be more likely to agree with the position when it is ascribed to the band than when it is not.

The Tibet question elicited different responses in the hypothesized direction when looking at white rap fans only. They were examined because the celebrities who endorsed a position were white rap musicians, and therefore these musicians were most likely to exert sociopolitical influence over white rap fans. Respondents were much more likely to agree that the West should do more to help Tibet when they responded to those positions as endorsed by celebrities who perform their favorite kind of music. Looking at blacks only, the endorsement of *The Beastie Boys* has no significant impact on difference of opinion on the assistance to Tibet question. These data demonstrate the power of musicians to influence fans who are already emotionally invested in a band.

---

1   None of these questions, as well as the morality of homosexual lifestyles, was asked on the Irish, U.K., or Canadian surveys.

Table 7.6: Celebrity Endorsement and Help Tibet* (White Rap Fans Only)

West Should Do More to Help Tibet:	Non-Celebrity Endorsed	Celebrity Endorsed	Totals
Disagree	21.7%	7.3%	12.5%
Neutral	52.2%	36.6%	42.2%
Agree	26.1%	56.1%	45.3%
Totals	100.0%	100.0%	100.0%

Chi-square (2) = 6.229, sig. (one-tailed) = .022

Question: The Beastie Boys believe that other countries should do more to end the Chinese military occupation of neighboring Tibet. How do you feel about this issue?

More systematic thought about celebrity endorsements of political ideas is required. Unfortunately, little scholarly research has been done on the impact of celebrity endorsements on public opinion in general. However, Jackson and Darrow (2005) and Jackson (2007) demonstrate that celebrity endorsement of popular beliefs make those beliefs more popular among young people, while celebrity endorsements of unpopular beliefs do not lead to persuasion, but do reduce the level of disagreement among Canadian and U.S. youths. While there is not much other political science research on the impact of celebrities on public opinion, much research has been done by marketing scholars on the impact of celebrity endorsements of products, and political scientists have examined the influence of "experts" and other authority figures on public opinion.

Even a cursory glance at television, radio, and print advertising suggests businesses believe that celebrity endorsements of their products work to sell more of their merchandise, and there is evidence to suggest they are correct. Butler et al. (2004) show that Oprah Winfrey's endorsement of a book improves its position on the bestsellers list, while Garthwaite and Moore (2008) demonstrate that Winfrey's endorsement of Barack Obama gained him an additional one million votes during the primary season. On the other hand, through use of experimental data, Pease and Brewer (2008) find that exposure to news about Winfrey's endorsement led respondents to say they were more likely to vote for Obama, and to be more likely to believe he would win. Agrawal and Kamakura (1995) study the impact of the announcement of 110 celebrity-endorsement contracts on companies' stock values. They find, "a positive impact of celebrity endorsements on expected future profits." This evidence suggests the stock-market believes in the power of celebrity endorsements to improve a company's bottom line.

Scholars have developed several explanations of how the process of celebrity endorsement might work to convince people to buy products or agree with certain opinions. Early research found that the perceived "trustworthiness" of a source of information influenced the level of agreement with certain ideas. For example, Hovland and Weiss (1952) show that "high credibility" news sources are more persuasive than "low-credibility" sources of opinions. Media and politics scholars have noted the prevalence of "experts" on television news broadcasts, even while calling into question their reliability (Soley 1992). Nevertheless, scholars have observed that experts and news commentators influence public opinion (Page et al. 1987). Popular presidents may be perceived of as especially credible, and scholars have shown they are able to influence public opinion as well (Mueller 1973; Page et al. 1987).

Dholakia and Sternthal (1977: 230–231) observe that highly credible sources positively influence attitudes, but may actually reduce the likelihood of inducing certain behaviors, such as consenting to a product trial. Sternthal, Dholakia, and Leavitt (1978: 259) also find that recipients' predisposition toward an issue influenced the impact of sources, with those favorably disposed more influenced by a moderately credible source than a highly credible one. They also find that those predisposed negatively were more likely to be influenced by a highly credible communicator.

The physical attractiveness and likeability of the source have been assessed by scholars as well. In general, physically attractive endorsers are more effective (Kahle and Homer 1985), but this is not always the case. Baker and Churchill (1977: 553) note that attractive sources are not always more successful because unattractive models may be more convincing than attractive ones with regard to selling non-romantic items, such as coffee. McGuire (1985) finds that increased familiarity, likeability, and resemblance between endorser and perceiver increase a message's effectiveness.

McCracken (1989) offers the most comprehensive theory of celebrity endorsements. Broadly describing the models presented above as "source credibility" and "source attractiveness," and not finding them entirely satisfying, McCracken develops what he calls "meaning-transfer" theory. His major criticism of earlier theories is that their interpretation of the persuasiveness of celebrities has, "everything to do with the celebrity and nothing to do with the product" (p. 311). A better theory should also account for the characteristics of the celebrity and how these interact with those of the product. Not every celebrity endorsement is successful, and the intention of meaning transfer theory is to help predict when celebrity endorsements might succeed and when they would fail.

McCracken argues that the effectiveness of a celebrity endorser depends in part on the meanings he or she brings to the endorsement process, including social status, class, gender, age, personality, and lifestyle type. Every celebrity is a complicated mix of these characteristics and their meanings. An endorsement of a product will only succeed if an association is formed between appropriate aspects of the celebrity's meaning and the endorsed product. The consumer then transfers the meaning(s) from the product to themselves. Therefore there are two crucial transfers of meaning: from celebrity to product and then from product to consumer (p. 314). He suggests that those who are moving from one age category to another would be especially inclined to use the meanings created by celebrities.

Meaning-transfer theory predicts that celebrities will influence young people's political opinions and indicates why political opinions are successful "products" for celebrities to sell. According to McCracken, the celebrity world is one of experimentation and innovation in the creation of new cultural categories. McCracken's theory suggests young people are especially susceptible to influence by celebrities, and that celebrities offer young consumers new and interesting meanings of adolescence. Entertainment figures increasingly offer an image that includes adhering to a cause or speaking out about politics. Celebrities show their support for various causes through their artistic creations, public statements, and through the colorful array of ribbons they wear at awards shows.

The research presented above suggests some hypotheses about the impact of celebrity endorsements in the political realm. First, some celebrity endorsements of ideas ought to predict higher levels of agreement with those ideas among youths overall. Celebrities who are politically credible ought to be more successful at influencing public opinion than non-credible sources. Celebrity political credibility is not easy to define, but most people know it when they see it. The opinions of Paris Hilton on the AIDS crisis in Africa are unlikely to mean anything to anyone, while Irish rock star Bono's beliefs might, because for years he has been actively learning and lobbying about the issue.

Second, some celebrities will not exert influence over youths overall because they are not famous or well-liked enough. Instead, these celebrities will exert influence only over those who have heard of them or who like them. Celebrities who are famous or well-liked enough to exert an overall influence are expected to exert a greater influence over those who know and like them.

The Beastie Boys are a good place for this thinking to start because they were never superstars, but definitely attracted a sizable and devoted following, and despite the party-down ethos the band represented, they were also politically active. But is it reasonable to expect, as shown above, that white fans of rap music would be the most likely to be influenced in their political thinking by *The Beastie Boys'* beliefs? The bivariate relationship showed this to be the case, but a better method for examining the effect of celebrity endorsements is to use ordered logistic regression, because it allows us to measure the impact of our key independent variable, the celebrity endorsement, while controlling for other political and demographic characteristics of the respondents.

Table 7.7: Ordered Logit Equation for Level of Agreement with Doing More to Help Tibet, White Rap Fans Only

Variable	Coefficient (Std. Error)
Celebrity Endorsement	1.491*** (.549)
Ideology (1=Extremely Liberal)	-.821*** (.274)
Democrat	-.769 (.595)

table continued on next page

Male	.603 (.521)
Cut 1	-5.894
Cut 2	-4.226
Cut 3	-1.662
Cut 4	.041
Nagelkerke R2	.237
n	64.

* Significant at the .10 level. ** Significant at the .05 level. *** Significant at .01 level
****Significant at the .001 level. Significance levels are two-tailed.

Question: The Beastie Boys believe that other countries should do more to end the Chinese military occupation of neighboring Tibet. How do you feel about this issue?

The best way to interpret an ordered logistic regression is to hold the control variables constant at their central tendency (mode for Democrat and male, mean for ideology) and determine the change in probability of respondents' placing themselves at the five points on the agree/disagree scale based on having seen the celebrity endorsed version of the question versus having read the non-celebrity endorsed version.

Table 7.8: Predicted Probabilities of Level of Agreement with Helping Tibet, with Other Variables Held Constant at their Base Values

	Strong Disagree	Disagree	Neutral	Agree	Strongly Agree
Celebrity Endorsed	.01	.03	.30	.40	.26
Not Endorsed	.03	.12	.55	.23	.08

Clearly, respondents who read the Tibet statement as endorsed by *The Beastie Boys* are more likely to agree and agree strongly with it than those who saw it as endorsed by an anonymous someone. They are less likely to disagree or be neutral as well.

Rap and Politics

Clearly, the words of rap musicians and their sociopolitical beliefs as expressed outside their recordings influence the beliefs of young fans. Among white U.S. fans, rap preference indicates less acceptance for newer lifestyles, less tolerance for homosexuality, and more support for a political position when taken by a white rap artist.

Evidently, on issues of sexuality, whites who are positively influenced by rap's homophobia 'become more homophobic themselves. However, on the broader issue of support for newer lifestyles (which might include those most threatening to white men), whites are negatively influenced by rap. Conservative white men raised in strict parent homes especially will disapprove of this aspect of rap as reportage and implicit endorsement of the tough ghetto lifestyle.

Among blacks, rap predicts greater moral relativism, less support for women's equality, and more tolerance toward homosexuality. What do these findings mean? Perhaps more strongly than whites, black youths are able to see through rap's messages. In other words, rap and hip-hop are simultaneously more and less important to blacks. The experience with rap may be richer because it influences more aspects of life, but some of these are trivial and for entertainment only. Rap plays Lusane's (1993) educational, subversive, and farcical roles and also is a place for relationships between the sexes to be worked out. It seems that blacks are more easily able to take or leave rap's messages, as we would expect of children raised in nurturing parent homes (or with little parenting), whereas whites seem more likely to take rap's messages seriously all the time. Is rap the voice of the oppressed? Perhaps it is, but it's also much more than that. It is a medium where fans imagine their community, especially relationships between men and women. It is fun, temporary diversion, and it is worthy of continued serious investigation.

8

The Influence
of Alternative Rock

In this chapter the investigation continues into the ways in which young people who prefer different styles of music are politically distinct from each other. More specifically, the history and meaning of "alternative rock" are examined and survey evidence is presented which suggests that young people who prefer "alternative rock" are politically different in a consistent pattern from other youths in English-speaking Canada, the United States, the United Kingdom, and Ireland. First, the history of the alternative rock genre is explored, with careful attention paid to the social and political content of the music's lyrics and the public statements of musicians. Survey evidence which indicates the existence of significant and consistent political differences between fans of alternative rock and others is presented. Next, the influence of alternative rock on creating and maintaining these differences is considered. Finally, we examine the effect of alternative rock stars' endorsement of political ideas on respondents' levels of agreement with those ideas.

As discussed in previous chapters, more than traditional political attitudes are involved with young people's musical preferences. Youths may be identified as members of various subcultures, which are defined in part by musical preference. While music is only one element around which subcultures may be built, Roe (1990) suggests many youthful subcultures use some form of music to cement their group identity. Alternative rock has long been identified as a subculture which includes a number of distinctive practices and beliefs. For example, Kruse (1993) examines the alternative rock subculture in Champaign, Illinois and finds, "to some degree everyone I interviewed . . . implicitly defined themselves as 'alternative' by making claims about the uniqueness of their music or their audience: no one else was doing what they were doing" (35). To be part of the alternative scene is to demonstrate how different you are from everyone else.

Alternative Rock's History and Politics

Alternative rock is a term used to describe bands that formed after the punk period of the 1970s and early 80s. Alternative rock brings together diverse strands of musical influence into one larger sound. Will Straw (1991) describes this process as "the eclectic revival and transformation of older musical forms" (375) and suggests that alternative rock culture has developed a "stable canon of earlier musical forms—1960s trash psychedelia, early 1970s metal, the dissident rock tradition of the Velvet Underground and others—which serves as a collective reference point" (378). The appropriation and transformation of these styles has led to the development of a vibrant and popular musical style.

The development of alternative rock followed different paths in the U.S. and Britain. Some bands became quite popular in both countries (e.g., R.E.M.), whereas some bands were popular in just one (e.g., Pearl Jam's U.S. popularity). Alternative rock traces its roots to the punk movement, new wave and progressive rock. The punk movement began in the early 1970s to become aggressively modern and distance itself from the popular rock and roll music of the 1970s. Former Sex Pistols manager Malcolm McLaren said, "punk rock had to come along because the rock scene had become so tame that acts like Billy Joel and Simon and Garfunkel were being called rock and roll, when to me and other fans, rock and roll meant this wild and rebellious music." Punk songs often contained political messages in their lyrics, were short, fast, hard, and played with stripped down instrumentation (a reaction against the common addition of strings and horns in '70s music). In the United States the biggest influence on Punk music was The Ramones who began the music scene at the popular club, CBGB, in New York City. In Britain, it was bands like the Sex Pistols and The Damned that formed the punk scene.

Other popular genres that that had a major influence on alternative rock were new wave and post-punk. New wave music was initially marketed as a more commercial and chart friendly version of punk (Savage 2005). It provided a less noisy and more pop-oriented sound. The term "new wave" could be applied to any band with an attitude that did not embrace the simplistic and loud-fast playing style of punk music, including Elvis Costello, The Police, Devo, The Go Gos, Talking Heads, and so on. Post-punk music branched off the punk music scene by continuing the anti-establishment stance but by becoming more experimental in the type of music played. The bands were more introverted, complex, arty, and experimental than classic punk rock and new wave music (Post-Punk).

Alternative rock originated by taking many pieces from these different genres. Starting in the 1980s, alternative rock grew from the push to make something outside the so-called "mainstream" and not to be as concerned with popularity as measured by record sales. It was equally as political as punk music but with more complicated music behind the lyrics. Early alternative bands toured relentlessly in support of low-budget records, which helped to build sizeable followings for a number of them, even with limited air-play. This helped to develop a closer relationship between fans and bands, which one might hypothesize would increase musicians' abilities to influence fans on matters not related to musical preferences, such as political beliefs. Also, new bands would form from the influence of previous groups, and would create a considerable alternative rock circuit in the U.S. Each stop on the circuit developed into its own unique scene, with place names like Athens, Georgia and Minneapolis, Minnesota coming to represent different sounds of alternative rock.

R.E.M. could be considered the first American alternative band. Their first full-length album in 1983, *Murmur*, received critical praise and broke into the top 40 album chart. Their style of music helped other similar bands to follow. This style combined punk influences with folk music and music popular in the mainstream. This music was more melodic, with more guitar distortion and complicated lyrics. They achieved their success both commercially and musically by non-stop touring throughout the 1980s. R.E.M. also released an album each year, which helped expand their fan base. This helped them set the stage for their 1987 breakthrough album, *Document*, which put them on the path to mainstream success. R.E.M. is considered an alternative rock band because they took the message of the punk movement and put better music behind it. The members of R.E.M. have become politically engaged over the years as well, with perhaps their most public politicking taking place in 2004 when they played on the Vote for Change tour in support of Democratic Presidential nominee John Kerry.

After the initial framework was established, multiple bands became major contributors to the alternative rock scene, including groups like *The Pixies, Dinosaur Jr., Sonic Youth*, and others. Some of these bands achieved success on major labels while others did not. Starting in the 1990s, the Seattle grunge scene, which synthesized heavy metal and hardcore punk music dominated alternative rock. In 1991, *Nirvana's* second and most successful album *Nevermind* and *Pearl Jam's* breakthrough debut *Ten* were released. *Nirvana's* surprise successes with *Nevermind* led to more airplay on mainstream stations for alternative rock (Rosen 1992). After the commercial successes of these bands, record labels broadened the definition of alternative rock to include bands that did not have punk or post-punk influences. These included pop-punk bands like *Green Day* and the *Offspring*, singer-songwriter Tracey Chapman, and heavy metal band *Living Colour*.

British alternative rock is different from the U.S. variant in two major ways. First, it is more pop-oriented. Second, it more freely acknowledges the music of dance and club culture. Many British alternative rock groups frequently experiment with dance rhythms and textures (Erlewine 2001). Like *R.E.M* in the U.S., *The Smiths* may be the beginning of alternative rock in Britain. In fact, they are considered by some to be the most important alternative rock band to emerge from the British music scene of the 1980s. Their guitar-pop was influenced by groups like *The Kinks* and *The Beatles*. What made them so popular were singer Morrissey's unusual, witty, and controversial lyrics and their lead guitarist Johnny Marr's music (Reynolds 2005). As with R.E.M. in the United States, *The Smiths* followed the punk movement with more interesting music behind their lyrics.

From there, the British alternative rock scene was dominated by the goth rock of *The Cure* and the dance-rock of *New Order* in the later part of the 80s. *The Cure* presented slower tempos, droning guitars and often morbidly depressing lyrics. They appealed to some of *The Smiths'* audience but were gloomier and less pop-oriented. *New Order* was at the other end of the spectrum. They experimented with dance, disco, and club beats. They created a fusion between rock and dance, which proved to be both commercially successful and musically influential (Erlewine 2001). However, the most significant British band of the late 80s and early 90s was the *Stone Roses*. Like *The Smiths*, they specialized in an updated version of 60s guitar pop. But, they came from psychedelic guitar pop not mainstream pop and experimented with club beats. They influenced multiple bands.

After the initial framework, British alternative rock became more local. The new alternative rock, called "Britpop" by the media, strove to be different from America and more "British" (Hasted). Bands like *Oasis* and *Blur* became the British equivalent of the grunge explosion in America (but with major stylistic differences). Britpop not only propelled alternative rock in Britain but also centered on the revitalization of British youth culture. Britpop has since faded but post-Britpop bands like *Radiohead* and *Coldplay* have achieved great success.

Other countries, like Canada and Australia have produced a number of alternative bands and become important centers for current alternative rock. National origin of alternative bands matters because bands may more than reflect the ideas of the times during which they are successful. Cloonan argues, "(a)t a minimum it seems that popular music has a continuing role to play in constructing national identity. At one level this is mere marketing or scene-making, but at another popular musicians have been said to encapsulate something about the nation." Britpop may have played a role in constructing a certain kind of British identity (see Cloonan 1997, 1999 for a full examination of this possibility). Scholars such as Jackson (2005) have also shown how Canadian bands have influenced the perspective on their country of their fans.

Alternative music was so named because it served as an alternative to rock music that was deemed excessively commercial or performed to please a broad audience. The bands did not want to be seen as rock stars, but rather as living on the same level as their fans. *R.E.M.* guitarist Peter Buck was asked how he thought bands could get popular and he responded by saying, "The reason we we're successful is that we were good, and we persevered, and we really didn't give much of a fuck about radio or selling records" (Nabors 1993). Their songs expressed the concerns of those fans and the attitudes of the songs were often angry and depressed (Charlton 1998). Most alternative music had elements of the antiestablishment push of the punk movement. Also, many alternative performers used the pounding beat and distorted guitars reminiscent of the *Sex Pistols* or *Ramones*. Also, there was more concentration on music and lyrics that were more individualistic and would not appeal to a wide array of people.

Alternative rock success is not defined by album sales. Some alternative rock bands are very popular, while others labor in relative obscurity. Some begin their careers as relative unknowns, but then achieve spectacular success. *R.E.M.* and *U2* are the quintessential examples of this. Bands that make it big are often accused of "selling out" when they become popular. This attack can take many forms, from claims the music and lyrics have changed to appeal to a mass audience to arguments the band members have stopped taking controversial stands on political and social issues.

The important role of women in alternative rock's development must not be ignored either. Punk, post-punk, new wave, and alternative rock offered women some of their first opportunities to front bands that performed their own words and music. From early punk band leaders like *Siouxsie Sioux of Siouxsie and the Banshees* to new wave band leader Debbie Harry (*Blondie*), women either led or played important roles in hundreds of bands (for a comprehensive collection and categorization of women's contribution to punk and new wave see "Rockin' Rina's Women of 1970s Punk" page at http://www.comnet.ca/~rina/). The taken-for-granted nature of women band leaders and creative contributors in both alternative rock and the music that inspired it would lead us to expect that fans of alternative rock would have different views about the proper role of women than would fans of other music.

From its inception, alternative rock has been connected with politics. In 1977, *The Sex Pistols* released the anti-monarchist punk rock anthem "God Save the Queen," and much politically oriented alternative rock followed. English band *The Clash* was one of the most politically oriented punk/alternative bands ever. In 1980 they released a 36-track triple-album entitled "Sandinista." The album contains a number of political songs including "Washington Bullets," with lyrics such as, "Sandinista! / For the very first time ever / When they had a revolution in Nicaragua / There was no interference from America / Human rights in America."

More recently, alternative rock musicians have made political comments both in their lyrics and public statements. Zack De La Rocha of the important 1990s alternative band *Rage Against the Machine*, said, "What passes for democracy today is a sham. It's all about raising money and owing favors to the wrong people." *Rage Against the Machine* was one of the most politically active bands of the late 1990s, espousing socialism in their lyrics and encouraging activism among their fans. They campaigned for the release from prison of AIM activist Leonard Peltier and Black Panther Mumia Abu-Jamal.

English band *Radiohead* were also politically active. For example, vocalist Thom Yorke said of U.S. President George W. Bush and British Prime Minister Tony Blair, "These men are liars. We have the right to call them such, they are putting our children's future in jeopardy. They are not controlling the terrorist threat, they are escalating it." Yorke has also been active in the environmental movement, and while he has been compared to U2 lead singer and activist Bono, Yorke cringes at the notion of insider politics, preferring instead to play the role of outside (and therefore independent) agitator.

Canadian alternative acts have not shied away from politics either. Prominent alternative rocker Alanis Morissette publicly opposed U.S. President George W. Bush's Energy Program because she believed it disregarded environmental protection and failed to support conservation and renewable energy programs. Deryck Whibley, leader of the band *Sum 41* said, "George W. Bush is probably one of the worst presidents we'll ever have, or have had. . . . I just don't know how, so far, he's gotten away with everything he's done." While his use of the phrase "we'll ever have" is odd in reference to a leader of another country, the left/liberal stance of the position is clear.

From the above research and the issue-position questions available on the surveys, a number of hypotheses are generated:

1. Ideology: Alternative rock fans will self-identity their political ideology as being further left than fans of other forms of music.
2. Alternative Lifestyles: Alternative rock fans will be more tolerant of alternative life styles. This study explores explore tolerance toward homosexuality.
3. Women's Roles: Alternative rock fans will be more accepting of non-traditional roles for women.
4. National Cultural Pride: Alternative rock fans will be more likely to support the culture and music of their nation.
5. Marijuana: Alternative rock fans will be more likely to support the legalization of marijuana.
6. Political Engagement: Alternative rock fans will display higher levels of political engagement.

Alternative Rock Fans' Political Beliefs

Overall Ideology

It is reasonable to hypothesize that fans of alternative rock will on average describe themselves as more left/liberal than others, and the evidence suggests this is at least partly true. On the seven point scale where seven represents extremely liberal, Canadian alternative fans average 5.07 compared with 4.85 for fans of other music and the difference is significant ($t = 1.319$, sig. (one-tailed) = .095). Also, U.K. respondents who prefer alternative rock average 4.50 on a 10-point left/right continuum where one represents extremely left, while others average 5.02 ($t=2.460$, sig. (two-tailed) = .015). There were no overall ideological differences between alternative fans and others in the U.S. and Irish samples, although an analysis of white U.S. respondents showed white alternative fans to be more liberal than other white respondents, but the difference was not statistically significant.

Alternative Lifestyles: Homosexuality

Greater tolerance for "newer" and homosexual lifestyles is expected from fans of alternative rock. Among U.S. respondents, the data show a strong relationship between preference for alternative rock and a lack of concern that "newer lifestyles contribute to the breakdown of society." Whereas 32.9% of U.S. alternative fans disagree with the statement, only 25.5% of non-alternative fans do. Moreover, only 42.2% of U.S. alternative fans agree with the statement, whereas 53.9% of non-fans agree. These relationships are significant (Chi-square (2) = 7.297, sig. (two-tailed) = .026).

The data are, however, even more striking on the relationship between alternative rock and the moral acceptability of homosexuality among U.S. respondents. Agreement with the statement that homosexual lifestyles are morally acceptable was far higher among U.S. alternative fans than others. Whereas 48% of U.S. alternative rock fans believe that homosexual lifestyles are morally acceptable, only 30.6% of U.S. non-fans believe this. Moreover, the difference is significant (Chi-square (2) = 19.867, sig. (two-tailed) = .000).

Canadian, U.K. and Irish respondents were not asked the questions analyzed above, but instead were asked about gay marriage. U.K. fans of alternative rock are more likely than fans of other music to strongly agree that gays should be allowed to marry (61% to 43.8%, chi-square (3) = 13.891, sig. (two-tailed) = .003). Canadian alternative fans were more supportive of gay marriage than others, but the differences were not large enough to become statistically significant.

Women's Roles

Fans of alternative rock should be more supportive than fans of other kinds of music of women's equality, and this appears to be the case. Among U.S. respondents, on a seven-point scale where one indicates a belief in gender equality and seven represents a belief that a woman's place is in the home, alternative fans average 1.65 while others average 1.92. This .27-point difference is significant at the .01 level.

Canadian alternative fans are more likely to at least somewhat disagree with the statement that society would be better off if more women stayed at home (83% to 73.7%, chi-square (3) = 4.044, sig. (two-sided) = .044). There appear to be no statistically significant relationships between beliefs about the role of women and alternative preferences among British and Irish respondents, although British respondents are slightly more likely to disagree with the claim women should stay at home.

National Cultural Pride

Among Irish respondents, fans of alternative rock are less likely to strongly or somewhat agree that Irish music and TV are not as good as American music and television (11.8% to 19.4% and 35.3% to 43.5% respectively, chi-square (3) = 8.941, sig. (two-tailed) = .030). Among U.K. respondents, those who prefer alternative rock are much less likely to strongly agree and are more likely to disagree that British music and television is not as good as American (1% to 10.8% and 82% to 68% respectively, chi-square (3) = 15.481, sig. (two-tailed) = .001). Canadian respondents who prefer alternative rock are less likely to agree that Canadian music and television is inferior to U.S. productions, but the differences are not statistically significant, and impressions of the quality of a nation's popular culture were not asked on the U.S. surveys.

Marijuana

Because of the libertarian bent of alternative rock, it is expected that its fans will be more likely than others to agree that marijuana possession should not be a criminal offense. Irish fans of alternative rock were more likely to somewhat and strongly agree that smoking marijuana should not be a criminal offense (58.8% to 30.6% and 23.5% to 16.1% respectively, chi-square (3) = 7.119, sig. (two-tailed) = .068).

U.K. alternative fans are more likely to strongly and somewhat agree that smoking marijuana should not be a criminal offense (25.7% to 22.6% and 41.6% to 33.2% respectively, chi-square (3) = 5.254, sig. (one-tailed) = .077). The question was not asked on the U.S. survey, and while Canadian alternative fans were more supportive of the proposition that marijuana smoking ought not be a criminal offense, the differences were not statistically significant.

Political Engagement

Because of the political content of the lyrics of much alternative rock and the calls to participate by so many alternative musicians, fans of the genre ought to be more politically active than others, and there is some evidence this is the case. Among U.S. respondents, alternative fans are more likely to place themselves on the extremes in terms of how frequently they talk with their family and friends about politics. While 41.7% of alternative fans report zero hours of conversation per day, only 35.9% of non-alternative fans report this level of disengagement. However, 14.9% of alternative fans report talking with their family and friends two to three hours per day, while only 10.8% of non-fans report this much (chi-square (4) = 6.985, sig. (two-tailed) = .137).

U.K. respondents were asked to report how many days in the past week they talked about politics with family and friends (as opposed to the hours per day measure used for U.S. respondents). U.K. alternative fans averaged 3.51 days to others' 2.96, and the difference is significant (t=2.097, sig. (two-tailed) = .038). There were no statistically significant differences with regard to levels of political engagement of Canadian or Irish respondents.

Summary of Results

Table 8.1 summarizes the findings. It provides five separate classifications for each hypothesis: whether the result is in the predicted direction (i.e. in agreement with our hypotheses), whether the result is statistically significant, and whether the question was asked in all countries. On every issue except political engagement, the differences between alternative rock fans and others were in the right direction and significant or at least in the right direction in at least three of the four countries examined. Importantly, in no country was the difference in the opposite of the expected direction and also significant. Further, while in a few instances the results were in the opposite direction from what was expected, they were never large, and may be due to other factors. For example, in the case of ideology among U.S. respondents, the "wrong" differences disappear when race is controlled for. Also, while the difference between Irish alternative fans and others on the question of gay marriage is in the wrong direction, 82.3% of alternative fans agree it should be legal while 83.6% of others do—hardly an earth-shattering difference in the wrong direction.

Table 8.1: Alternative Rock Preference and Political Beliefs

	Ideology	Homosexuality	Women's Roles	National Pride	Marijuana	Political Engagement
Agreement & Signif.	U.K., Can	U.K., U.S.	U.S., Can	U.K., Irl	U.K., Irl	U.K., U.S.
Agreement w/o Signif.	Irl	Can	U.K.	Can	Can	None
No Agree & Signif.	None	None	None	None	None	None
No Agree w/o Signif.	U.S.	Irl	Irl	None	None	Can, Irl
Question not asked	—	—	—	U.S.	U.S.	—

The Influence of Alternative Rock Stars

As done when looking at the effect of white rappers *The Beastie Boys* in chapter seven, ordered logistic regression will be utilized to examine the influence of several alternative rockers in a number of the countries being examined in this book.

Zack De La Rocha and the USA

As mentioned earlier, Zack De La Rocha, was the front-man for popular California hard-rock band *Rage Against the Machine*. The band was among the more politically-oriented of the 1990s, and took decidedly leftist positions on issues. The band included footage of Green party presidential candidate Ralph Nader in their 2000 music video for the song "Testify," and played at concerts supporting abortion rights and the freeing from prison of native American activist Leonard Peltier, as well as protesting the Free Trade Area of the Americas and the 2000 Democratic National Convention. Their sound was abrasive and their politics tended toward the extreme. While this may make them less likeable or attractive to older fans, the young males who predominate in the world of hard rock and punk fans are likely to find the band's sound and style appealing, and perhaps their politics as well.

The two versions of the statement from De La Rocha are:

Zack De La Rocha of *Rage Against The Machine*, said, "What passes for democracy today is a sham. It's all about raising money and owing favors to the wrong people." How do you feel about his comments?

Some people believe that, "What passes for democracy today is a sham. It's all about raising money and owing favors to the wrong people." How do you feel about this position?

Table 8.2: Ordered Logit Equations for Level of Agreement with Democracy is a Sham, Alternative Rock Fans Only

Variable	Coefficient (Std. Error)
Celebrity Endorsement	.642* (.382)
Ideology (7=Extremely Conservative)	-.253* (.135)
Republican	.520 (.429)
Male	1.073**** (.337)
Income	-.097 (.140)
Black	-2.452** (1.139)
Cut 1	-5.516
Cut 2	-2.428
Cut 3	-.920
Cut 4	1.715

* Significant at the .10 level. ** Significant at the .05 level. *** Significant at .01 level ****Significant at the .001 level. Significance levels are two-tailed.

Zack De La Rocha's endorsement of the belief that democracy in the U.S. is a sham appears to predict higher levels of agreement among young fans of alternative rock. When Zack De La Rocha claims democracy in the U.S. is a sham, young fans of alternative rock are less likely to disagree with the statement or to be neutral, while they are more likely to agree or strongly agree.

Table 8.3: Predicted Probabilities of Level of Agreement, with Other Variables Held Constant at their Base Values

	Strong Disagree	Disagree	Neutral	Agree	Strongly Agree
De La Rocha Question					
Celebrity Endorsed	.01	.13	.28	.49	.09
Not Endorsed	.01	.22	.35	.37	.05

Avril Lavigne, Deryck Whibley, Alanis Morissette, and Canada

Avril Lavigne is a very popular musician, both in Canada and the United States. Her debut album sold 14 million copies and earned eight Grammy nominations. Lavigne released the album *Under My Skin* in 2004, and it quickly climbed to number one in Canada, the United States, the United Kingdom, and Australia ("Avril Lavigne: Definition, Meaning, Explanation"). Only 24 years old, Lavigne is the youngest of the celebrities included in the Canadian survey, and her age matches the mean age of the survey's respondents. Lavigne celebrates adolescence, and teenagers are drawn to her because of it (Fuchs 2004). Her songs send a message of teenage angst and empowerment.

When Lavigne signed her first contract at the age of 16, the industry was enthusiastic about this newest teen sensation ("Avril Lavigne: Definition, Meaning, Explanation"). She was a beautiful teenager with a bad-girl attitude, and therefore a marketing dream. The industry believed they could make Lavigne into a sex symbol, much as they had done with Britney Spears. Lavigne, though, defied the marketers and has rejected displaying "hypersexual femminess," (Fuchs 2004), choosing instead to stress self-respect and defiance of authority. While she has not sold her sexuality as blatantly as Britney Spears or Christina Aguilera, she has still become a sex symbol. Lavigne was listed in the *FHM Magazine* "100 Sexiest Women in the World" in 2003 and 2004 ("Avril Lavigne: Definition, Meaning, Explanation" Retreived 2009). This may send the message to young women that they can be beautiful while standing up for themselves. Lavigne's impact was demonstrated when her image as a "skater-chick" became a fashion trend among her fans.

Alanis Morissette

Alanis Morissette differs from the two other musicians in the study because of her age, 34. Most of the young adults in our study are not old enough to remember her character on *You Can't Do That on Television*, a children's program seen mostly in Canada and during the early years of Nickelodeon. Morissette began her musical career as a pop princess in the mode of Debbie Gibson. Then she changed her image in 1995 with the release of "Jagged Little Pill," which contained the angry rantings of a jilted lover in the form of the hit single, "You Oughtta Know," which won a Grammy for song of the year.

Morissette sings of female empowerment, and recently she appeared in an off-Broadway production of the *Vagina Monologues*, which portrays how women feel about their sexual organs. She has stated she does not want to adhere to the conventional stereotype of how a woman should look (Sullivan 2004). Her resulting simple, hard-working on-stage image is one of striving and unadorned beauty.

As Morissette's career has matured, she has maintained her opinionated and independent persona, but added a new degree of spirituality ("Alanis Morissette" 2005), projecting meanings such as introspective aggressiveness, feminine strength, and independence. She is also generous with her money, setting aside at least ten percent of her earnings per year for charity and other humanitarian efforts (Sullivan 2004).

Alanis may represent what Avril Lavigne will yet become, and comparisons between the stars are common, even though Lavigne bristles at them. "I think I get compared to her just (because) she's Canadian and she's not some pop chick, she's a rocker, and I'm not a pop chick, and I'm a rocker, " Lavigne said (Fuchs 2004). The influence of Morrissette ought to be more muted among young fans, because she has made a transition in her career from screaming at arena-sized crowds of young people, to entertaining theater-sized audiences of grown-ups.

Deryck Whibley

At just 28 Whibley is the handsome young leader of a Canadian pop/punk band known as *Sum 41*. Whibley attracts attention for his wild antics, both off and on the stage (Edwards 2001). He has been in several high-profile romantic relationships with other celebrities, including Avril Lavigne, whom he married in 2006. Whibley's age is an important element of his meaning. Although 28, he does not look a day older than 15, which allows him to connect with his fans. He is near their age and is making millions of dollars doing something he loves to do, and which they would love to do. He often autographs R-rated body parts of female fans after concerts (Edwards 2001). One meaning transferred from Whibley to his fans is of adolescent lust for everything young heterosexual men lust for: beer-fueled mayhem and the company of women.

Offstage, *Sum 41* is known for one major contribution to the party-punk musical lifestyle: destruction of property. This may result from the angst of a life on the road and stage, but the band's lyrics are angst-ridden as well (Harvilla 2001). Other rock bands have been known to trash and damage hotel rooms, but Sum 41 seems to personify the word "destruction," even though lately they have sought to be taken more seriously.

Before the release of a recent album, *Sum 41* took a humanitarian trip to the war-torn Democratic Republic of Congo in association with the charity War Child Canada. While in the Congo, the band members filmed a documentary for the organization, which outlined issues of the six-year civil war including human-rights violations, refugee camp conditions, the role of child-soldiers, and the demand for a mineral which is used in the production of electronics, which is considered to be one of the major reason for war. Fighting broke out outside the hotel in which they were staying, and the band, along with 40 other guests, had to be evacuated and escorted to a nearby United Nations compound. When the band reached relative safety at the compound, a unanimous decision was made to name their upcoming album "Chuck" after Canadian U.N. peacekeeper Chuck Pelletier, the man who led them to safety. The first single released from the album was penned immediately after that eye-opening experience, eventually entitled "We're All to Blame."

In an interview with MTV, Whibley explained the song's meaning and purpose. "It's about the state of the world, and how it's come to be like this, (and) directly or indirectly, everyone is somehow to blame one way or another. Whether you have direct involvement or you just choose to be ignorant, we all have some kind of involvement" (D'Angelo 2004). With the release of "We're All to Blame," there is evidence of a maturing by Whibley and the band. Whibley now represents humanitarian awareness, and that it is "cool" even for party-oriented punk bands to think about the world and have political opinions.

The respondents were asked to agree or disagree, on a four-point scale from strongly disagree (1) to strongly agree (4), with a series of political statements that had in fact been made by the celebrities discussed above. Through a random distribution, half of the sample was given a version of the statement with the celebrity's name attached, while the other half was presented the statement as having been said by an anonymous "someone."

Each of the statements related to the United States—specifically the policies of President George Bush—with two of the statements critical of U.S. policy, and one a positive statement about the Canadian government's decision not to go to war in Iraq. The exact wording of each question follows:

> Avril Lavigne recently said, "I don't have respect for the people that made the decisions to go with the war. I don't have much respect for Bush. He's about war, I'm not about war—a lot of people aren't about war . . . I'm really proud that our Prime Minister didn't fight." How do you feel about these statements?

> Deryck Whibley of the band *Sum 41* said recently, "George W. Bush is probably one of the worst presidents we'll ever have, or have had. . . . I just don't know how, so far, he's gotten away with everything he's done." How do you feel about these comments?

> Alanis Morissette opposed U.S. President George W. Bush's Energy Program because she believed it disregarded environmental protection and failed to support conservation and renewable energy programs. How do you feel about this?

Table 8.4: Ordered Logit Equations for Level of Agreement with Political Statements

	Lavigne Question	Morissette Question	Whibley Question
Celebrity Endorsement	.305* (.205)	-.053 (.206)	1.412*** (.473)
Ideology	.546**** (.072)	.402**** (.073)	.570*** (.183)
USA Temperature Rating	-.035**** (.004)	-.028**** (.004)	-.053**** (.012)
Canada Temperature Rating	.026**** (.007)	.008 (.007)	.011 (.018)
Male	-.357* (.211)	.093 (.211)	-.608* (.464)
Quebec	-.566** (.422)	.613* (.443)	-1.640** (.961)
Ontario	.067 (.351)	-.127 (.358)	-2.235*** (.776)
Prairies	.407 (.414)	.055 (.416)	-.293 (.956)
Alberta	-.658* (.448)	.272 (.466)	-4.638**** (1.081)
British Columbia	-.860** (.423)	.103 (.443)	-2.891*** (.930)
Cut 1	-.336	-2.498	-4.736
Cut 2	.994	-1.217	-2.932
Cut 3	3.049	1.617	.219
Chi-square	182.525	112.366	73.866
Nagelkerke R2	.392	.279	.568
n	456	456	113

*Significant at the .10 level (one-tailed). ** Significant at the .10 level (two-tailed). *** Significant at the .05 level (two-tailed). **** Significant at the .001 level (two-tailed).*

When other political and demographic variables are controlled for, celebrity endorsement increases the probability of the respondent's agreeing with the statement in two of the three cases.[1] In each case, ideology and U.S. temperature rating predict changes in the expected direction. Those with warmer feelings toward the U.S. are less likely to agree with the anti-Bush sentiments. For ideology, liberals are more likely to agree with anti-Bush statements. Canadian temperature rating, gender, and region are controlled for as well, and do not appear to produce a patterned influence on levels of agreement.

Avril Lavigne's endorsement of the position that it is good Canada did not join the U.S.-led war in Iraq predicts both slightly less disagreement with the position and more strong agreement. Deryck Whibley's endorsement of the position that President Bush is the worst President ever moves respondents from mere agreement to strong agreement. Alanis Morissette's impact appears almost non-existent.

Table 8.5: Predicted Probabilities of Level of Agreement, with Other Variables Held Constant at their Base Values

	Strongly Disagree	Disagree	Agree	Strongly Agree
Lavigne Question				
Celebrity Endorsed	.02	.05	.30	.63
Not Endorsed	.03	.07	.35	.56
Morissette Question				
Celebrity Endorsed	.02	.05	.50	.42
Not Endorsed	.02	.05	.49	.44
Whibley Question				
Celebrity Endorsed	.00	.00	.06	.94
Not Endorsed	.00	.01	.21	.78

Thom Yorke's Influence in the United Kingdom

Thom Yorke is a unique political celebrity who brings a very different set of meanings to the endorsement process and a distinct kind of credibility as well. Isolation in his youth pushed Yorke towards music, and after his family settled in Oxford, Yorke

1   We report two-tailed significance levels for celebrity effect in three of the four models, but in one (Avril Lavigne) the effect was only significant if we utilized a one-tailed test. Because we are confident we know the expected direction of the relationship, this is an acceptable practice. Note that we are also more muted in our discussion of the impact of Ms. Lavigne, because of this relative weakness of her impact. Also, there are no collinearity problems in any of the models, as no correlation coefficient between any of the independent variables exceeds .323.

attended the Abingdon School, where he met guitarist Ed O'Brien and bassist Colin Greenwood. The boys eventually added drummer Phil Selway and Greenwood's younger brother Jonny, and the band "On A Friday" was formed (Prato). The band changed its name to *Radiohead* after the title of a song on *Talking Heads*' album *True Stories*.

In 1993 the band released their first full-length album, *Pablo Honey*. The first single, "Creep," became a surprise hit on U.S. radio and MTV. Rolling Stone columnist Rob Sheffield commented that, "according to the script, Radiohead was supposed to disappear . . . leaving only fond memories of Thom Yorke's Martin-Short-after-electroshock yodel and that wukka-wukka guitar hook." But then *Radiohead* released their second album, *The Bends*. The album won critical acclaim as well as commercial success, prompting Sheffield to remark that "U2 would have sold crack to nuns to make this record."

After *The Bends*, the band released OK Computer in 1997, which won a Grammy for Best Alternative Album ("About Radiohead"). Their futuristic sound and darkly emotional ballads appealed to a wide audience. The band's members became involved in political and humanitarian events as their fame grew, including the Amnesty International Concert in Paris in 1998, and the Tibetan Freedom Concert in Amsterdam ("About Radiohead").

Radiohead released *Kid A* in 2000. The album debuted at the top of the U.S. charts despite the absence of the release of a single or a video (Prato). The album also won a Grammy Award for Best Alternative Album ("About Radiohead"). A year later, the band released the second half of *Kid A* entitled *Amnesiac*. *Radiohead*'s next and final studio album thus far, *Hail to the Thief*, was released in 2003.

The title of the album raised some controversy in the U.S., when some interpreted it as a reference to the 2000 Presidential election. In the June 2003 issue of Spin magazine, however, Yorke commented that, "if the motivation for naming our album had been based solely on the U.S. election, I'd find that to be pretty shallow" ("About Radiohead").

In 2004, the band members separated to pursue individual projects. In 2006, Yorke released his first solo album, *The Eraser* (Prato). Rob Sheffield sums up Yorke and *Radiohead*'s career to date by saying, "Topping the charts with zero airplay, refusing to kiss a square inch of ass, too busy rewriting the rules to follow anyone else's, *Radiohead* remains king."

Yorke has also become a political and social activist. During a concert in 2001, he dedicated the song "No Surprises" to George W. Bush. The song contains the lyrics "Bring down the government / They don't speak for us". He is also very open about his dislike of former British Prime Minister Tony Blair. Yorke was given the opportunity to meet with Tony Blair and refused on the basis that Blair has "no environmental credentials" (Duerden).

Thom Yorke has also been active in the environmental movement, urging for legislation and action to combat climate change. He is an ambassador for the environmental organization Friends of the Earth. He joined "The Big Ask" campaign to push for a three percent yearly curb on carbon emissions ("The Big Ask: Thom Yorke"). According to the organization, The Big Ask shuns what it believes is the blatant consumerism of Bono's "Product Red" campaign and instead focuses on lobbying the government directly to reform the laws on climate change.

In May of 2006, Friends of the Earth held a benefit concert named "The Big Ask Live," featuring Yorke and *Radiohead* guitarist Jonny Greenwood as the headliners (McLean 2006). However, Yorke and *Radiohead* refused to play Live8 in 2005, claiming, "it was a form of distraction. A convenient political sideshow to what was probably the most important G8 meeting . . . Holding a big rock concert and reducing the issues to bare essential levels, I think, ultimately, was to the detriment of the [Make Poverty History] campaign." (McLean 2006)

Because of his political involvement, Yorke is often compared to Bono, but the view that Yorke and Bono are similar in their beliefs may be misguided. Yorke sees himself as the opposite of Bono. In an interview with Brian Draper, referring to his and Bono's political involvement, Yorke said:

> The difference between me and Bono is that he's quite happy to go and flatter people to get what he wants and he's very good at it, but I just can't do it. I'd probably end up punching them in the face rather than shaking their hand, so it's best that I stay out of their way. I can't engage with that level of bullshit . . . I admire the fact that Bono can, and can walk away from it smelling of roses.

York may be seen as the opposite of Bono, relying for his credibility on an image as a tough, straight-talking outsider.

Let us now examine through regression analysis the potential influence of Thom Yorke on the U.K. sample. Many independent variables are controlled for including U.S. temperature rating, Bush temperature rating, left/right placement, and gender. We will add the temperature ratings for Tony Blair and for the U.K. as well. Moreover, in the U.K. surveys respondents were asked if they were familiar with the celebrities in question and how warmly they felt toward them, which eliminates the necessity of dividing the sample between fans of the celebrity's musical form, and others.

Table 8.6: Ordered Logit Equations for Level of Agreement with Claim Bush and Blair are Liars1

	Overall	At Least Somewhat Familiar with Yorke*Celebrity	Warm toward Yorke*Celebrity	Both Familiar with and Warm toward Yorke*Celebrity
Celebrity Endorsed	-.032 (.212)	-.008 (.283)	-.473 (.334)	-.301 (.357)
Bush Temper ature	.019**** (.006)	.019**** (.006)	.018**** (.016)	.019**** (.006)
Blair Temp	.045**** (.005)	.044**** (.005)	.045**** (.006)	.045**** (.005)

table continued on next page

U.S. Temperature	.015*** (.006)	.015*** (.006)	.016*** (.006)	.016*** (.006)
Great Britain Temp.	.008 (.007)	.008 (.007)	.007 (.007)	.008 (.007)
Left Right Placement	.143*** (.058)	.143** (.059)	.133** (.059)	.135** (.059)
Female	-.049 (.216)	-.051 (.218)	-.089 (.218)	-.080 (.219)
Cut 1 (strongly agree)	3.623	3.637	3.484	3.537
Cut 2 (somewhat agree)	6.331	6.345	6.204	6.251
Cut 3 (somewhat disagree)	8.289	8.304	8.163	8.211
Nagelkerke R2	.456	.456	.460	.457
n	365	365	365	365

* Significant at the .10 level. ** Significant at the .05 level. *** Significant at .01 level ****Significant at the .001 level. Significance levels are two-tailed. [1]Negative coefficients indicate greater level of agreement due to the way the responses were coded (1=strongly agree).

It appears that in none of the models does Thom Yorke's endorsement move agreement level among respondents with his belief that Bush and Blair are liars. However, the celebrity endorsement variable coupled with giving Thom Yorke a temperature rating of over 50 is nearly significant, and if the significance level for that variable (.158) is divided in half, which is permissible because the direction of the expected relationship (negative) is know, it is significant at the .10 level. Therefore it is worth determining the substantive effect of that interactive variable in the model.

Table 8.7: Predicted Probabilities of Level of Agreement with Blair and Bush are Liars, with Other Variables Held Constant at their Base Values

	Strongly Agree	Somewhat Agree	Somewhat Disagree	Strongly Disagree
Warm Toward Yorke				
Celebrity Endorsed	.359	.536	.089	.016
Not Endorsed	.259	.582	.133	.026

It appears that among those who feel warmly toward him, Mr. York's endorsement increases the probability of a respondent's strongly agreeing with the statement while decreasing the other three categories. This suggests that warmth is an essential component of celebrity endorsement effectiveness, because among the general sample, Yorke's endorsement had no effect. In the case of Yorke, familiarity and warmth are quite strongly related as well, with those who are more familiar with him also feeling more warmly toward him.

Bono: Beloved Insider

Bono (whose birth name is Paul Hewson) is the lead singer of the Irish rock band U2, which was founded in 1978 by the band's drummer Larry Mullen Jr., and includes Adam Clayton on bass and The Edge (David Evans) on guitar. As the band became increasingly famous in the early and mid-1980s, their politics began to take center stage, along with the Christian spirituality of the band's lyrics. Their politics were not confined to their lyrics, but included action as well, such as participation in the Live-Aid concert at London's Wembley Stadium in 1985.

According to Bono, during the band's early concerts in the US, "people were throwing money on stage during the Bobby Sands hunger strike. But what was that money for? Those dollars were arriving in the streets of Belfast and Derry as weapons and bombs. Some things are black and white—but the troubles in Northern Ireland are not. I know: I'm the son of a Protestant mother and a Catholic father" (Miller 1984; 61). Even early in U2's career, Bono was conscious of and concerned about the audience's perception of the political beliefs of the band. Clearly he did not want the audience to assume any support by U2 for Sinn Fein or the Irish Republican Army (IRA).

While the band's lyrics are often political, or at least concern important world events and public figures, critics have noticed vagueness in them. David Plotz (2002) suggests U2's unlikely 25 year run as one of the world's most important rock bands has been facilitated in part by U2's, "pretend[ing] that it is a political rock band." While admitting the band has written about such political topics as Ireland's troubles, Martin Luther King's civil rights struggles, US policy in Latin America, and Burmese democracy activist Aung San Suu Kyi, Plotz still argues, "U2 is perhaps the world's vaguest band."

While U2's political focus started with US involvement in Irish issues, over time it has expanded to include broad justice issues. After U2 performed in 'Live-Aid,' which raised $200 million for African assistance, Bono spent a month working in Ethiopia in a relief camp (Leland 2000). After recognizing in the late 1990s that $200 million amounted only to the debt payments of African nations for a few days, Bono came to be most strongly associated with the issue of third world debt relief. The movement has appeared to achieve a number of successes, including the G-8 nations' pledging to forgive $100 billion of the $356 billion it was owed (Leland 2000), and pledges of increased aid and trade after the G-8 summit in Gleneagles, Scotland in 2005. Bono has formed a policy advocacy group called DATA, which stands for 'Debt AIDS Trade Africa' (Traub 2005), and in 2005 he launched a brand of products and services called "Red," from which a portion of the proceeds are contributed to the group. He has lobbied for debt relief among G-8 leaders both in their capitals and at G-8 summits and has helped fellow rocker Bob Geldof organize the *Live 8* benefit concerts in 2005. According to economist Robert J. Barro, who is critical of the value of debt relief, "Bono was as successful with conservatives, such as Senator Jesse A. Helms . . . as he was with liberals" (Barro 2001).

Bono combines massive celebrity with self-deprecating irony, knowledge of the issues, and commitment to very un-glamorous causes. According to Traub, he is "the most politically effective figure in the recent history of popular culture" (2005: 82). He demonstrates that it is possible to be a number of potentially contradictory things: a Christian, a rock star, and a deeply committed activist for the world's least well-off people.

Bono's Influence in the United Kingdom

We are able to control for a number of other variables that may influence the respondents' beliefs on this issue. They include Bush Temperatue Rating, USA Temperature Rating, Left/Right, Sex, and of course the Celebrity Endorsement. We present four versions of the celebrity endorsement variable. The first is a dichotomous variable coded "1" for the presence of Bono's endorsement, while the other three models include an interactive variable. The second column shows the effect of the celebrity endorsement among those who are at least "somewhat familiar" with Bono. The third column shows the effect of the celebrity endorsement model among those who give Bono more than 50 degrees. The final column shows the effect of the celebrity endorsement combined with familiarity and warmth for Bono. The variables cannot be included in the same model because of collinearity issues.

Table 8.8: Ordered Logit Equations for Level of Agreement with Claim Bush Has Done an Incredible Job on AIDS[1]

	Overall	At Least Somewhat Familiar with Bono*Celebrity	Warm toward Bono*Celebrity	Both Familiar with and Warm toward Bono*Celebrity
Celebrity Endorsed	-.640**** (.199)	-.808**** (.203)	-.788*** (.249)	-.767*** (.255)
Bush Temperature	-.024**** (.005)	-.025**** (.005)	-.023**** (.005)	-.023**** (.005)
US Temperature	-.008* (.005)	-.008* (.005)	-.008* (.005)	-.009* (.005)
Left Right Placement	-.152*** (.053)	-.154*** (.053)	-.153*** (.053)	-.153*** (.053)
Female	.152 (.198)	.132 (.199)	.197 (.198)	.188 (.198)

table continued on next page

Cut 1 (strongly agree)	-6.464	-6.543	-6.252	-6.253
Cut 2 (somewhat agree)	-2.89	-2.953	-2.688	-2.692
Cut 3 (somewhat disagree)	-.942	-.982	-.736	-.744
Nagelkerke R2	.196	.210	.196	.193
n	375	375	375	375

* Significant at the .10 level. ** Significant at the .05 level. *** Significant at .01 level ****Significant at the .001 level. Significance levels are two-tailed.

Question: "President Bush has done an incredible job on AIDS. And 250,000 Africans are on antiviral drugs. They literally owe their lives to America." How do you feel about these comments?

[1]Negative coefficients indicate greater level of agreement.

In each of the models celebrity endorsement is significant. With just Bono's endorsement and without controlling for likeability or warmth of feeling the coefficient is the smallest, -.640. However, when we limit Bono's endorsement to only those who are at least somewhat familiar with Bono, the coefficient increases to -.808. When we limit Bono's endorsement to only those who gave Bono more than 50 degrees the coefficient drops to -.788, but is still higher than the overall number. Finally, when controlling for both likeability and Familiarity, Bono's coefficient drops to -.767, but is still greater than the coefficient for just his endorsement in the overall sample.

In order to determine the substantive effects of Bono's endorsement on respondents' levels of agreement with the statement about President Bush and AIDS, it is necessary to determine the probability of the respondent placing him or herself at each point on the scale of agreement as Bono's endorsement occurs, and each control variable is kept constant at its base value, which are the mean for Bush and USA temperature ratings and left/right placement, and zero (male) for female (Liao 1994).[2] These results are presented in Table 2.

Table 8.9: Predicted Probabilities of Level of Agreement, with Other Variables Held Constant at their Base Values

	Strongly Agree	Somewhat Agree	Somewhat Disagree	Strongly Disagree
Overall				
Celebrity Endorsed	.016	.344	.438	.202
Not Endorsed	.008	.220	.447	.325

table continued on next page

2   Actual calculations were performed using "*X Post*: Post-Estimation Interpretation Using Excel," written by Simon Cheng and Scott Long, http://www.indiana.edu/~jslsoc/xpost.htm.

Familiar With Bono				
Celebrity Endorsed	.017	.375	.430	.178
Not Endorsed	.008	.216	.450	.326
Warm Toward Bono				
Celebrity Endorsed	.022	.417	.407	.153
Not Endorsed	.010	.253	.452	.285
Fam. and Warm to Bono				
Celebrity Endorsed	.022	.422	.404	.151
Not Endorsed	.010	.260	.452	.277

In all four models Bono's effect is similar. His endorsement slightly increases the probability of a respondent strongly agreeing that President Bush has done an incredible job on AIDS. In each model Bono's endorsement also increases the likelihood of a respondent somewhat agreeing, and reduces the likelihood of strongly disagreeing. It appears that familiarity with Bono increases his influence, but warmth toward him does not add much. His temperature rating and familiarity are only slightly correlated, so these variables are in fact measuring distinct characteristics of respondents' attitudes toward him.

Bono, Rowling, and Ireland

Among the Irish respondents there are sufficient numbers of respondents to perform the overall regression regarding Bono's potential influence. However, because 97.3% of respondents are at least somewhat familiar with Bono (only 81.9% of U.K. respondents were at least somewhat familiar) and 66.7% feel warmly toward him (only 37% of U.K. respondents do) it does not make sense to combine familiarity, warmth and celebrity endorsement. The overall model is presented in the table below.

Table 8.10: Ordered Logit Equations for Level of Agreement with Claim Bush Has Done an Incredible Job on AIDS, Irish Respondents only[1]

	Overall
Celebrity Endorsed	-2.046**** (.578)
Bush Temperature	-.053*** (.017)

table continued on next page

US Temperature	.013 (.014)
Left Right Placement	-.165 (.158)
Female	-.067 (.596)
Cut 1 (strongly agree)	-6.571
Cut 2 (somewhat agree)	-3.146
Cut 3 (somewhat disagree)	-.914
Nagelkerke R2	.426
n	59.0

* Significant at the .10 level. ** Significant at the .05 level. *** Significant at .01 level
****Significant at the .001 level. Significance levels are two-tailed.
[1]Negative coefficients indicate greater level of agreement.

The Irish results are quite impressive, with Bono's endorsement appearing to move young Irish opinion on President Bush's handling of AIDS substantially. Again, substantive effects are determined by holding all other variables constant at their base (the mean for Bush Temperature, US Temperature and Left/Right placement, and the mode (female) for the gender category). These results are presented in the table below.

Table 8.11: Predicted Probabilities of Level of Agreement with Bush Had Done Incredible Job on AIDS, with Other Variables Held Constant at their Base Values, Irish Respondents Only

	Strongly Agree	Somewhat Agree	Somewhat Disagree	Strongly Disagree
Celebrity Endorsed	.004	.466	.430	.098
Not Endorsed	.031	.109	.405	.456

The probability of a respondent somewhat agreeing with the statement when Bono endorses it is nearly four times greater than when his endorsement is absent, while the likelihood of a respondent strongly disagreeing is four times less likely when Bono endorses it.

Alternative Rock and Politics

There are a number of interesting parallel results in the data presented above. What is striking is that in every case where there were statistically significant results, except for level of political engagement and national pride, the differences between alternative rock fans and others each indicate alternative rock fans preferring more left/liberal positions than others. While not demonstrating that listening to alternative rock is the cause of these differences, the data suggest the existence of a sub-culture of fans of alternative rock in four mainly English-speaking countries who hold different political opinions than others, and may find those beliefs reinforced by the lyrics and political statements of alternative rock musicians.

Popular music scholar Simon Frith (1996) argues that scholars who focus on the potential influence on listeners of the lyrical content of pop songs miss the point, because songs are best understood as the expressions of these ideas.[3] In other words, alternative rock bands are not necessarily getting young people to agree with their messages by influencing them through specific lyrical and other appeals, but instead are offering listeners expressions of their shared beliefs, which may take the form of singing along with bands' recordings, or in concerts with tens of thousands of others. Frith's skepticism about the impact of lyrics may be right, but that would not mean that the political differences mentioned above are false or non-existent. It could simply mean that for some youths, membership in the alternative rock subculture means adhering to a different set of political beliefs than others hold. Moreover, the politics of alternative rock analyzed in this paper are not confined to lyrics, but include the public comments and activities of musicians as a crucial element as well. Alternative rock musicians almost always take political stands on the left/liberal side of the spectrum, therefore it should not come as a surprise that their fans differ from the rest of youths in this direction.

Another, more general way to examine the question of alternative musicians and political beliefs is to look at responses to a question on the surveys that asked respondents to name an actor or musician whose opinions on politics they respect, which was asked of Canadian, Irish, and British respondents. In response to this question 206 Canadian respondents offered a name, and 99 different names resulted. In total, 233 discrete respondent mentions of celebrities were obtained, because a few named more than one. U2 lead singer Bono received 24% of these mentions. The next most frequently mentioned celebrity was alternative rocker Matthew Good, who received 5.2% of the mentions. Alternative rockers Dave Matthews and Eddie Vedder also received considerable numbers of mentions. Clearly, however, Bono is the musician Canadian respondents respect with regard to political beliefs.

---

3   There is also the concern that young people do not correctly interpret the political messages of lyrics. Greenfield et al. (1987) demonstrated that even among older youths (12th graders and university students) misunderstanding of lyrics does take place, but likelihood of understanding increases substantially with age.

As the lead singer of U2—one of the bands which led the alternative rock revolution in the 1980s—Bono has stood for religious and political reconciliation in Northern Ireland, and debt relief and AIDS treatment in Africa. Jackson (2007) has explored the relationship between Bono's politics and his fans,' and found their selection of him as a celebrity whose opinions they respect to be an expression of internationalism, left-liberalism, and subtle anti-Americanism—their political beliefs are significantly different from other respondents in a left/liberal direction.

British and Irish respondents together produced 313 total answers to the question of a celebrity whose opinions on politics they respect. Forty-one of these (13.1%) were Irish alternative rocker and aid-concert organizer Bob Geldof. Bono was a close second with 11.8% of mentions. Interestingly, among Canadian respondents Bob Geldof did not come up even a single time, even though he is just as active on the same issues as Bono. This difference in celebrity status between Europeans and North Americans is worthy of further investigation, as is the apparent lack of political differences among young Irish and British youths who respect Bono, Geldof, and others. No significant ideological differences could be found between these groups among Irish and British youths, while large and significant differences appeared among Canadian respondents who respected Bono, and other young Canadians. This contrast too is worthy of further investigation.

The research presented above indicates the possibility of a trans-national youth sub-culture of devotees of the same or similar music, whose political beliefs are different from other youths. The research presented here demonstrates political differences at the group level between fans of alternative rock and others. Focus group research is the next logical step in the process of determining how individual young people select the political music to which they listen, and what impact such music has on the development of their own beliefs. This research also demonstrates that alternative rock musicians' endorsements of several positions leads to greater agreement with the popular ones and less strong disagreement with the unpopular ones.

9

The Influence of Classic Rock and Country Music on Young Adults' Political Beliefs

Classic Rock[1]

It is not easy to ascertain what effect, if any, listening to classic rock ought to have on young fans today. For the purposes of this research, classic rock is defined as the rock 'n' roll music from the mid-1960s onward. The rock of the 1950s and early 1960s is generally thought of as "oldies" now. Moreover, it is clear that this is how the survey respondents think of it, too. When those U.S. respondents who identified themselves as fans of classic rock identified their favorite musical artist, there were a total of 51 answers. Of these, seven (13.7%) were for *Led Zeppelin*, a major English hard rock act who had their origins in the late 1960s. The next most popular were *The Beatles* and *Pink Floyd*, who each received 4 votes (7.8%). Little needs to be said about the importance of *The Beatles* in the history of rock 'n' roll. *Pink Floyd* is the quintessential classic rock band. As these responses indicate, clearly when young Americans say they prefer classic rock they are indicating they prefer the rock of the late 1960s and 1970s, as very often for the music of British acts.

---

1   Only U.S., Canadian,s and U.K. respondents will be considered here because there are an insufficient number of Irish classic rock fans to permit analysis.

The political content of popular music was very high during the classic rock period. As indicated in chapter 1, cultural studies scholars, historians, social scientists, and musicologists began taking the sociopolitical influence of mass-marketed American popular music recordings seriously at this time, too. Whereas it is not entirely clear what influence one ought to expect classic rock to have on its young listeners, there are some reasonable hypotheses.

One would expect fans of classic rock to be more liberal/left overall and also more progressive on issues than fans of other kinds of music for several reasons. First, it was during the 1960s and 1970s when classic rock was still contemporary rock 'n' roll that politics first became prominent in mass-marketed American popular music recordings. During the 1960s and 1970s, rock musicians frequently wrote songs with political themes, and almost all of them from the liberal perspective. From Phil Ochs's antiwar songs of the 1960s to Crosby, Stills, Nash, and Young's antiviolence, anti-Nixon, antiracism anthems of the 1970s, the music now known as classic rock is replete with liberal political messages. Moreover, the musicians in this genre frequently wrote of doing one's own thing in terms of sex and drugs and over-the-top individualism. If young people prefer this music over other, more contemporary music, it is expected it will influence them in a liberal direction. As demonstrated earlier, however, U.S. fans of classic rock are not more likely to be more liberal than fans of other music, and in fact fans of classic rock are pretty evenly split among liberals, moderates, and conservatives. Moreover, classic rock fans are the least likely to be Democrats. Even so, classic rock fans are the most likely to be more liberal than their parents. This is because U.S. classic rock fans, perhaps ironically, are the most likely to have conservative parents. Thus their movement toward greater liberalism may not show up as actual liberalism or progressive stances on issues. For example, classic rock preference has no influence on abortion position, conformism, newer lifestyles, or moral relativism. However, classic rock does influence positions on some issues.

Furthermore, fans of classic rock should be more supportive of women's equality. This was a major theme of the liberal and progressive political movements of the 1960s and 1970s, and it is often sung about by classic rock performers. Moreover, there are several strong female performers in classic rock such as Janis Joplin, Grace Slick, and Joni Mitchell, each of whom still today is respected for her pioneering work for women in rock. Unfortunately, the relationship is the opposite of the expected one. On a 7-point scale where 1 indicates a belief in gender equality and 7 represents a belief that a woman's place is in the home, U.S. classic rock fans average 2.49 while others average 1.80. Moreover, this .69-point difference is significant at the .000+ level.

Clearly, U.S. fans of classic rock are less supportive of equal roles for women than are nonfans. Why this is the case is puzzling, except that classic rock fans have more conservative parents and parental influence may be more discernible on this issue than on others. Moreover, not all classic rock is progressive on women's issues. *Led Zeppelin* and *The Rolling Stones* were two classic rock bands who came in for much criticism in the 1960s and 1970s for the misogyny of some of their lyrics and antics (Frith and McRobbie 1990).

One would expect classic rock fans to be more cynical about politics than non-fans. This should be so because classic rock contains a prevalence of messages critical of the U.S. government and its domestic and international policies during the 1960s and 1970s. The anticipated result though does not materialize as Table 9.1 indicates.

Table 9.1: Classic Rock Preference and Cynicism*

Government Run For:	Non Classic Fans	Classic Fans	Totals
Benefit of All	22.2%	42.0%	24.0%
A Few Big Interests	77.8%	58.0%	76.0%
Totals	100.0%	100.0%	100.0%

Chi-square (1) = 9.776, sig. (two-tailed) = .002

*Question: Would you say the government is pretty much run by a few big interests looking out for themselves or that it is run for the benefit of all the people?

While more cynical than not, classic rock fans are nearly twice as likely as non-fans to believe that the government is run for the benefit of all. Furthermore, as Table 9.2 shows, classic rock fans are much more likely than nonfans to believe that not many government officials are crooked. They are less likely to believe that quite a few are. Again, this result indicates a greater faith in government among classic rock than nonfans that requires explanation. It is important to note that those who believe hardly any government officials are corrupt are statistically significantly more likely to say they plan to vote than those who believe quite a few officials are corrupt (94.4% compared with 85.1%).

One possible explanation for these results is that classic rock fans draw a favorable contrast between the relatively benign governmental leaders and policies of their own youths and those experienced by their parents and the focus of massive protest demonstrations. In addition, they have more conservative parents than do fans of other types of music.

Table 9.2: Classic Rock Preference and Corruption in Government*

Corrupt Officials	Non Classic Fans	Classic Fans	Totals
Hardly Any	2.9%	1.8%	2.8%
Not Many	28.9%	45.5%	30.4%
Quite a Few	68.2%	52.7%	66.8%
Totals	100.0%	100.0%	100.0%

Chi-square (2) = 6.519, sig. (two-tailed) = .038

*Question: Do you think that QUITE A FEW of the people running the government are crooked, NOT VERY MANY are, or do you think HARDLY ANY of them are crooked?

Finally fans of classic rock are expected to be more supportive of the morality of homosexuality. However, as the following table indicates, the findings on homosexuality are mixed.

Table 9.3: Classic Rock Preference and Morality of Homosexuality*

Homosexuality Acceptable:	Non Classic Fans	Classic Fans	Totals
Disagree	45.7%	49.2%	46.0%
Neutral	20.2%	8.2%	19.1%
Agree	34.1%	42.6%	34.8%
Totals	100.0%	100.0%	100.0%

Chi-square (2) = 5.471, sig. (two-tailed) = .065
*Question: Homosexual lifestyles are morally acceptable.

U.S. classic rock fans are more likely than nonfans to agree or disagree on homosexual lifestyles, and less likely to take a neutral or moderate position. What this increased polarization within this group of fans means, if anything, is a puzzle. It seems like classic rock has some sociopolitical influence on its young fans, but the relationships are frequently not at all those expected, nor are they easily explained.

In terms of support for gay marriage, women's place in society, and moral relativism, Canadian classic rock fans are no different from other respondents, and the other issue positions reported on above were not asked of them. However, Canadian classic rock fans are, as expected, more likely to agree that smoking marijuana should not be a criminal offense. However, they are less likely to agree that only police should have guns. This is a bit of a puzzling finding. There are no relationships on any of these questions in the U.K. sample. These disparate findings suggest that, unlike as was the case with alternative rock, with classic rock there is no coherent set of beliefs that fans of the music hold.

Frampton Comes Alive for John Kerry

Peter Frampton was born in Beckenham England in 1950, and came to the music world's attention first with his band *Humble Pie*, and the legendary 1976 live album *Frampton Comes Alive*. Having appeared on Rolling Stone's cover shirtless, Frampton lost credibility as a musician. "That cover essentially said, 'Goodbye musician, hello teenybopper star," he said ("New Music and Politics"). His career fizzled in the 1980s until David Bowie took him on tour as a guitarist, and in 2007 his instrumental album "Fingerprints" won the Grammy for Best Pop Instrumental Album ("49th Annual Grammy"). In 2000, Frampton moved to suburban Cincinnati, Ohio and has become an American citizen ("New Music and Politics"). He performed at a private fundraising concert for Democratic Presidential nominee John Kerry in 2004, as well as at a Toledo, Ohio concert with Neil Young and *Pearl Jam* as part of the Vote for Change tour ("New Music and Politics"). Among his fans, Frampton may represent maturity and dedication.

In order to determine Peter Frampton's effect on young UK respondents, we ran a binary logistic regression with our dependent variable set at "1" if the respondent indicated he/she would have voted for John Kerry in 2004. We control for Left/right placement, gender, Bush temperature rating, as well as the four versions of the celebrity endorsement variable used in the regressions above, which interact the celebrity endorsement with respondents' familiarity and affect for Frampton.

Table 9.4: Binary Logit Equations for Hypothetical Kerry Vote in 2004

	Overall	At Least Somewhat Familiar with Frampton* Celebrity	Warm toward Frampton* Celebrity	Both Familiar with and Warm toward Frampton* Celebrity
Celebrity Endorsed	.164 (.220)	.857* (.483)	1.372* (.846)	
Bush Temperature	-.025**** (.005)	-.024**** (.005)	-.025**** (.005)	
Left Right Placement	-.113** (.058)	-.114** (.058)	-.118** (.058)	1
Female	-.559*** (.223)	-.556*** (.058)	-.545*** (.058)	
Nagelkerke R2	.142	.152	.151	
n	432	432	432	

* Significant at the .10 level. ** Significant at the .05 level.

*** Significant at .01 level ****Significant at the .001 level. Significance levels are two-tailed.
[1] Cannot be run because there is complete separation: all those warm and familiar with Frampton would have voted for Kerry

It would appear that being familiar with and/or warm toward Peter Frampton is a necessary precondition for an effect of his endorsement. His endorsement alone seems to have no influence on hypothetical 2004 presidential vote, but among those who are either familiar with or warm toward Frampton there does appear to be an effect. To determine the substantive effect we need to determine the probability of a hypothetical Kerry vote holding the other variables constant, which for Bush Temperature and Left/Right placement is the mean and female is the mode, or "0" (male).

Table 9.5: Predicted Probabilities of Hypothetical Kerry Vote, with Other Variables Held Constant at their Base Values

	Would Have Voted for Kerry	Would Have Voted for Some Other Candidate
Familiar With Frampton		
Celebrity Endorsed	.815	.185
Not Endorsed	.652	.348
Warm Toward Frampton		
Celebrity Endorsed	.883	.117
Not Endorsed	.656	.344

Peter Frampton's endorsement of John Kerry matters among those who are familiar with or warm toward him. His endorsement of Kerry makes the already popular position even more popular.

Country and Western Music[2]

Are fans of country and western music different politically from nonfans?

Country music is the more conservative and traditional of the favorite kinds of music mentioned, as Jon Pareles (1995) stated when he wrote, "When modern country does venture to suggest a community, it envisions honest working men (and, much more rarely, working women) who long for the good old days when harmonious families lived in idealized small towns. It's the same all-American mythos conjured up by Republican rhetoric." It is expected that fans' politics reflect this concept. Table 9.4 demonstrates the relationship between preference for country music and conformity.

Both country and noncountry fans are overwhelmingly in favor of conducting oneself according to one's own standards; however, whereas 86.1% of noncountry fans support this position, only 77.5% of country fans do. The difference, however, is not statistically significant. However, as pointed out in chapter 5, those who are nonconformist may be more likely to vote. The traditional values often espoused in country music tend to support conformity. There are fixed and unchanging moral standards that one ought to learn and follow. Living in a small town in the North or the South

---

2   Only U.S. data will be analyzed here because there are an insufficient number of Canadian, Irish, and U.K. fans of country music to achieve statistically significant relationships.

typically requires conformity to the beer swilling, C & W music listening, blue-collar job, pick-up truck driving lifestyle or becoming an outcast.

Table 9.6: Country and Western Preference and Fitting In*

	Non Country Fans	Country Fans	Totals
Better to Fit In	13.9%	23.1%	14.5%
Use Own Standards	86.1%	76.9%	85.5%
Totals	100.0%	100.0%	100.0%

Chi-square (1) = 2.488, sig. (two-tailed) = .115

*Question: Which of the following two statements comes closer to your own views? You might agree to some extent with both, but we want to know which one is CLOSER to your views. ONE, is it better to fit in with people around you; or TWO, is it better to conduct yourself according to your own standards even if it makes you stand out?

Country music preference seems to explain some differences of opinion on the abortion question as well, with country fans (as expected) taking the more conservative position. Table 9.5 demonstrates this relationship.

Table 9.7: Country/Western Preference and Abortion*

Abortion:	Non CW Fans	CW Fans	Totals
Never Permit	10.2%	7.7%	10.0%
Permit in Rape/Incest	31.4%	61.5%	33.1%
Permit/Prove Need	13.2%	10.3%	13.0%
Permit All Abortion	45.2%	20.5%	43.8%

Chi-square (1) = 2.488, sig. (two-tailed) = .115

*Question: Which comes closer to your views on abortion?
- By law, abortion should never be permitted
- The law should permit abortion only in the case of rape, incest, or when the woman's life is in danger
- The law should permit abortion for reasons other than rape, incest, or danger to the woman's life, but only after the need for the abortion has been clearly established
- By law, a woman should always be able to obtain an abortion as a matter of personal choice.

Country fans are half as likely as nonfans to believe that abortion should be permitted in all circumstances. Moreover, country fans are almost twice as likely as non-country fans to permit abortion only in cases of rape or incest, which is certainly a strict limitation on the availability of the procedure.

Patriotism as a political theme is prevalent in country music as well. It is likely that country fans are less supportive of the legality of flag burning than noncountry fans. Table 9.6 demonstrates that this is in fact the case, although the relationship again only approaches statistical significance.

Table 9.8: Country/Western Preference and Flag Burning*

	Non Country Fans	Country Fans	Totals
Against the Law	64.8%	77.2%	65.5%
Legal	35.2%	22.9%	34.5%
Totals	100.0%	100.0%	100.0%

Chi-square = 2.239, sig. (one-tailed) = .068

*Question: Should burning or destroying the American flag as a form of political protest be LEGAL or should it be AGAINST THE LAW?

The patriotism of country music fans manifests itself in their opposition to the legality of flag burning. Whereas nearly 65 % of noncountry fans oppose it, 77.2 % of country fans do, but the difference is not statistically significant. However, this is only a piece of the patriotism puzzle. Country fans are less cynical and less likely to believe that people in government are corrupt. Those who are very patriotic may be less disposed to be cynical about politics and government than others. Table 9.7 shows the relationship between country music and cynicism, and table 9.8 shows the relationship between country music and belief in the crookedness of government officials.

Country fans are nearly twice as likely as noncountry fans to believe that the government is run for the benefit of all. Furthermore, more country fans believe that hardly any government officials are corrupt and fewer believe that quite a few are. Troublingly, however, a majority of both groups believes that quite a few government officials are corrupt. However, those who believe hardly any government officials are corrupt are statistically significantly more likely to say they plan to vote than those who believe quite a few officials are corrupt (94.4% compared with 85.1%).

Table 9.9: Country and Western Preference and Cynicism*

Government Run For:	Non Country Fans	Country Fans	Totals
Benefit of All	22.7%	45.2%	24.0%
A Few Big Interests	77.3%	54.8%	76.0%
Totals	100.0%	100.0%	100.0%

Chi-square (1) = 8.075, sig. (two-tailed) = .004

*Question: Would you say the government is pretty much run by a few big interests looking out for themselves or that it is run for the benefit of all the people?

Table 9.10: Country Preference and Corruption in Government*

Corrupt Officials:	Non Country Fans	Country Fans	Totals
Hardly Any	2.5%	9.7%	2.8%
Not Many	30.4%	29.0%	30.4%
Quite a Few	67.1%	61.3%	66.8%
Totals	100.0%	100.0%	100.0%

Chi-square (2) = 5.612, sig. (two-tailed) = .060

*Question: Do you think that QUITE A FEW of the people running the government are crooked, NOT VERY MANY are, or do you think HARDLY ANY of them are crooked?

Country Star Tim McGraw and American Farmers

Are country fans, like fans of other kinds of music, influenced by celebrity endorsements? What are the differences in level of agreement with political positions when taken by a country musician versus the same position when not endorsed by a musician?

Tim McGraw scored major hits in the mid and late 1990s. In typical country and western-star fashion, he has presented an image of himself as a simple and sincere country boy. No song demonstrates this image more clearly than his number one hit from 1994 entitled, "Down on the Farm." The song is a paean to the simple pleasures of being farmers and farmers' children looking for a good time on the weekend. McGraw has supported a number of very non-controversial charities over his career, including zoos, an organization to help the victims of the bombing of the U.S.S. Cole, and the baseball little league in his hometown in Northeast Louisiana ("McGraw Charities"). He is married to Faith Hill, another country superstar. His influence ought to be most pronounced among fans of country and western music. His likeability is high, and as a country musician who was raised in a rural area, his credibility on farm issues may be higher than that of musicians from other genres and backgrounds.

Respondents were asked two versions of a question about increased government support for farmers. The first read, "Tim McGraw has performed at a concert designed to raise money for American farmers. Many believe that the government should do more to help these farmers. How do you feel about this?" while the other version deleted McGraw's endorsement.

As table 9.10 shows, among U.S. country music fans, celebrity endorsement is the only significant variable explaining respondent's level of support for increased aid to farmers, even controlling for ideology, sex, partisanship, and income. Moreover, they were much more likely to believe the government should do more.

Table 9.11: Ordered Logit Equations for Level of Agreement with Doing More to Help Farmers, Country Fans Only

Variable	Coefficient (Std. Error)
Celebrity Endorsement	3.897*** (1.557)
Ideology (7=Extremely Conservative)	-.560 (.657)
Republican	.306 (2.029)
Male	1.280 (1.539)
Income	-.443 (.524)
Cut 1	-4.385
Cut 2	-1.908
Nagelkerke R2	.394
n	32

* Significant at the .10 level. ** Significant at the .05 level. *** Significant at .01 level ****Significant at the .001 level. Significance levels are two-tailed.

In order to determine the substantive effects of celebrity endorsement on respondents' levels of agreement with the political statements, it is necessary to determine the probability of the respondent placing him or herself at each point on the scale of agreement as celebrity endorsement occurs, and each control variable is kept constant at its base value, which are the mean for ideology and income, and zero for male and Republican.[3] These results are presented in Table 9.10 and are consistent with expectations regarding the musicians.

Table 9.12: Predicted Probabilities of Level of Agreement, with Other Variables Held Constant at their Base Values

	Gov't Do Less	Gov't Do Same	Gov't Do More
McGraw Endorsed	.01	.07	.92
Not Endorsed	.26	.55	.19

Young country and western fans are much less likely to say the U.S. ought to spend less on farm subsidies when country star Tim McGraw is shown as supporting

---

3   Actual calculations were performed using "*XPost:* Post-Estimation Interpretation Using Excel," written by Simon Cheng and Scott Long, http://www.indiana.edu/~jslsoc/xpost.htm.

farmers, and they are substantially more likely to say we ought to spend more when they know McGraw thinks so too.

Conclusion

Classic rock fans seem to be more conservative than nonfans. Moreover, they are more patriotic, less supportive of equal roles for women, and more extreme on the abortion question. This could be the case for a couple of reasons. First, perhaps the young fans of classic rock are missing the liberalizing messages and merely enjoying the music as kitsch and nostalgia. In other words, like many young people in the 1960s and 1970s, perhaps they are just going along for the ride. Furthermore, the questionnaire did not offer the respondents a choice of "rock 'n roll" in terms of music preference. Rock 'n' roll, both the classic and contemporary variants, is macho, male dominated music. Fans of this music are expected to be more conservative, patriotic, and less supportive of equal roles for women. Perhaps fans of politics-free, misogynistic rock 'n' roll selected classic rock as the category nearest their actual preference.

Country and western music fans are politically different from nonfans as well. They are more likely to believe it is better to fit in than other youths do. They are less supportive of abortion rights than others. Moreover, they are less cynical about the national government than others. Finally, as with the other kinds of music, country musicians may be able to influence their fans on political issues, such as assistance to farmers.

What does this mean for the values that youths will hold in the future? Liberal youths will continue to have their liberal values reinforced when they listen to most types of popular music. Conservative youths' relatively durable values may weaken and perhaps change over time due to the absence of reinforcement, especially as they distance themselves from their parents. Although some elements of the popular culture do reinforce conservative values (i.e., country music), they are less prominent than elements of the popular culture that reinforce liberal values or no widely accepted values at all.

Having attended concerts where interest groups had set up information tables predicts which youths are more liberal than their parents, independently of music preference and use levels. Music preference and use levels matter as well, though. The more time fans of alternative and classic rock spend listening to alternative or classic rock music, then the more likely they are to be influenced by it and become more liberal than their parents. White rap fans are also more likely than other youths to be more liberal than their parents.

As suggested previously, the attempt by interest groups to communicate with and influence young people through concerts is a new means of political communication that political scientists ought to take seriously. Apparently in some cases the groups have their desired effect, namely, influencing youths to greater liberalism than their parents. Naturally, groups that try to influence the ideology of young Americans are not interested in political persuasion alone. They are also interested in action. Are interest groups able to influence youths, e.g., through access to them in the concert setting, to vote, or to vote for different candidates and parties than they had initially intended? Are they able to influence youths to call or send letters to elected officials, participate in protest demonstrations, or lobby elected officials in person? These are some of the questions future research ought to aim to answer.

Young people do not think about ideology in traditional ways. One way that young people perceive ideology differently relates to beliefs about lifestyle issues, and as such is relevant to concern with the so-called "culture wars" over beliefs about basic values. That white rap fans are more likely than others to be more liberal than their parents might indicate that another aspect of the "culture wars" influences their perceptions about ideology. This other front in the "culture war" relates to the growth of identity politics, multiculturalism, and tolerance of different cultures. Perhaps white rap fans view themselves as more liberal than their parents not only because they view themselves as more permissive on lifestyle issues, but also because they view themselves as more tolerant of different cultures than their parents are. In other words, conservatives may be losing on both fronts of the "culture war."

10

Learning Theory, Values Conflict, and Cultural Imperialism Revisited

This book offers a theory of the political socialization process that includes the entertainment media as important agents of socialization. Data have been gathered from surveys of undergraduate college students in the U.S., English-speaking Canada, Ireland, and the U.K. to demonstrate a number of important political effects of the entertainment media. These effects are important because they are linked with the ongoing conflict over the basic values that define the political community, the conflict some call the "culture war," and also because they show us how a refined version of cultural imperialism theory still makes sense.

Political scientists generally believe parents, schools, churches, and the news media politically socialize children, and roughly in that order of importance. Whereas each of these has an impact, researchers who focused exclusively on these agents of socialization at times came up with very tenuous results, or no significant results at all. Thus, if parents have little enduring significance, it suggests that there may be no answer to the question of how young people learn about politics. But this is not the case. Political socialization research is difficult because there are so many independent variables (agents) that influence the acquisition and holding of political values by young people. This complexity, rather than arguing that political socialization research ought to abate, instead suggests that it ought to continue, but with more realistic expectations.

Social scientists search for the smallest number of independent variables to explain the largest amount of variation in a dependent variable. This method is not always the best to apply to socialization research. Certainly there are independent variables that explain a fair amount of young people's sociopolitical values, and to a large extent these have been identified. One of the best examples is the influence of parents' party attachments on their children's party preferences. However, the effects thus far accounted for are not very large, and thus much remains to be explained. Popular media may not be the sole or even the key factor in explaining young people's political attitudes. It seems likely that nothing will soon replace parents, the schools, churches, peer groups, and so on in the pantheon of relevant agents of socialization. However, the information presented in the preceding chapters clearly demonstrates that the sociopolitical content of the entertainment media and public positions taken by performers do influence young people in some circumstances. The entertainment media may not be the most important agents, but they do matter—especially to the extent that they influence young people to deviate from the beliefs promoted by parents and parentally selected agents of socialization.

Political socialization is defined as the process by which young people acquire and hold political values. Inglehart's work concerning the shift to postmaterialism in an industrial society employs this definition because it helps to explain how young people conceive of politics, how they define political ideology, and to which political issues current in the popular culture they pay attention. A focus on political values helps shed light on why young people might perceive politics in the personalistic and individualistic ways the data indicate that they do. It helps explain levels of patriotism and nationalism felt by young people. It assists in explaining increased attention to environmental and other supranational concerns. It explains why young people conceive of politics in terms of individual moral choices, rather than of politics in terms of collective or public choices. It sheds light on the importance of "lifestyle liberalism" and "culture wars" issues among the young. It explains why young Americans believe Madonna, who has expressed few political beliefs, is more liberal than Eddie Vedder, who helped convince Congress to investigate Ticketmaster's alleged monopoly over concert ticket distribution.

Young people think about politics in ways that the traditional political science continuum of "liberal" and "conservative" does not fully account for. The "culture war" in the U.S., and the "lighter" version of the struggle between traditional and more liberal views in other societies, is primarily seen (by conservatives especially) as a battle for the hearts and minds of youths over competing positions a wide variety of issues including abortion, homosexuality, violence, women's rights, drug use, promiscuity, single parenting, and so on. Conservatives believe that permissive attitudes on these issues are prevalent in the entertainment media, and the data presented above indicate that in many cases they are correct—or at least that young observers see and hear the same messages. Believers in traditional values in countries other than the U.S. examined in this book rightly see U.S. entertainment media as supportive of values with which they profoundly disagree.

Conservatives seem also to assume that the entertainment media do influence youths' values, rather than taking the possibility of influence as a claim requiring elaboration and defense. Based on the research presented here, it is undoubtedly true that the entertainment media influence young people's sociopolitical beliefs, but influence is very complex, and determining the effects of the entertainment media on young people's politics is no easy process. If determining the influence of parents proved elusive to scholars from the 1950s to the 1990s, why should we expect that determining the influence of entertainment in the twenty-first century ought to be any easier?

Usually, the conflicts presented in the popular culture involve several value distinctions—hedonism versus delayed gratification, individualism versus family and community, equality versus authority and hierarchy. That violence and sex in the popular media are commonplace demonstrates the widespread appeal of hedonism, even if one is only a spectator. Religion, with its focus on morality and punishment, is more often presented as the source of problems, rather than the solution. Sexual intercourse is presented as a recreational activity to enjoy with many partners or to use as one more tool to achieve success, whereas monogamy, children, and long-term relationships are rarely endorsed. For example, daytime and prime-time soap operas depict a great deal of bed-hopping not only for fun, but manipulation as well. Class distinctions are blurred or misunderstood, which is as expected in a postmaterialist culture. The legitimacy of institutions, the need for hierarchy, and respect for authority are mocked in much of the popular culture. The individual's needs and desires are paramount, whereas the community's needs are neglected or overlooked. The popular culture emphasizes individual rights, not responsibility, family, friends, and community. There is certainly more alternative rock, rap, and classic rock music singing the praises of individualism than the virtues of community, family, and neighborhood.

These are the distinctions that define the culture wars in the U.S., and the less virulent conflict between traditionalism and modernism in other nations. Popular culture presents messages that fit on each side of these dichotomies, but the preponderance appear to fit on the side of hedonism, individualism, equality, and fun. The research presented above demonstrated that different kinds of young people are influenced by these competing messages in different ways. Not all young people approach the popular culture in the same way. In other words, young people are "pre-socialized" before they are influenced by popular culture. Depending on when they start watching television, listening to music, or going to the movies young people have already been subject to the other agents of socialization. Thus, the popular culture either contradicts or reinforces existing political values more than it instills new ones.

As argued in chapter 2, learning theory helps explain the influence of the entertainment media on young people's political values. Thorndike's law of effect (Skinner 1974) describes operant learning, whereby behavior is shaped and maintained by its consequences. Behavior that is rewarded increases, whereas unrewarded behavior tends to decrease in frequency and may eventually disappear. Most importantly, contingencies in the social environment determine whether a particular behavior is rewarded or punished.

Agents of socialization (parents, schools, churches, peers, news, and entertainment media) have some degree of control over the contingencies of reinforcement to which youths are subjected. For example, a parent may offer smiles and kind words of support when a child parrots the parent's political beliefs, and this positively reinforces the child's budding ideology. Similarly, a young person may experience rewards through experience with the popular culture. One could witness a behavior in a movie, television program, or song that makes a political or moral statement. If the message contradicts the individual's political, ethical, or moral beliefs that is an unpleasant experience and thus constitutes negative reinforcement. Just as touching a hot stove teaches a child through pain that the choice to do so was wrong, when rapper L'il Kim sings that she sells for money, her behavior contradict a conservative youth's belief in the sanctity of sexuality. The individual thereafter avoids repeating the unpleasant experience by avoiding the element of the popular culture that led to the unpleasant experience.

Conversely, should other components of the social environment (e.g., peers) provide positive reinforcement for initially unpleasant experiences, the individual's ethical and moral beliefs might change over time. In other words, there are two different ways to avoid the unpleasant experience of popular culture that contradicts one's values. One can avoid the popular culture that produces the unpleasant experience, which while probably the more likely behavior, becomes more difficult everyday as entertainment culture permeates almost every aspect of daily life in the West. Alternatively, one could change values. The initial negative experience might not be so negative that the individual makes an all-out effort to avoid the popular culture completely. The individual may know the messages are "wrong," based on his/her existing values, but still find the message sufficiently reinforcing due to its fictional rendering of the consequences of promiscuity, drug use, violence, and so on. Repeated exposure and peer support might break down the initial opposition to the messages. How frequently the message must be repeated and/or how much support from other elements of the young person's social world the new message requires before sinking in requires longitudinal and true experimental research.

Conversely, if the message of the popular culture agrees with the young person's values, this is pleasure, and thus triggers positive reinforcement of the individual's beliefs and behavior. When a parent promises a child his favorite dessert for cleaning up his room and then delivers it, this is pleasure. When a young adult suspects that the U.S. is a greater force for evil in the world than good and sees a movie like *Fahrenheit 9–11* which presents a compelling case against Bush administration policies, the youth experiences pleasure and has his values reinforced, and will likely seek out similarly reinforcing experiences.

Children are simultaneously susceptible and resistant to parental efforts at shaping their beliefs and behavior. In general, a parent and child both share a common interest in the child's success and welfare. However, there may be conflicts of interest as well (Trivers 1974). Parental manipulation of children generally should be directed at encouraging children to behave in ways that will lead to the children becoming successful in raising children of their own.

To what extent do parents actually instruct children on appropriate models of behavior? As argued previously, Lakoff (1996) has identified two polar models of parenting—strict parent and nurturing parent. The strict parent model is controlling, establishes clear-cut contingencies of reinforcement, and makes frequent use of rewards and punishments. The nurturing parent model is less controlling. Parents protect children from clear-cut dangers, but rely more upon contingencies of reinforcement in the larger social world to shape children's behavior.

What kind of socialization children benefit from most cannot be solved here. In other words, it is unclear which model is "right" in an objective sense. However, entertainment media attract large audiences of youths to sell them products by depicting behaviors that are contrary to traditional conservative values—the values taught to children under the strict parent model. The entertainment media tend to reinforce promiscuous sex, drugs, hedonism, and so on. In effect, the entertainment media tell youths raised under the strict-parent model that their parents and other agents of socialization are wrong about the negative consequences of these behaviors. Thus, there is a competition for influence of young people between parents, the church, the school, and other traditional agents of socialization on the one hand, and much of the popular media, on the other. Competition takes the form of entertainment media either challenging or complementing preexisting values. The competition is seen as especially fierce by children raised under the strict-parent model.

Cultural imperialism theory has also informed our understanding of the impact of U.S. popular culture in other countries. In its early formulations, the theory suggested saturation of other countries with U.S. cultural products would overwhelm these nations' young people into an acceptance of American values. Scholars came to recognize over time, however, that U.S. culture was not monolithic, as well as the important and active role played by audiences in constructing their own meanings from the raw materials provided by foreign cultures. Research has show how different non-Americans view cultural products from the U.S. as diverse as the TV shows *Dallas* and *The Simpsons* in ways that work for them, while the research presented here shows how even U.S.-produced cultural products, such as Michael Moore's films, can lead to a reinforcing of anti-American attitudes.

The young people in the U.S., English-speaking Canada, the U.K., and Ireland surveyed for this book clearly think about the political messages in the popular culture do so, and in ways related to their previous socialization. For example, strong majorities of each sample have ever agreed or disagreed with the messages of the entertainment media, but often from very different perspectives. Some conservatives likely have their conservatism hardened by limited exposure to unpleasantly liberal messages in the entertainment media. Some might be experiencing the first steps of change. Liberals might experience a hardening of their liberalism. The anti-Americanism of some non-U.S. consumers of American popular culture may be reinforced by repeated exposure to it in US. productions, or domestic ones for that matter. On the other hand, many respondents saw much pro-U.S. content in our entertainment media. Most didn't like such content, but it is possible that repeated exposure could change their minds.

The Influence of Movies on Political Socialization

Young people do watch movies, and a large percentage of the movies they watch are Hollywood blockbusters. The movies, however, do not appear to have a great influence on the political beliefs of young people. Even so, there is some influence. For example, U.S. women are less likely than men to disagree with the message of a movie. Perhaps this is because they see women characters who, whereas engaging in reprehensible behavior by the standards of traditional morality, are nonetheless strong and successful. For their part, men may be more likely to disagree because they see women who are powerful, manipulative, and independent—the very opposite of what they are naturally attracted to—that is, women who are submissive and dependent.

Canadian conservatives are more likely to have ever disagreed with the message of a movie, and they are slightly more likely to have ever agreed with one too. There are no differences with regard to gender in terms of young Canadians ever having agreed or disagreed with the political message of a movie. There are no statistically significant differences in ideology between disageers and non-disagreers in either Ireland or the U.K. The same is true for ever having agreed with a movie's political message. Irish men, however, are significantly more likely to have ever disagreed with the message of a film.

A significant number of American youths, both black and white, placed themselves ideologically closer to actors rather than to their mother. This might mean that they are projecting their ideology onto the actors. Nevertheless, some parents offer their children a smorgasbord of ethical and political choices and allow their children to make their own selections. Other youths may have once more closely identified with parents, but after they have moved away from home, K-12 education, and perhaps even the church, other agents of socialization (such as the movies and actors) have stepped in to replace the traditional ones. Of course a longitudinal study is needed to prove this point.

While movies may not seem to exert much of a measurable influence on young people's political beliefs, they are at least as capable as other elements of the popular culture of providing images and plots to frame how Americans understand political dilemmas. As Delli Carpini and Williams (1996) showed, Americans make use of televised docudramas when thinking about solutions for environmental pollution. More research is needed, but it is reasonable to conclude that how Americans think about myriad other policy areas is influenced by images and plots from movies. Naturally, the terrorist attacks of 11 September 2001, are an obvious example of this possibility, when Americans used images and plots from Hollywood movies to comfort themselves in the wake of unprecedented foreign attacks on the U.S. mainland that America would prevail over its enemies (because they did so in the movies!).

The surveys also indicated that British and Irish youths were more likely to dis-agree with a U.S. production than to agree with one. This finding is important because it demonstrates both the extent to which Hollywood movies permeate other English-speaking cultures, but also because it demonstrates the active role played by those being socialized in terms of selecting and interpreting the meaning of the films they watch.

Regarding Canadian responses to movies, the most interesting finding involves the films of Michael Moore. Canadians watch his movies, and those who seem prone to anti-Americanism, or at least to opposition to some then-current American poli-cies had their beliefs reinforced. While the sample was smaller, some U.K. respon-dents seemed to experience something similar with themes in movies with which they agreed and disagreed, finding pro-U.S. themes objectionable and anti-U.S. themes to their liking.

The Influence of Television on Political Socialization

Television influences young people's political values, both in ways that were antici-pated and ways that were not. First, there is a great deal of sociopolitical content on television, even in the programs especially popular with youths. Young Americans recognize this political content and frequently disagree with it. Homosexuality, sexual freedom, and racism are the dominant themes with which young people disagree.

Moreover, those Americans who disagree with these messages are the more con-servative youths, which is consistent with the theory of socialization developed in this work. Whether or not these youths will soften their attitudes with repeated exposure or peer pressure remains an open question and is answerable only through a longitu-dinal study.

Canadian conservatives are more likely to have ever disagreed with the message of a TV program; interestingly, they are also more likely ever to have agreed with one. There are no differences with regard to gender in terms of young Canadians ever hav-ing agreed or disagreed with the political message of a TV show.

There are no relationships between ideology and ever having agreed or disagreed with the message of a TV show among Irish and U.K. respondents. Irish men are more likely than women to have ever disagreed with the political message of a TV show, and U.K. women are more likely than men ever to have agreed.

As discussed above, television's political messages are primarily liberal and toler-ant. Does TV use influence U.S. viewers to become more liberal and tolerant? There is a small negative and statistically significant relationship between the number of hours per day of entertainment television watched and support for the morality of homosexuality (more television watching means less support for the morality of homo-sexuality). It appears that repeated exposure to entertainment television among self-identified liberals actually influences them to become less tolerant of homosexual lifestyles, whereas for conservatives it has no influence. Among liberals, increased television use correlates with an increased belief that women's place is in the home.

There is no relationship among conservatives. Among self-identified liberals, increased entertainment television use correlates with an increasingly strong belief that newer lifestyles contribute to the breakdown of society. Among conservatives, it appears that entertainment television use influences young conservatives to become more tolerant of newer lifestyles and young liberals to become less tolerant. Interestingly, in terms of abortion, conservatives' views become more liberal with increased entertainment television, whereas for self-identified liberals there is no impact.

What conclusions can be drawn from these disparate findings, especially in light of the theory this book explores? This analysis demonstrates that, whereas television may reinforce beliefs in those who have already acquired them from earlier agents of socialization, it may also lead to change. It also demonstrates that what is viewed may be just as important or more so than how much television is watched.

Preference for certain programming among U.S. respondents appears to correlate with certain political beliefs. Fans of the situation comedy *Seinfeld* are more conformist than nonfans, whereas fans of *The Simpsons* are less conformist than nonfans. Fans of *E.R.* are more tolerant of homosexuality than nonfans. Fans of television programs that present promiscuity (including among women) as the norm are more favorable toward women's equality than nonfans. The differences remain large and significant when only women fans are examined. Thus, television watching does not make all youths more conservative, just those who are already conservative. Liberals, however, seem to become more liberal from watching liberal programming (e.g., *E.R.* and the dramas with promiscuous female characters).

Television is unique. Popular programs last for many seasons and develop loyal fans. Fans select programs they like for various reasons. Certainly some of this selection, whether conscious or not, is based on whether or not the values supported by the program conform to those of the fan. Thus conservatives probably will not watch the sexually explicit shows, thus limiting these programs' influence over them. Women who want to see strong female characters will watch the sexy soap operas. Those who prefer to fit in and go along with the crowd will be attracted to *Seinfeld*, whereas individualists will seek out programming like *The Simpsons*. This will limit the ability of these programs to influence nonfans or casual watchers; people who do not like a program will not watch it consistently. However, these programs do have the power to reinforce beliefs and values among their fans. This pattern of behavior and its political significance is consistent with the theory of this study. Young liberals probably seek out programs they believe will be consistent with their values. Young conservatives, finding little television consistent with their values, watch television and find their conservatism hardened by exposure to liberal messages with which they disagree. In defense of this claim, there do seem to be differences between conservatives and liberals with regard to favorite television programs. For example, 4.7% of liberals report the African-American comedy *Martin* as their favorite television program, whereas only 1.5% of conservatives do. Interestingly, nearly four times as many conservatives (8.1%) as liberals (2.1%) report *Beverly Hills, 90210* as their favorite. The differences are not exactly as expected, but they do indicate that future research ought to look into differences in television preference among liberals and conservatives when constructing interactive models of political socialization.

Television watching not only influences political attitudes and beliefs but also activities as well. As expected, entertainment television use positively correlates with watching the news, but not with political knowledge. Entertainment television use positively correlates with listening to music, both on the radio and from one's own personal collection. Most interestingly, entertainment television use negatively correlates with talking to others about politics. The dying art of intelligent political conversation is being hurried to its grave by increased use of entertainment television. Moreover, blacks watch more television than whites, and each of the relationships mentioned above, with the exception of news television use, increases in strength when looking at African-Americans only. Entertainment television might be more important to the black community whereas simultaneously being more damaging to it.

Similar relationships occurred in the Canadian data. There is a significant and negative correlation between time spent with entertainment TV and time spent talking with family and friends about politics. There is a positive and significant relationship between news and entertainment TV use. There are also small and statistically significant correlations between time spent at news sites on the internet and time spent talking to others about politics, watching news on TV, and reading a newspaper. Evidently, some young people are just "news junkies" and utilize multiple sources for information.

Among Irish respondents, only watching news TV and entertainment TV were statistically significantly correlated. The same was the case for U.K. respondents. However, among U.K. respondents time spent looking at news sites on the internet is positively and statistically significantly correlated with talking about politics with friends and family, reading a daily newspaper, and watching news on TV, again indicating the existence of a cadre of highly news-interested young people.

Canadian respondents were asked how often they viewed Canadian stations, as well as to rate various countries/provinces on the standard 100 degree temperature scale (where higher temperature ratings mean the individual feels more warmly about the place). There is small, significant correlation between increased watching of Canadian stations and temperature rating of Quebec, which was expected. This is a very significant finding, because one of the missions of the Canadian Broadcasting Corporation is to promote national unity, and this is evidence they are succeeding at this.

There was also a significant negative correlation between Canadian station watching and U.S. temperature rating. Those who watch Canadian stations the least rate the U.S. at 51.7 degrees, while those who watch Canadian stations most of the time rate the U.S. at only 36.2 degrees. It is not a stated goal of any Canadian public or private broadcasters to worsen Canadians' feelings about the U.S., but nonetheless that appears to be happening.

Similar results obtain for the Irish and U.K. samples. Among Irish respondents, watching Irish stations more frequently leads to higher temperature ratings of

Northern Ireland. Among U.K. respondents, increased viewing of U.K. stations correlates with higher temperature ratings of both the U.K. and Ireland. Watching local stations has no effect on Irish or U.K. respondents' ratings of the U.S.

The Influence of Music on Political Socialization

Music influences young people's politics as well. In terms of overall exposure, young people spend a great deal of time listening to the radio and their own personal music collections. Increased music listening correlates with ideology, especially on the extremes of the 7-point liberal-conservative scale. Moreover, greater music listening predicts less agreement with the claim that newer lifestyles are contributing to the breakdown of society. Furthermore, greater music use correlates with an increased belief in moral relativism. Each of these relationships is as expected.

A majority of young Americans has disagreed with a political message in a song. European Americans are more likely than African Americans to have done so, whereas men are more likely than women. There are no significant differences in likelihood of agreeing or disagreeing with the message of a song among Canadian respondents when controlling for sex. Male Irish respondents are much more likely to have disagreed than are women (81.3% to 57.9%). Among the Irish there are no significant differences in likelihood of having agreed when controlling for sex. Among U.K. respondents there are no significant differences in likelihood of having agreed or disagreed with a song with regard to sex. Canadian conservatives are more likely ever to have disagreed with the message of a song; liberals are more likely to have ever agreed with one. For Irish and U.K. respondents there is no statistically significant relationship between ideology and ever having agreed or disagreed with the message of a song.

Violence is the theme with which respondents most frequently disagreed. It is followed by anti-religion, anti-women's rights and pro-premarital sex, and promiscuity. Conservatives are more likely to disagree with themes from a conservative orientation than liberals are to disagree from a liberal orientation. Conservatives tend to be raised by strict parents and find more to object to in music than liberals raised in homes where parents are more nurturing and teach their children to sort out on their own all the various influences on their political values.

It is not surprising that conservative white males do not like violence and promiscuity in popular culture. This may be the case because violence by nonwhites and female sexual power are perceived by conservative white males as attacks on the legitimacy of white male dominance of economic, social, and political life.

Young Americans' perception of the political orientations of popular musicians appears to influence their politics as well. Generally black musicians have a greater influence on blacks, and white musicians have a greater influence on whites. Music preference has some impact in this area as well. Generally fans of the kind of music performed by the musician in question are more influenced by the musician. Sometimes the influence seems to eclipse that of parents. This condition is expected to occur with children raised by nurturing parents because such parents do not insulate their children from the popular culture. For example, among alternative rock fans, music preference is more than just an expression of musical taste. It is also a choice to join a distinctive subculture of friends who dress, talk, and probably think alike. It is not improbable that such a closely knit community could take the place of parents.

Interestingly as well, U.S. country fans and rap fans show much higher correlations with parents than do alternative fans. Some speculation as to why this might be true is in order. Country fans are more likely raised by strict parents. Therefore, in the short term they show a greater correlation with their parents' ideology because they have been exposed less frequently to contrary agents of socialization. These individuals would be an interesting group to watch over time because as the distance from parents increases, and other agents of socialization contrary to parents emerge, sudden changes in values may occur as well.

Race may be a factor in why U.S. rap fans are more closely connected with parents. Blacks show a greater correlation with each parent's ideology than do whites. The correlation between youth and mother's ideology for blacks is .573 (sig. two-tailed = .000). and the correlation between youth and father's ideology for blacks is .405 (sig. two-tailed = .000). The correlation between youth and mother's ideology for whites is .404 (sig. two-tailed = .000). The correlation between youth and father's ideology for whites is .327 (sig. two-tailed = .000). That blacks are more closely related to parents' ideology and make up a plurality of rap fans probably explains why rap fans appear to be more closely related to parents.

In terms of young Americans who are more liberal than their parents, both listening to music on the radio and listening to their own collections positively correlate with the likelihood of holding such an ideological position. More interestingly, having attended concerts where interest groups had set up information booths positively correlated with the likelihood of being more liberal than one's parents, too. This is as expected. The musicians who allow interest groups are more liberal as are the interest groups invited to disseminate information.

Music preference appears to influence the politics of young Americans as well. Music preference predicts ideology, but only among whites. Alternative rock fans are the most liberal, whereas country fans are the least liberal. Party preference is also influenced by music choice as well, but only among blacks. Country fans are the least likely to be more liberal than parents, whereas classic and alternative rock fans are the most likely. Classic rock fans may be more liberal than parents because their parents are more conservative than other parents. Mothers of classic rock fans and alternative fans are the most conservative, whereas fathers of classic rock fans are the most conservative. These differences are significant. Country fans, though, are more likely to be Democrats and less likely to be liberal, possibly because country fans are lifestyle conservatives and prounion economic liberals, and this distinction does not appear on the blunt seven-point scale.

Rap music and race together have a great deal of influence on young Americans' political orientations. Rap fans are a little less likely to believe that newer lifestyles contribute to the breakdown of society. White rap fans are more likely to agree strongly with the claim than nonfans, whereas black rap fans are only slightly more likely to agree. Rap may be a cynical statement that society has broken down, but it does not demonstrate support for the breakdown.

Moral relativism, rap preference, and race are related as well. White rap fans are less morally relativistic than white nonfans, whereas black rap fans are more morally relativistic than black nonfans. This is because white rap fans approach rap somewhat voyeuristically in terms of the socially pathological messages, but remain fairly strongly opposed to them and to moral relativism. African Americans are more morally relativistic than European Americans, but this fact does not explain why black rap fans would be more relativistic than non-rap fans. It may be defensive. Black rap fans take an "anything goes" attitude in terms of the music because they may perceive as racist white elite complaints against the music. Rap musicians are able to influence their fans. White rap acts are able to influence white fans, and black rap acts are probably more easily able to influence black fans. In terms of women's equality, rap and race combine to have a significant influence. Black rap fans are significantly less supportive of women's equality than black non-rap fans. Rap has no influence on white fans' views on women's equality.

Fans of alternative rock are more in favor of women's equality than nonfans. They are more likely to believe it is better to live by one's own standards. Alternative fans do not believe that newer lifestyles are contributing to the breakdown of society and they tend to be more in favor of homosexuality than nonfans. Moreover, fans of the music are more likely than nonfans to agree with political positions when taken by performers in the genre.

Among Canadian respondents, there is a small but statistically significant relationship between hours listening to music on the radio and ideology: more hours correlates with increased conservatism. Also unexpectedly, there were negative correlations between hours listening to the radio and support for gay marriage and marijuana legalization. More in the expected direction, increased listening to one's own collection correlates with greater support for moral relativism, support for gay marriage, and the legalization of marijuana.

Among Irish respondents, there are no significant correlations between listening to music on the radio and the various political beliefs. Among U.K. respondents, increased listening correlates with less support for the legalization of marijuana and less support for using British troops in U.N. peacekeeping operations. Among Irish respondents, the more frequently they listen to their own collections the more supportive they are of marijuana legalization, gay marriage, and moral relativism. Among U.K. respondents, increased listening to one's own collection correlates with less support for the idea that women should stay home, increased support for gay marriage, and with increased leftism on the seven point ideology scale.

Canadian youths who have attended concerts where information tables had been set up by political groups are more likely than other youths to be more liberal than both parents. Among Irish respondents, there is no such relationship, while U.K.

youths who report having attended such concerts are also more likely to be more left than both parents.

Canadian alternative rock and rap fans are much more likely than country fans to prefer the Liberal Party or the social democratic New Democratic Party. Country and Western fans are more likely than these others to prefer the Conservative Party. There were no statistically significant relationships between music preference and political party in the Irish or U.K. samples, although alternative rock and rap fans were more likely to prefer the Labour Party than were others.

Fans of alternative rock are especially worthy of future consideration for a number of reasons. First, the music is the most political in terms of content and activism by musicians. Second, its popularity is growing. Usually more than one station in each major market is dedicated to it exclusively. Recently the Detroit market had three stations playing alternative rock, but now there are two. Finally, in every case where there were statistically significant results for the differences in beliefs between fans of alternative rock and others, except for level of political engagement and national pride, the differences each indicate alternative rock fans preferring more left/liberal positions than others. While this does not prove that listening to alternative rock is the cause of these differences, the data suggest the existence of a sub-culture of fans of alternative rock in four mainly English-speaking countries who hold different political opinions than others, and may find those beliefs reinforced by the lyrics and political statements of alternative rock musicians. These phenomena are definitely worthy of future consideration.

U.S. classic rock fans are basically more conservative than nonfans as well, but they are more likely to be more liberal than their parents. This is not attributable to the content of classic rock because its fans are generally more conservative. The fans of macho rock 'n' roll may have selected classic rock on the questionnaire because it was the category closest to their actual music preference. Country and western music fans are politically different from nonfans as well. They tend to be more likely than other youths to believe it is better to fit in. They are less supportive of abortion rights and legalized flag burning than others. Moreover, they are less cynical about the national government than others. Finally, as with the other kinds of music, country musicians are able to influence country fans on important political issues, such as assistance to farmers.

Celebrity Endorsements

In each of the samples from the four countries studied, when celebrities from the entertainment culture were shown as endorsing a specific political belief, the level of agreement increased compared with the same statement as said by an anonymous someone, if the statement were already popular. Regarding unpopular positions, celebrity endorsements tempered the severity of respondents' disagreement.

Young American country and western fans were more likely to agree that more should be done to help farmers when country star Tim McGraw endorsed the position. Young American alternative rock fans were more likely to agree with musician Zack De La Rocha's claim that democracy in the U.S. is a sham, than an anonymous someone's exact same statement. U.S. white rap fans are more likely to agree with helping Tibet when white rap stars *The Beastie Boys* say it.

Young Canadian fans of alternative rock are more likely to agree with the statement that Bush is one of the worst presidents ever when Deryck Whibley of the band *Sum 41* says it. Young Canadians are also more likely to agree with a statement of pride in Canada for not joining the Iraq war coalition when the claim is made by pop star Avril Lavigne.

Young British respondents are more likely to say they would have voted for John Kerry if given the chance when they know that classic rocker Peter Frampton supported Kerry. Irish rock star Bono consistently influences the British and Irish samples. Respondents are less likely to disagree strongly and more likely to somewhat agree with a very unpopular belief that President Bush has done an incredible job on AIDS. Thom Yorke's endorsement of the popular belief that Blair and Bush are liars increases support for that position among U.K. respondents.

These findings are among the most significant of the work because they offer the clearest causal evidence that celebrities' political beliefs as expressed outside their work influence the beliefs of fans. For some lesser celebrities, their influence is great only among fans of their genre, or of them specifically. Other celebrities—Bono, for example—is so famous that his influence is comprehensive. These results have implications not only for basic research in the social sciences, but should also be considered by candidates and leaders of causes when they select their celebrity spokespersons.

Why Political Scientists Must Continue to Study the Influence of Pop Culture

So, in the final analysis, are young people's political attitudes the products of experience with popular culture, or does the pop culture merely reflect back to young people the values they already hold? Clearly the evidence marshaled in this book indicates that it is more of the former and less the latter. While young people's beliefs are not only the products of popular culture, but instead are influenced by a myriad of sources, that is a better description of the actual case than the claim that the pop culture merely reflects what its producers think is already happening in the world. Of course the interactive model discussed in chapter two remains the most reasonable explanation.

Clearly the popular culture influences the political values of young people. Music is the most significant influence, with television second and movies third. This order exists for a number of reasons. Movies are seen usually only once or twice. For an agent of socialization to have great effect, repeated exposure helps. Television programs are watched repeatedly. However, no element of the popular culture is experienced more repetitively than music. Many young people are able to remember the words of dozens of songs at a time as a result of repeated listening. Very few if any remember all the words to a television program or movie.

There is a greater variety of music, and young people do more self-selection of songs as well. There are fewer movies than television programs at any time, and there are fewer television programs than songs. Thus, young people have a wider variety of songs to choose from that will reaffirm their preexisting values. Moreover, there is a greater chance that they will be randomly exposed to songs that challenge their values than there is of being randomly exposed to movies and television programs that do so.

Furthermore, music resonates more emotionally than the other aspects of the popular culture. Songs define a time and dredge up long-term memories much more than do television programs and movies. This may be because of the shorter lengths of songs and that they usually have one simple theme. The increased emotional connection gives them greater influence.

Finally, music preference helps create communities among people. As suggested earlier, just preferring alternative rock as a musical choice can be a reason for young people to form social groups. The young people who prefer classic rock often dress in 1970s fashion as a way of further bonding.

The data do not conclusively prove my claims about the differences between strict parents and nurturing parents. However, the data are consistent with the theory. In addition, young American conservatives are more likely to disagree with messages in the popular culture. Young conservatives are more likely to disagree from the conservative perspective than liberals are to disagree from the liberal perspective. Conservative Americans raised by conservative parents recoil against the popular culture and liberals raised by liberal parents take the entertainment media as just another influence. A longitudinal study would be required to determine whether young conservatives, as they move further from the influence of parents, will be more influenced by the entertainment media, whereas young liberals will have more stable orientations and will not be so influenced.

Canadian, British, and Irish consumers of popular culture are able to critically evaluate it as well, and are in no way passive victims of cultural imperialism. These findings too lend credence to the active and interactive models of socialization which suggest a significant role of the individual being socialized in choosing the cultural products consumed.

Finally, the popular culture helps provide metaphors and frameworks that help people, young ones especially, to understand the political world. Nothing demonstrated this more clearly than the 11 September 2001 terrorist attacks on the United States. Grappling for language to understand these horrific events, man Americans turned to movies and television, which until then had been the only place where they had seen such terrible images and plots. Social scientists should examine the utility of these media produced understandings. Do they help Americans understand political reality, or do they instead cloud our judgments with cartoonish enemy images, false dichotomies, and easy solutions?

There has been much speculation about the influence of the entertainment media over young people's values, political and otherwise. Unfortunately, not enough research has been done to test whether our worst fears or greatest hopes about media influence are correct. The research presented here indicates a middle path is the more reasonable. Determining the influences on young people is a phenomenally complicated process. Demonstrating the influence of parents, the agreed upon strongest influence over young people, is difficult. Demonstrating the influence of entertainment media is even more difficult. Even though, they clearly have an influence, especially as a secondary influence challenging or confirming the preexisting values that other agents of socialization have instilled.

APPENDIX A

The Survey Instruments

The Survey of U.S. Students

◎ Which of the following two statements comes closer to your own views? You might agree to some extent with both, but we want to know which one is CLOSER to your views. ONE, It is better to fit in with people around you; or TWO, it is better to conduct yourself according to your own standards, even if it makes you stand out?
- ONE comes closer to my opinion.
- TWO comes closer to my opinion
- Don't Know

◎ Which is closer to your views on abortion? (Please circle one response.)
- By law, abortion should never be permitted.
- The law should permit abortion only in the case of rape, incest, or when the woman's life is in danger.
- The law should permit abortion for reasons other than rape, incest, or danger to the woman's life, but only after the need for the abortion has been clearly established.
- By law, a woman should always be able to obtain an abortion as a matter of personal choice.

◎ Recently there has been a lot of talk about women's rights. Some people feel that women should have an equal role with men in running business, industry and government. Suppose these people are at one end of a scale, at point 1. Others feel that a woman's place is in the home. Suppose these people are at the other end, at point 7. And, of course, some people have opinions somewhere in between at points 2, 3, 4, 5, or 6.

○ Where would you place yourself on this scale? (Please circle one number.)

1	2	3	4	5	6	7

Women and Men should   A woman's place
have an equal role   is in the home

○ Zack De La Rocha of *Rage Against The Machine*, said, "What passes for democracy today is a sham. It's all about raising money and owing favors to the wrong people." How do you feel about his comments? (Please circle one response.)
- Agree strongly
- Agree somewhat
- Neither agree nor disagree
- Disagree somewhat
- Disagree strongly

○ Should burning or destroying the American flag as a form of political protest be LEGAL or should it be AGAINST THE LAW? (Please circle one response.)
- Legal
- Against the law
- Don't know

○ Recently some people have raised concerns about low wages and poor working conditions at Nike shoe factories overseas. Michael Jordan, who has a product endorsement deal with Nike has said that he's not concerned about the issue. He said, "I don't know the complete situation. Why should I? I'm trying to do my job. Hopefully Nike will do the right thing, whatever that may be." How do you feel about Michael Jordan's comments? (Please circle one response.)
- Agree strongly
- Agree somewhat
- Neither agree nor disagree
- Disagree somewhat
- Disagree strongly

○ Do You FAVOR or OPPOSE the death penalty for persons convicted of murder?
- Favor
- Oppose
- Don't know

○ The newer lifestyles are contributing to the breakdown of society.
- Agree strongly
- Agree somewhat
- Neither agree nor disagree

- Disagree somewhat
- Disagree strongly

◎ The world is always changing and we should adjust our view of moral behavior to those changes.
- Agree strongly
- Agree somewhat
- Neither agree nor disagree
- Disagree somewhat
- Disagree strongly

◎ Homosexual lifestyles are morally acceptable.
- Agree strongly
- Agree somewhat
- Neither agree nor disagree
- Disagree somewhat
- Disagree strongly

◎ Would you say the government is pretty much run by a few big interests looking out for themselves or that it is run for the benefit of all the people? (Please circle one response.)
- For the benefit of all
- For a few big interests
- Don't know

◎ Do you think that QUITE A FEW of the people running the government are crooked, NOT VERY MANY are, or do you think HARDLY ANY of them are crooked? (Please circle one response.)
- Hardly any
- Not many
- Quite a few
- Don't know

◎ Please write in the space provided the name of the public figure you most respect
-

◎ Do You plan to vote in the next elections? (Please circle one response):
- Yes
- No

◎ Tim McGraw has performed at a concert designed to raise money for American farmers. Many believe that the government should do more to help these farmers. How do you feel about this? (Please circle one response.)
- The government should do more
- The government is doing just about enough
- The government should do less
- Don't know

◎ The Beastie Boys believe that other countries should do more to end the Chinese
    military occupation of neighboring Tibet. How do you feel about this issue?
    (Please circle one response.)
    • Agree strongly
    • Agree somewhat
    • Neither agree nor disagree
    • Disagree somewhat
    • Disagree strongly

◎ Here is a set of questions concerning various public figures. We want to see how
    much information about them gets out to the public from television, newspapers,
    and the like. In the space next to the names, please write in what job or political
    office the person now holds.
    • Al Gore
    • Sandra Day O'Connor
    • Trent Lott
    • William Rehnquist
    • Dennis Archer (Ohio version: Michael White)
    • John Engler (Ohio version: George Voinovich)
    • Carl Levin (Ohio version: Michael DeWine)
    • Newt Gingrich
    • Stephen Yokich
    • David Bonior (Ohio version: March Kaptur)
    • Maryann Mahaffey (Ohio version: Carty Finkbiner)

◎ If you know what political party your mother/legal guardian prefers, please circle
    the name of that party:
    • Republican
    • Independent
    • No Preference
    • Other Party
    • Democrat
    • Don't Know

◎ If you know what political party your father/legal guardian prefers, please circle
    the name of that party:
    • Republican
    • Independent
    • No Preference
    • Other Party
    • Democrat
    • Don't Know

◎ How many days in the PAST WEEK did you talk about politics with your family
    or friends?
    • 0 (none)

- 1 day
- 2 days
- 3 days
- 4 days
- 5 days
- 6 days
- 7 (every day)

◎ How many days in the PAST WEEK did you read a daily newspaper?
- 0 (none)
- 1 day
- 2 days
- 3 days
- 4 days
- 5 days
- 6 days
- 7 (every day)

◎ How many days in the PAST WEEK did you watch the news on TV?
- 0 (none)
- 1 day
- 2 days
- 3 days
- 4 days
- 5 days
- 6 days
- 7 (every day)

◎ On average how many HOURS PER DAY do you spend listening to music on the radio?
- less than 1 hour
- more than 1 hour, but less than 2 hours
- more than 2 hours, but less than 3 hours
- more than 3 hours

◎ If you talk to others about politics, with whom do you talk about politics most frequently? (please circle one response)
- mother
- father
- brother
- sister
- teacher
- minister/pastor/church leader
- other; please specify

◎   On average how many HOURS PER DAY do you spend watching TV?
- less than 1 hour
- more than 1 hour, but less than 2 hours
- more than 2 hours, but less than 3 hours
- more than 3 hours

◎   If you own your own music collection, on average how many HOURS PER DAY do you spend listening to it? (please circle one response)
- less than 1 hour
- more than 1 hour, but less than 2 hours
- more than 2 hours, but less than 3 hours
- more than 3 hours

◎   If you have your own music collection, about how many compact discs, cassette tapes and records do you own?
-

◎   What kind of music is your favorite? (please circle one response)
- Country
- Jazz
- Classic Rock
- Alternative Rock
- Rap/Hip-Hop
- Other (specify)

◎   Do you remember the name and artist of the first piece of recorded music you purchased? If you do please write them in he space provided:
-

◎   Who is your favorite musical artist?
-

◎   What is the name and artist of your favorite song ever?
-

◎   Who is your favorite actor/actress?
-

◎   What is the name of your favorite movie?
-

◎   What is the name of your favorite TV program?
-

◎   Sometimes artists say things about politics, ethics, morality, and so on in their songs. Have you ever disagree with the message of a song? (please circle one response):
- Yes
- No

◉ If you have ever disagreed with the message of a song and can remember the title of the song and the artist, please name them and briefly explain why you disagreed with the song in the space provided.

•

◉ Sometimes actors and writers say things about politics, ethics, morality, and so on in their movies. Have you ever disagreed with the message of a movie? (Please circle one response.):
  • Yes
  • No

◉ If you have ever disagreed with the message of a movie and can remember the title of the movie, please write it in the space provided and briefly explain why you disagreed with the message.

•

◉ Sometimes actors and writers say things about politics, ethics, morality, and so on in their television programs. Have you ever disagreed with the message of a television program? (please circle one response):
  • Yes
  • No

◉ If you have ever disagreed with the message of a television program and can remember the name of the program, please write it in the space provided and briefly explain why you disagreed with the message.

•

◉ Please list a few songs you like right now and who sings them

•

◉ Please list a few movies you like right now:

•

◉ Please list a few television programs you like right now:

•

◉ Please list a few magazines you like to read:

•

◉ How would you describe your political beliefs? (Please circle one response.)
  • extremely liberal
  • liberal
  • slightly liberal
  • moderate; middle of the road
  • slightly conservative
  • conservative
  • extremely conservative

◎ How would you describe your mother/legal guardian's political beliefs? (Please circle one response.)
  - extremely liberal
  - liberal
  - slightly liberal
  - moderate; middle of the road
  - slightly conservative
  - conservative
  - extremely conservative

◎ Have you ever been to a musical performance where political organizations had set up information tables?
  - yes
  - no

◎ If you have been to a musical performance where political organizations had set up information tables and you can remember the name of the organization, the issue they were interested in, or any other information about them, please write it in the space below.
  -

◎ How would you describe your father/legal guardian's political beliefs? (Please circle one response.)
  - extremely liberal
  - liberal
  - slightly liberal
  - moderate; middle of the road
  - slightly conservative
  - conservative
  - extremely conservative

◎ De La Soul
  - extremely liberal
  - liberal
  - slightly liberal
  - moderate; middle of the road
  - slightly conservative
  - conservative
  - extremely conservative

◎ Zack De La Rocha:
  - extremely liberal
  - liberal
  - slightly liberal
  - moderate; middle of the road
  - slightly conservative

- conservative
- extremely conservative

◎ Madonna:
  - extremely liberal
  - liberal
  - slightly liberal
  - moderate; middle of the road
  - slightly conservative
  - conservative
  - extremely conservative

◎ Garth Brooks:
  - extremely liberal
  - liberal
  - slightly liberal
  - moderate; middle of the road
  - slightly conservative
  - conservative
  - extremely conservative

◎ Eddie Vedder:
  - extremely liberal
  - liberal
  - slightly liberal
  - moderate; middle of the road
  - slightly conservative
  - conservative
  - extremely conservative

◎ Arnold Schwarzenegger:
  - extremely liberal
  - liberal
  - slightly liberal
  - moderate; middle of the road
  - slightly conservative
  - conservative
  - extremely conservative

◎ Will Smith:
  - extremely liberal
  - liberal
  - slightly liberal
  - moderate; middle of the road
  - slightly conservative
  - conservative
  - extremely conservative

◎ Jim Carrey:
- extremely liberal
- liberal
- slightly liberal
- moderate; middle of the road
- slightly conservative
- conservative
- extremely conservative

◎ Bruce Willis:
- extremely liberal
- liberal
- slightly liberal
- moderate; middle of the road
- slightly conservative
- conservative
- extremely conservative

◎ Your Age
-

◎ High School Attended
-

◎ State you are from
-

◎ Town/City you are from
-

◎ Year in College:
- Freshman
- Sophomore
- Junior
- Senior

◎ Sex (please circle one):
- Male
- Female

◎ Race (please circle one):
- African American
- White, Non-Hispanic
- Hispanic
- Other

◎ High School Grade Point Average (on a 4.0 scale):
-

◎ What is your mother/legal guardian's occupation?
  •

◎ What is your father/legal guardian's occupation?
  •

◎ What is your best guess about your family income? (please circle one response)
  • under $20,000
  • $20,000 to $49,999
  • $50,000 to $74,999
  • $75,000 to $99,999
  • $100,000 or more

◎ What is your religious affiliation? (please circle one response)
  • Protestant
  • Catholic
  • Jewish
  • Muslim
  • Other, please specify
  • none

◎ How often do you attend religious services?
  • Never
  • A few times a year
  • Monthly
  • Once a week
  • More than once a week

◎ Did your high school have student government? (Please circle one response.):
  • Yes
  • No

◎ If your high school did have student government, did you participate? (Please circle one response.):
  • Yes
  • No

◎ If so, what did you do? (circle any that apply):
  • ran for office
  • campaigned for another candidate
  • voted
  • other (specify)

◎ Generally speaking, do you think of yourself as a Republican, a Democrat, an Independent, or what? (Please circle one response.)
  • Republican
  • Independent
  • No Preference

- Other Party
- Democrat
- Don't Know

Did you participate in organized sports in high school? (Please circle one response.)
- Yes
- No

If you did participate in athletics in high school, which sport(s) did you play?
-

Amy Ray and Emily Saliers of *The Indigo Girls* believe that Native American communities ought to have more political control over issues that are important to them, and that the Federal Government ought to have less influence. How do you feel about this? (Please circle one response.)
- Agree strongly
- Agree somewhat
- Neither agree nor disagree
- Disagree somewhat
- Disagree strongly

Some people say that because of past discrimination it is sometimes necessary for colleges and universities to use different admissions standards for black students. Others oppose such preferences because they say preferences give blacks advantages they haven't earned. What about your opinion? Are you FOR or AGAINST preferences to admit black students? (please circle one response)
- For
- Against
- Don't Know

Our society should do whatever is necessary to make sure that everyone has an equal opportunity to succeed.
- Agree strongly
- Agree somewhat
- Neither agree nor disagree
- Disagree somewhat
- Disagree strongly

We have gone too far in pushing equal rights in this country.
- Agree strongly
- Agree somewhat
- Neither agree nor disagree
- Disagree somewhat
- Disagree strongly

The Survey of Canadian Students

◎ Quebec has the right to separate no matter what the rest of Canada says
  - strongly agree
  - somewhat agree
  - somewhat disagree
  - strongly disagree

◎ Overall, free trade has been good for the Canadian economy
  - strongly agree
  - somewhat agree
  - somewhat disagree
  - strongly disagree

◎ Canadian music and television is not as good as American music and television
  - strongly agree
  - somewhat agree
  - somewhat disagree
  - strongly disagree

◎ Smoking marijuana should not be a criminal offence
  - strongly agree
  - somewhat agree
  - somewhat disagree
  - strongly disagree

◎ Society would be better off if more women stayed home with their children
  - strongly agree
  - somewhat agree
  - somewhat disagree
  - strongly disagree

◎ Only the police and the military should be allowed to have guns
  - strongly agree
  - somewhat agree
  - somewhat disagree
  - strongly disagree

◎ Gays and lesbians should be allowed to get married
  - strongly agree
  - somewhat agree
  - somewhat disagree
  - strongly disagree

◎ The world is always changing and we should adjust our view of moral behavior to those changes
  - strongly agree
  - somewhat agree

- somewhat disagree
- strongly disagree

◎ Canada should participate in peacekeeping operations abroad even if it means putting the lives of Canadian soldiers at risk
- strongly agree
- somewhat agree
- somewhat disagree
- strongly disagree

◎ Sometimes artists say things about politics, ethics, morality, and so on in their songs. Have you ever DISAGREED with the message of a song? (please circle one response):
- Yes
- No

◎ If you have ever DISAGREED with the message of a song and can remember the title of the song and the artist, please name them and briefly explain why you disagreed with the song in the space provided.
-

◎ Sometimes artists say things about politics, ethics, morality, and so on in their songs. Have you ever AGREED with the message of a song? (please circle one response):
- Yes
- No

◎ If you have ever AGREED with the message of a song and can remember the title of the song and the artist, please name them and briefly explain why you agreed with the song in the space provided.
-

◎ If you know what political party your mother/legal guardian prefers, please circle the name of that party
- Liberal
- Conservative
- N.D.P.
- Green
- Bloc Quebecois
- Another Party

◎ If you know what political party your father/legal guardian prefers, please circle the name of that party
- Liberal
- Conservative
- N.D.P.
- Green

- Bloc Quebecois
- Another Party

◎ How many days in the PAST WEEK did you talk about politics with your family or friends?
- 0 (none)
- 1 day
- 2 days
- 3 days
- 4 days
- 5 days
- 6 days
- 7 (every day)

◎ How many days in the PAST WEEK did you read a daily newspaper?
- 0 (none)
- 1 day
- 2 days
- 3 days
- 4 days
- 5 days
- 6 days
- 7 (every day)

◎ How many days in the PAST WEEK did you watch the news on TV?
- 0 (none)
- 1 day
- 2 days
- 3 days
- 4days
- 5 days
- 6 days
- 7 (every day)

◎ Sometimes actors and writers say things about politics, ethics, morality, and so on in their movies. Have you ever DISAGREED with the message of a movie? (Please circle one response.):
- Yes
- No

◎ If you have ever DISAGREED with the message of a movie and can remember the title of the movie, please write it in the space provided and briefly explain why you disagreed with the message.
-

- Sometimes actors and writers say things about politics, ethics, morality, and so on in their movies. Have you ever AGREED with the message of a movie? (Please circle one response.):
  - Yes
  - No

- If you have ever AGREED with the message of a movie and can remember the title of the movie, please write it in the space provided and briefly explain why you agreed with the message.
  -

- On average how many HOURS PER DAY do you spend reading news sites on the internet?
  - less than 1 hour
  - more than 1 hour, but less than 2 hours
  - more than 2 hours, but less than 3 hours
  - more than 3 hours

- On average how many HOURS PER DAY do you spend listening to music on the radio?
  - less than 1 hour
  - more than 1 hour, but less than 2 hours
  - more than 2 hours, but less than 3 hours
  - more than 3 hours

- On average how many HOURS PER DAY do you spend watching entertainment programming on TV?
  - less than 1 hour
  - more than 1 hour, but less than 2 hours
  - more than 2 hours, but less than 3 hours
  - more than 3 hours

- Do you watch Canadian stations all of the time, most of the time, some of the time, or none of the time? (please circle one response)
  - all of the time
  - most of the time
  - some of the time
  - none of the time
  - don't know

- If you own your own music collection, on average how many HOURS PER DAY do you spend listening to it? (please circle one response)
  - less than 1 hour
  - more than 1 hour, but less than 2 hours
  - more than 2 hours, but less than 3 hours
  - more than 3 hours

◎ If you have your own music collection, about how many compact discs, cassette tapes, and records do you own?

•

◎ About what percentage of the recordings in your collection would you say are Canadian?

•

◎ What kind of music is your favourite? (please circle one response)
- Country & Western
- Jazz
- Classic Rock
- Alternative Rock
- Rap/Hip-Hop
- R & B
- Classical Music
- Other (specify)

◎ Who is your favourite musical artist?

•

◎ What is the name and artist of your favourite song ever?

•

◎ Who is your favourite actor/actress?

•

◎ What is the name of your favourite movie?

•

◎ What is the name of your favourite TV program?

•

◎ How would you describe your political beliefs? (Please circle one response.)
- extremely liberal
- liberal
- slightly liberal
- moderate; middle of the road
- slightly conservative
- conservative
- extremely conservative

•

◎ How would you describe your mother/legal guardian's political beliefs? (Please circle one response.)
- extremely liberal
- liberal
- slightly liberal
- moderate; middle of the road

- slightly conservative
- conservative
- extremely conservative

◎ Have you ever been to a musical performance where political organizations had set up information tables?
- yes
- no

◎ If you have been to a musical performance where political organizations had set up information tables and you can remember the name of the organization, the issue they were interested in, or any other information about them please write it in the space below.
-

◎ How would you describe your father/legal guardian's political beliefs? (Please circle one response.)
- extremely liberal
- liberal
- slightly liberal
- moderate; middle of the road
- slightly conservative
- conservative
- extremely conservative

◎ How would you describe the political beliefs of the following people/groups? (Please circle one; if you don't know please do not circle anything.)

◎ Don Cherry
- extremely liberal
- liberal
- slightly liberal
- moderate; middle of the road
- slightly conservative
- conservative
- extremely conservative

◎ Gord Downie
- extremely liberal
- liberal
- slightly liberal
- moderate; middle of the road
- slightly conservative
- conservative
- extremely conservative

◎ Sarah McLachlan
  - extremely liberal
  - liberal
  - slightly liberal
  - moderate; middle of the road
  - slightly conservative
  - conservative
  - extremely conservative

◎ Avril Lavigne
  - extremely liberal
  - liberal
  - slightly liberal
  - moderate; middle of the road
  - slightly conservative
  - conservative
  - extremely conservative

◎ Generally speaking which political party do you prefer?
  - Liberal
  - Conservative
  - N.D.P.
  - Green
  - Bloc Quebecois
  - Another Party

◎ Do you think Canada's ties with the United States should be:
  - much closer
  - somewhat closer
  - about the same as now
  - more distant
  - much more distant
  - don't know

◎ We'd like to get your feelings on some countries in the news these days. We'd like you to rate them using what is known as the feeling thermometer. Ratings between 50 degrees and 100 degrees mean that you feel favorable and warm towards that country. Ratings between 0 and 50 degrees mean that you don't feel favorable towards that country. If you rate the country at the midpoint, 50 degree mark, that means that you don't have any particular feelings towards that country.
  - Great Britain
  - France
  - The United States
  - Canada

- China
- Quebec

◎   Here is a list of FOUR goals. Which goal is MOST important to you personally?
- fighting crime
- giving people more say in important government decisions
- maintaining economic growth
- protecting freedom of speech

◎   On the whole how satisfied are you with the way democracy works in Canada?
- very satisfied
- fairly satisfied
- not very satisfied
- not satisfied at all

◎   Please describe in the space provided Canadian achievements of which you are particularly proud.
-

◎   In the space provided please name a song besides *O Canada!* that makes you feel proud to be Canadian
-

◎   Avril Lavigne recently said, "I don't have respect for the people that made the decisions to go with the war. I don't have much respect for Bush. He's about war, I'm not about war—a lot of people aren't about war... I'm really proud that our Prime Minister didn't fight." How do you feel about these statements? (please circle one response)
- strongly agree
- somewhat agree
- somewhat disagree
- strongly disagree

◎   In the space provided please name an actor or musician whose opinions on politics you respect.

◎   Deryck Whibley of the band *Sum 41* said recently, "George W. Bush is probably one of the worst presidents we'll ever have, or have had. ... I just don't know how, so far, he's gotten away with everything he's done." How do you feel about these comments? (please circle one response)
- strongly agree
- somewhat agree
- somewhat disagree
- strongly disagree

◎ Alanis Morissette opposed U.S. President George W. Bush's Energy Program because she believed it disregarded environmental protection and failed to support conservation and renewable energy programs. How do you feel about this? (please circle one response)
- strongly agree
- somewhat agree
- somewhat disagree
- strongly disagree

◎ Please write in the space provided the name of the public figure you most respect
-

◎ Sometimes actors and writers say things about politics, ethics, morality, and so on in their television programs. Have you ever DISAGREED with the message of a television program? (please circle one response):
- Yes
- No

◎ If you have ever DISAGREED with the message of a television program and can remember the name of the program, please write it in the space provided and briefly explain why you disagreed with the message.
-

◎ Sometimes actors and writers say things about politics, ethics, morality, and so on in their television programs. Have you ever AGREED with the message of a television program? (please circle one response):
- Yes
- No

◎ If you have ever AGREED with the message of a television program and can remember the name of the program, please write it in the space provided and briefly explain why you agreed with the message.
-

◎ Which statement best describes your ability to speak and understand French? (please circle one response)
- I can speak French well enough to conduct a fairly long conversation on different topics
- I can speak French well enough to get by in a predominantly French speaking environment
- I understand some French, but I would be uncomfortable in a French speaking environment
- I understand very little or no French

◎ How often do you listen to music in French? (please circle one response)
- Frequently

- Occasionally
- Rarely or Never

◎ Your Age
-

◎ In what province do you live?
- Newfoundland
- PEI
- Nova Scotia
- New Brunswick
- Quebec
- Ontario
- Manitoba
- Saskatchewan
- Alberta
- British Columbia

◎ Sex (please circle one):
- Male
- Female

Survey of British and Irish Students:

◎ Northern Ireland has the right to separate no matter what the rest of the United Kingdom says
- strongly agree
- somewhat agree
- somewhat disagree
- strongly disagree

◎ Overall, free trade has been good for the British economy
- strongly agree
- somewhat agree
- somewhat disagree
- strongly disagree

◎ British music and television is not as good as American music and television
- strongly agree
- somewhat agree
- somewhat disagree
- strongly disagree

◎ Smoking marijuana should not be a criminal offence
- strongly agree
- somewhat agree

- somewhat disagree
- strongly disagree

◎ Society would be better off if more women stayed home with their children
  - strongly agree
  - somewhat agree
  - somewhat disagree
  - strongly disagree

◎ Only the police and the military should be allowed to have guns
  - strongly agree
  - somewhat agree
  - somewhat disagree
  - strongly disagree

◎ Gays and lesbians should be allowed to get married
  - strongly agree
  - somewhat agree
  - somewhat disagree
  - strongly disagree

◎ The world is always changing and we should adjust our view of moral behavior to those changes
  - strongly agree
  - somewhat agree
  - somewhat disagree
  - strongly disagree

◎ Britain should participate in peacekeeping operations abroad even if it means putting the lives of British soldiers at risk
  - strongly agree
  - somewhat agree
  - somewhat disagree
  - strongly disagree

◎ Sometimes artists say things about politics, ethics, morality, and so on in their songs. Have you ever DISAGREED with the message of a song? (please circle one response):
  - Yes
  - No

◎ If you have ever DISAGREED with the message of a song and can remember the title of the song and the artist, please name them and briefly explain why you disagreed with the song in the space provided.
  -

⊚ Sometimes artists say things about politics, ethics, morality, and so on in their songs. Have you ever AGREED with the message of a song? (please circle one response):
- Yes
- No

⊚ If you have ever AGREED with the message of a song and can remember the title of the song and the artist, please name them and briefly explain why you agreed with the song in the space provided.
-

⊚ If you know what political party your mother/legal guardian prefers, please circle the name of that party
- Liberal
- Conservative
- Labour
- SNP
- Plaid Cymru
- Another Party

⊚ If you know what political party your father/legal guardian prefers, please circle the name of that party
- Liberal
- Conservative
- Labour
- SNP
- Plaid Cymru
- Another Party

⊚ How many days in the PAST WEEK did you talk about politics with your family or friends?
- 0 (none)
- 1 day
- 2 days
- 3 days
- 4 days
- 5 days
- 6 days
- 7 (every day)

⊚ How many days in the PAST WEEK did you read a daily newspaper?
- 0 (none)
- 1 day
- 2 days
- 3 days
- 4 days

- 5 days
- 6 days
- 7 (every day)

◎ How many days in the PAST WEEK did you watch the news on TV?
- 0 (none)
- 1 day
- 2 days
- 3 days
- 4 days
- 5 days
- 6 days
- 7 (every day)

◎ In politics, people sometimes talk of left and right. Where would you place yourself on the scale below?

1	2	3	4	5	6	7	8	9	10
Left									Right

◎ Sometimes actors and writers say things about politics, ethics, morality, and so on in their movies. Have you ever DISAGREED with the message of a movie? (Please circle one response.):
- Yes
- No

◎ If you have ever DISAGREED with the message of a movie and can remember the title of the movie, please write it in the space provided and briefly explain why you disagreed with the message.
-

◎ Sometimes actors and writers say things about politics, ethics, morality and so on in their movies. Have you ever AGREED with the message of a movie? (Please circle one response.):
- Yes
- No

◎ If you have ever AGREED with the message of a movie and can remember the title of the movie, please write it in the space provided and briefly explain why you disagreed with the message.
-

◎ On average how many HOURS PER DAY do you spend reading news sites on the internet?
- less than 1 hour
- more than 1 hour, but less than 2 hours
- more than 2 hours, but less than 3 hours
- more than 3 hours

◎ On average how many HOURS PER DAY do you spend listening to music on the radio?
- less than 1 hour
- more than 1 hour, but less than 2 hours
- more than 2 hours, but less than 3 hours
- more than 3 hours

◎ On average how many HOURS PER DAY do you spend watching entertainment programming on TV?
- less than 1 hour
- more than 1 hour, but less than 2 hours
- more than 2 hours, but less than 3 hours
- more than 3 hours

◎ We'd like to find out how well-known are some of our political leaders and other people who are in the news these days. After you read each of the following names, please fill in the box corresponding to the response that indicates how familiar you are with the person.

◎ Tony Blair
- Very familiar
- Somewhat familiar
- Not too familiar
- Not at all familiar

◎ Bono
- Very familiar
- Somewhat familiar
- Not too familiar
- Not at all familiar

◎ George W. Bush
- Very familiar
- Somewhat familiar
- Not too familiar
- Not at all familiar

◎ Mick Jagger
- Very familiar
- Somewhat familiar
- Not too familiar
- Not at all familiar

◎ David Beckham
- Very familiar
- Somewhat familiar
- Not too familiar
- Not at all familiar

◎ J.K. Rowling
  - Very familiar
  - Somewhat familiar
  - Not too familiar
  - Not at all familiar

◎ Peter Frampton
  - Very familiar
  - Somewhat familiar
  - Not too familiar
  - Not at all familiar

◎ Sir Ian Holm
  - Very familiar
  - Somewhat familiar
  - Not too familiar
  - Not at all familiar

◎ Thom Yorke
  - Very familiar
  - Somewhat familiar
  - Not too familiar
  - Not at all familiar

◎ Madonna
  - Very familiar
  - Somewhat familiar
  - Not too familiar
  - Not at all familiar

◎ Do you watch British stations all of the time, most of the time, some of the time or none of the time? (please circle one response)
  - all of the time
  - most of the time
  - some of the time
  - none of the time
  - don't know

◎ If you own your own music collection, on average how many HOURS PER DAY do you spend listening to it? (please circle one response)
  - less than 1 hour
  - more than 1 hour, but less than 2 hours
  - more than 2 hours, but less than 3 hours
  - more than 3 hours

◎ If you have your own music collection, about how many compact discs, cassette tapes, and records do you own?
  -

◎ About what percentage of the recordings in your collection would you say are British?

•

◎ What kind of music is your favourite? (please circle one response)
- Country & Western
- Jazz
- Classic Rock
- Alternative Rock
- Rap/Hip-Hop
- R & B
- Classical Music
- Other (specify)

◎ How would you describe your political beliefs? (Please circle one response.)
- extremely left
- left
- slightly left
- moderate; middle of the road
- slightly conservative
- conservative
- extremely conservative

◎ How would you describe your mother/legal guardian's political beliefs? (Please circle one response.)
- extremely left
- left
- slightly left
- moderate; middle of the road
- slightly conservative
- conservative
- extremely conservative

◎ Have you ever been to a musical performance where political organizations had set up information tables?
- yes
- no

◎ If you have been to a musical performance where political organizations had set up information tables and you can remember the name of the organization, the issue they were interested in, or any other information about them please write it in the space below.

•

◎ How would you describe your father/legal guardian's political beliefs? (Please circle one response.)
- extremely liberal

- liberal
- slightly liberal
- moderate; middle of the road
- slightly conservative
- conservative
- extremely conservative

◎ Generally speaking which political party do you prefer?
- Liberal
- Conservative
- Labour
- SNP
- Plaid Cymru
- Another Party

◎ Do you think Britain's ties with the United States should be:
- much closer
- somewhat closer
- about the same as now
- more distant
- much more distant
- don't know

◎ We'd like to get your feelings on some countries in the news these days. We'd like you to rate them using what is known as the feeling thermometer. Ratings between 50 degrees and 100 degrees mean that you feel favorable and warm towards that country. Ratings between 0 and 50 degrees mean that you don't feel favorable towards that country. If you rate the country at the midpoint, 50 degree mark, that means that you don't have any particular feelings towards that country.
- Great Britain
- France
- The United States
- Canada
- China
- Quebec
- Ireland
- Northern Ireland

◎ We'd like to get your feelings toward some of our political leaders and other people who are in the news these days. We'd like you to rate that person using something we call the feeling thermometer. The feeling thermometer can rate people from 0 to 100 degrees. Ratings between 50 degrees and 100 degrees mean that you feel favorable and warm toward the person. Ratings between 0 degrees and 50 degrees mean that you don't feel favorable toward the person. Rating the person at the midpoint, the 50 degree mark, means you don't feel particularly warm or cold toward the person. If you come to a person whose name you don't recognize, please don't rate that person. Just move on to the next one.

- Tony Blair
- Bono
- George W. Bush
- Mick Jagger
- David Beckham
- J.K. Rowling
- Peter Frampton
- Sir Ian Holm
- Thom Yorke
- Madonna

◎ On the whole how satisfied are you with the way democracy works in Britain?
- very satisfied
- fairly satisfied
- not very satisfied
- not satisfied at all

◎ Someone said, "President Bush has done an incredible job on AIDS. And 250,000 Africans are on antiviral drugs. They literally owe their lives to America." How do you feel about these comments?
- strongly agree
- somewhat agree
- somewhat disagree
- strongly disagree

◎ In the space provided please name an actor or musician whose opinions on politics you respect.
-

◎ Someone said, "Many Americans have no idea of what has been the foreign policy of their country. If you don't know about something, you can't understand what is going on." How do you feel about these comments?
- strongly agree
- somewhat agree
- somewhat disagree
- strongly disagree

◎ Please write in the space provided the name of the public figure you most respect
-

◎ Sometimes actors and writers say things about politics, ethics, morality and so on in their television programs. Have you ever DISAGREED with the message of a television program? (please circle one response):

- Yes
- No

◎ If you have ever DISAGREED with the message of a television program and can remember the name of the program, please write it in the space provided and briefly explain why you disagreed with the message.

-

◎ Sometimes actors and writers say things about politics, ethics, morality and so on in their television programs. Have you ever AGREED with the message of a television program? (please circle one response):

- Yes
- No

◎ If you have ever AGREED with the message of a television program and can remember the name of the program, please write it in the space provided and briefly explain why you agreed with the message.

-

◎ Some authors have urged their publishers to print their books on recycled paper. How do you feel about this?

- strongly agree
- somewhat agree
- somewhat disagree
- strongly disagree

◎ If you could have voted in the U.S. in 2004, which candidate would you have voted for?

- George W. Bush
- John Kerry
- Some other candidate

◎ Someone recently said, "I just don't want American troops to be in Iraq, period." How do you feel about these comments?

- strongly agree
- somewhat agree
- somewhat disagree
- strongly disagree

◎ Someone said of U.S. President George W. Bush and British Prime Minister Tony Blair, "These men are liars. We have the right to call them such, they are putting our children's future in jeopardy. They are not controlling the terrorist threat, they are escalating it." How do you feel about these comments?

- strongly agree
- somewhat agree
- somewhat disagree
- strongly disagree

◎ Your Age
   •

◎ In which nation do you live?
   • England
   • Scotland
   • Wales
   • Northern Ireland

◎ Sex (please circle one):
   • Male
   • Female

References

"2007 Year-End Shipment Statistics," *RIAA*, retrieved 16 February 2009 from http://76.74.24.142/81128FFD-028F-282E-1CE5-FDBF16A46388.pdf

"2008–09 National Top Program Reports Archive." *BBM*, retrieved 13 February 2009 from http://www.bbm.ca/en/national_archive.html

Acock, Alan, and Vern Bengston. 1978. On the Relative Influence of Mothers and Fathers: A Covariance Analysis of Political and Religious Socialization. *Journal of Marriage and Family* (Aug): 519–30.

Adams, William C., Allison Salzman, William Vantine, Leslie Suelter, Anne Baker, Lucille Bonvouloir, Barbara Brenner, Margaret Ely, Jean Feldman, and Ron Ziegel. 1985. The Power of "The Power of The Right Stuff": A Quasi–Experimental Field Test of the Docudrama Hypothesis. *Public Opinion Quarterly* 49(3): 330–39.

Adelman, Shonagh. 1989. Representations of Violence against Women in Mainstream Film. *Resources for Feminist Research* 18(2): 21–26

"Alanis Morissette." 2005. <http://www.rollingstone.com/artist/bio/_/id/5702/alnismorissette?pageid=rs.Artistcage&pageregion=artistHeader> (accessed Dec. 28, 2004).

All in the Family. 1971–1979. CBS.

Anderson, Benedict. *Imagined Communities: Reflections on the Origin and Spread of Nationalism.* New York: Verso.

Armageddon. 1998. Dir. Michael Bay. Perf. Bruce Willis, Billy Bob Thornton, Ben Affleck, Liv Tyler. Touchstone.

"Avril Lavigne: Definition, Meaning, Explanation." N.d.Free-DefinitionOnline.<http://www.free-definition.com/Avril-Lavigne.html. Retrieved 8 July 2009.

Ball, Terence, and Richard Dagger. 1998. *Political Ideologies and the Democratic Ideal.* New York: Longman.

Ball-Rokeach, Sandra J., Joel W. Grube, and Milton Rokeach. 1981. *Roots: The Next Generation: Who Watched and with What Effect. Public Opinion Quarterly* 45(1): 58–68.

Baran, Stanley J. 1976. Sex on TV and Adolescent Sexual Self-Image. *Journal of Broadcasting* 20(1): 61–68.

Baumgartner, Jody and Jonathan S. Morris, 2006. "The Daily Show Effect: Candidate Evaluations, Efficacy, and American Youth." *American Politics Research* 34(3): 341-367.

Beck, Paul Allen, and M. Kent Jennings. 1991. Family Traditions, Political Periods, and the Development of Partisan Orientations. *Journal of Politics* 53(3): 742–763.

Belovari, S., G. Look, J. Murphy, N. Nicholson, and J. Williamson. 1976. Political Orientations of Students in Southern Ontario. *History and Social Studies Teacher* 11: 33–42.

Bennett, Stephen Earl. 1998. Young Americans' Indifference to Media Coverage of Public Affairs. *PS: Political Science and Politics* 30(3): 535–41.

Bernard-Donals, Michael. 1994. Jazz, Rock 'n' Roll, Rap and Politics. *Journal of Popular Culture* 28: 127–38.

Bernardin, Marc. 2001. What about Videos? *Entertainment Weekly,* 28 September, p. 2.

Berti, Anna Emilia. 1988. The Development of Political Understanding in Children Between 6 and 15 Years Old. *Human Relations* 41(6): 437–46.

Beverly Hills 90210. 1990–2000. Fox.

Bindas, Kenneth J. 1993. The Future Is Unwritten: The Clash, Punk, and America, 1977–1982. *American Studies* 34(1): 69–89.

Bork, Robert. 1997. *Slouching Towards Gomorrah: Modern Liberalism and American ecline.* New York: Harper Collins.

"Boycotting the Booth." *USA Today.* 3 November 1992, D–2.

Boyd, Todd. 1994. Check Yo Self Before You Wreck Yo Self: Variations on a Political Theme in Rap Music and Popular Culture. *Public Culture* 7(1): 289–312.

Braveheart. 1995. Dir. Mel Gibson. Perf. Mel Gibson, Sophie Marceau. Paramount.

Braxton, Greg. 2000. Study Finds Blacks Seen Most on Comedies, New Networks; Report Sponsored by Screen Actors Guild Says African Americans Are Underused for Major Roles, *Los Angeles Times,* 25 February, section f, p. 24.

Brooks, Garth. 1989. "The Dance." By Tony Arata. *Garth Brooks.* EMD/Capitol.

Brooks, Garth. 1992. "We Shall Be Free." By Garth Brooks, Stephanie Davis. *The Chase.* EMD/Capitol.

Brooks, Stephen. 2006. *As Others See Us: The Causes and Consequences of Foreign Perceptions of America.* Peterborough, Ontario: Broadview Press.

Buckingham, David. 1999. "Young People, Politics and News Media: beyond political socialization." *Oxford Review of Education* 25(1 and 2): 171-184.

Burriss, Larry L. 1987. How Anchors, Reporters and Newsmakers Affect Recall and Evaluation of Stories. *Journalism Quarterly* 64: 514–19.

Buss, David M. 1995. *The Evolution of Desire: Strategies of Human Mating.* New York: Basic Books.

Butler, David and Donald Stokes. 1969. *Political Change in Britain.* London: Macmillan.

Calvo, Dana. 2001. Response to Terror: Hollywood Signs on to Assist War Effort. *Los Angeles Times*, 12 November, A1.

Calvo, Dana and Rachel Abramowitz. 2001. Uncle Sam Wants Hollywood, but Hollywood Has Qualms. *Los Angeles Times*, 19 November, Part 6, 1.

Campbell, Angus , Philip Converse, Warren Miller, and Donald Stokes. 1960. *The American Voter.* Ann Arbor: The University of Michigan Press.

Campbell, Bruce. 1980. A Theoretical Approach to Peer Influence in Adolescent Socialization. *American Journal of Political Science* 24(2): 324–44.

Campbell, John Creighton and John Strate. 1981. Are Old People Conservative? *The Gerontologist* 21(6): 580–91.

Cantor, Paul A. 1999. The Simpsons: Atomistic Politics and the Nuclear Family. *Political Theory* 27(6): 734–49.

Carmody, John. 1998. NBC Puts Its Money On *ER*: 3-Year, $850 Million Deal Sets a Series Record, *The Washington Post*, 15 January, B1.

Castaway. Dir. Robert Zemeckis. Perf. Tom Hanks, Helen Hunt. 20th Century Fox.

Chafee, Steven H., L. Scott Wood, and Leonard P. Tipton. 1970. Mass Communication and Political Socialization. *Journalism Quarterly* 47(Winter): 647–59.

Charlton, K. *Rock Music Styles: A History.* New York: McGraw Hill, 1998.

Christensen, Terry. 1987. *Reel Politics: American Political Movies from* Birth of a Nation *to* Platoon. New York: Blackwell.

Christenson, Peter G. and Donald F. Roberts. *It's Not Only Rock and Roll: Popular Music in the Lives of Adolescents.* Cresskill, NJ: Hampton Press, 1998.

Cloonan, Martin. 1997. "State of the Nation: 'Englishness,'" Pop, and Politics in the Mid-1990s." *Popular Music and Society* (Summer, 1997): 47–70.

Cloonan, Martin. 1999. "Pop and the Nation-State: Towards a Theorisation." *Popular Music* 18(1999): 193–207.

Clymer, Adam. 2000. College Students Not Drawn to Voting or Politics, Poll Shows. *New York Times*, 11 January, A14.

Combs, James, (ed.). 1993. *Movies and Politics: The Dynamic Relationship.* New York: Garland.

Combs, James. 1991. *Polpop2: Politics and Popular Culture in America Today.* Bowling Green, Ohio: The Popular Press.

Combs, James. 1990. *American Political Movies: An Annotated Filmography of Feature Films.* New York: Garland.

Conway, M. Margaret, Mikel L. Wyckoff, Eleanor Feldbaum, and David Ahern. 1981. The News Media in Children's Political Socialization. *Public Opinion Quarterly* 45(2): 164–78.

Cook, Timothy E. 1983. Another Perspective on Political Authority in Children's Literature: The Fallible Leader in L. Frank Baum and Dr. Seuss. *Western Political Quarterly* 36(2): 326–36.

The Cosby Show. 1984–1992. NBC.

Crowdus, Gary, (ed.). 1994. *The Political Companion to American Film.* Chicago: Lakeview Press.

Dash, Shrikant. 1992. Transmission of Ideology and Partisanship in India, Canada, and the United States. *Political Psychology*, 13(4): 709–726.

Days of Our Lives. 1965-Present. NBC.

Decker, Jeffrey Louis. 1993. The State of Rap: Time and Place in Hip Hop Nationalism. *Social Text* (34): 53–84.

Delli Carpini, Michael X., Scott Keeter, and J. David Kennamer. 1994. Effects of the News Media Environment on Citizen Knowledge of State Politics and Government. *Journalism Quarterly* 71(2): 443–56.

Delli Carpini, Michael X. and Bruce A. Williams. 1996. Constructing Public Opinion: The Uses of Fictional and Nonfictional Television in Conversations about the Environment. *The Psychology of Political Communication.* Ann Arbor: The University of Michigan Press.

De Moraes, Lisa. 2000. A Racial Divide in Viewing Habits. *The Washington Post,* 12 February, C7.

Denisoff, R. Serge. 1972. *Sing a Song of Social Significance.* Bowling Green, Ohio: Bowling Green University Popular Press.

"Diane Watts on Bill C-10," The National Post, retrieved 11 February 2009 from http://network. nationalpost.com/np/blogs/fullcomment/archive/2008/04/22/diane-watts- on-bill-c-10-holding-artists-accountable.aspx.

Die Hard with a Vengeance. 1995. Dir. John McTiernan. Perf. Bruce Willis, Samuel L. Jackson, Graham Greene, Jeremy Irons. 20th Century Fox.

Dirty Dancing. 1987. Dir. Emile Ardolino. Perf. Jennifer Grey, Patrick Swayze, Jerry Orbach. Vestron Pictures.

The Dixie Chicks. 1999. *Fly.* Sony/Monument.

Dixon, Wheeler Winston. 2004. "Something Lost: Film after 9/11." In *Film and Television after 9/11,* edited by Wheeler Winston Dixon.

Dodson, Debra L. 1990. Socialization of Party Activists: National Convention Delegates, 1972–81. *American Journal of Political Science* 34(4): 1119–41.

Dolan, Kathleen. 1995. "Attitudes, Behaviors, and the Influence of the Family: A Reexamination of the Role of Family Structure." *Political Behavior* 17(3, 1995): 251-264.

Doran, Charles F. and James Patrick Sewell. 1986. Anti-Americanism in Canada? *The Annals of the American Academy of Political and Social Science,* Vol. 497, No. 1, 105-119

Douglas, Susan J. 1994. *Where the Girls Are: Growing up Female with the Mass Media.* New York: Times Books.

Dowse, Robert E. and John Hughes. 1971. "The Family, the School, and the Political Socialization Process." *Sociology* 5(21): 21–45.

Dreyfuss, Joel. 1992. White Men on Black Power. *Essence* (November): 66.

Dyson, Michael Eric. 1996. *Between God and Gangsta Rap: Bearing Witness to Black Culture.* New York : Oxford University Press.

E.R. 1994–Present. ABC.

Edgar, Patricia M. and Donald E. Edgar. 1971. Television Violence and Socialization Theory. *The Public Opinion Quarterly,* 35(4): 608-612

Edsall, Thomas B. 1992. The "Values" Debate: Us vs. Them? At Issue Is Which Party Best Represents Heavily White Middle Class. *The Washington Post,* 31 July, A8.

Edwardson, Ryan. 2002–2003. "'Kicking Uncle Sam out of the Peaceable Kingdom': English-Canadian 'New Nationalism" and Americanization" *Journal of Canadian Studies,* 37(4).

Ehman, Lee H. 1980. The American School in the Socialization Process. *Review of Educational Research* 50(1): 99–119.

Ellen. 1994–1998. ABC.

Emberley, Peter C. and Walter R. Newell. 1994. *Bankrupt Education: The Decline of Liberal Education in Canada.* Toronto: University of Toronto Press.

Enemy of the State. Dir. Tony Scott. Perf. Will Smith, Gene Hackman. Touchstone.

Entman, Robert M. 1993. Framing: Toward Clarification of a Fractured Paradigm. *Journal of Communication* 43(4): 51–58.

Erlewine, S.T. (2001a). American Alternative Rock/Post-Punk. Retrieved March 3, 2007, from All-Music: http://www.allmusic.com/cg/amg.dll?p=amg&sql=19:T578.

Erlewine, S.T. (2001b). British Alternative Rock. Retrieved March 3, 2007, from All-Music: http://www.allmusic.com/cg/amg.dll?p=amg&sql=19:T579.

Erlewine, S.T. (2000). Post-Punk. Retrieved March 2, 2007, from All-Music: http://www.allmusic.com/cg/amg.dll?p=amg&sql=77:2636.

Essock-Vitale, Susan M., and Michael T. McGuire. 1988. What 70 Million Years Hath Wrought: Sexual Histories and Reproductive Success of a Random Sample of American Women. In *Human Reproductive Behavior: A Darwinian Perspective,* edited by Laura L. Betzig, Monique Borgerhoff Mulder, and Paul Turke. New York: Cambridge University Press.

Feder, Don. 2001. Hollywood's Patriotism Is All Staged. *The Boston Herald,* 19 November, 25.

Feldman, Stanley, and Lee Sigelman. 1985. The Political Impact of Prime-Time Television: "The Day After." *The Journal of Politics* 47(2): 556–78.

Fluck, Winfried. 1987. Popular Culture as a Mode of Socialization: Theory About Social Functions of Popular Culture Forms. *Journal of Popular Culture,* 21(3): 31–46.

Forrest Gump. 1994. Dir. Robert Zemeckis. Perf. Tom Hanks, Robin Wright, Gary Sinise. Paramount.

Fox, William S. and James Williams. 1974. Political Orientation and Music Preferences among College Students. *Public Opinion Quarterly* 38(3): 352–371.

Friday. 1995. Dir. F. Gary Gray Perf. Ice-Cube, Chris Tucker. New Line Cinemas.

Friends. 1993–2004. NBC.

Frith, Simon, and Angela McRobbie. 1990. Rock and Sexuality, in *On Record: Rock, Pop, and the Written Word* edited by Simon Frith and Andrew Goodwin. New York: Pantheon.

Frith, Simon. *Performing Rites: On the Value of Popular Music.* Cambridge: Harvard University Press, 1996.

Garman, Bryan. 2007. "Models of Charity and Spirit: Bruce Springsteen, 9/11, and the War on Terror." In *Music in the Post 9/11 World,* edited by Jonathan Ritter and J. Martin Daughtry. New York: Routledge.

Garthwaite, Craig and Timothy J. Moore. 2008. The Role of Celebrity Endorsements in Politics: Oprah, Obama and the 2008 Democratic Primary.

Gauntlett, David. 2005. *Moving Experiences: Media Effects and Beyond.* Eastleigh, Eng.: John Libbey Publishing.

Gerbner, George, Larry Gross, Michael Morgan, and Nancy Signorelli. 1984. Political Correlates of Television Viewing. *Public Opinion Quarterly,* 48(1B): 283–300.

Ghiglieri, Michael P. 1999. *The Dark Side of Man: Tracing the Origins of Violence.* New York: Perseus Books.

Ghost. 1990. Dir. Jerry Zucker. Perf. Patrick Swayze, Demi Moore, Whoopi Goldberg. Paramount Pictures.

Giglio, Ernest. 2000. *Here's Looking at You: Hollywood, Film, and Politics.* New York: Peter Lang.

Gibbins, Roger. 1995. *The New Face of Canadian Nationalism.* Kingston: Queen's University Press.

Ginsberg, Benjamin, and Martin Shefter. 1999. *Politics by Other Means: Politicians, Prosecutors and the Press from Watergate to Whitewater.* New York: W. W. Norton.

Girvin, Brian. 1997. Political culture, political independence and economic success in Ireland *Irish Political Studies,* 12 (1): 48 – 77.

Gitlin, Todd. 1983. *Inside Prime-Time.* New York: Pantheon.

Gitlin, Todd. 1995. *The Twilight of Common Dreams: Why America Is Wracked by Culture Wars.* New York: Owlet.

Goldsmith, Peter D. 1998. *Making People's Music: Moe Asch and Folkways Records.* Washington, D.C: Smithsonian Institution Press.

Graber, Doris A. 1990. Seeing Is Remembering: How Visuals Contribute to Learning from Television News. *Journal of Communication* 40(3): 134–55.

Granatstein, J.L. 1996. *Yankee Go Home?: Canadians and Anti-Americanism* New York: Harper Collins.

Gray, Jonathan. 2007. "Imagining America: *The Simpsons* Go Global." *Popular Communication* 5(2): 129–148.

Greenfield, Patricia M., Lisa Bruzzone, Kristi Koyamatsu, Wendy Satuloff, Karey Nixon, Mollyann Brodie, and David Kingsdale. "What is Rock Music Doing to the Minds of Our Youth? A First Experimental look at the Effects of Rock Music Lyrics and Videos." *Journal of Early Adolescence* 7 (1987): 315–329.

Greenstein, Fred I. 1965. *Children and Politics.* New Haven: Yale University Press.

Halstead, Ted. 1999. A Politics for Generation X. *The Atlantic Monthly,* August.

Hammer, Joshua, and Adam Wolfberg. 1992. Not Just Video Hits Anymore: MTV Energizes a Young—and Powerful—Electorate. *Newsweek,* 2 November, 92–93.

Happy Gilmore. 1996. Dir. Dennis Dugan. Perf. Adam Sandler. Universal Studios.

Hardiman, Niamh, and Christopher Whelan. 1998. "Changing Values." In *Ireland and the Politics of Change,* edited by William Crotty and David E. Schmitt. New York: Longman.

Hargrave, Andrea Millwood. 2003. *How Children Interpret Screen Violence.* Retrieved 6 February 2009 from http://www.ofcom.org.uk/static/archive/bsc/pdfs/research/how%20child.pdf.

Hendrickson, Matt. 1997. Revolution Rock. *Rolling Stone,* 4 September, 35–43.

Henn, Matt, Mark Weinstein and Sarah Forrest. 2005. "Uninterested Youth? Young People's Attitudes towards Party Politics in Britain." *Political Studies* 53: 556-578.

Henson, Lori. 2009. "The Dixie Chicks vs. Toby Keith: Country Music's Contested Ideologies and the Culture War in America" Retrieved 16 February 2009 from http://www.allacademic.com//meta/p_mla_apa_research_citation/1/7/2/8/5/pages172853/p172853-2.php.

Hershey-Webb, David. 1999. Number One with a Bullet: Songs of Violence Are Part of America's Folk Tradition. In *Mass Politics: The Politics of Popular Culture*, edited by Daniel Shay. New York: St. Martin's/Worth.

Hess, Robert, and Judith Torney. 1967. *The Development of Political Attitudes in Children*. Chicago: Aldine.

Holloway, Carson. 2001. *All Shook Up: Music, Passion and Politics*. Dallas: Spence Publishing Company.

Home Improvement. 1991–1999. ABC.

Huckfeldt, Robert, Eric Plutzer, John Sprague. 1993. Alternative Contexts of Political Behavior: Churches, Neighborhoods, and Individuals. *The Journal of Politics* 55(2): 365–81.

Huddy, Leonie and Nayda Terkildsen. "Gender Stereotypes and the Perception of Male and Female Candidates." *American Journal of Political Science* 37(1, 1993): 119-147.

Hyman, Herbert. 1959. *Political Socialization: A Study in the Psychology of Political Behavior*. Glencoe, Ill.: Free Press

Ice-T. 1992. "Cop-Killer." By Ice-T. *Body Count*. WEA/Warner Brothers.

Ingle, Roisin. 2000. Worshipping at the altar of Homer. *The Irish Times*, 24 June, 9.

Inglehart, Ronald. 1990a. *Culture Shift in Advanced Industrial Society*. Princeton, NJ: Princeton University Press.

Inglehart, Ronald. 1990b. Political Value Orientations. In *Continuities in Political Action*, edited by M. Kent Jennings, and J.W. van Deth . New York: Walter de Gruyter.

Inglehart, Ronald. 1997. *Modernization and Postmodernization: Cultural, Economic, and Political Change in 43 Societies*. Princeton, NJ: Princeton University Press.

Iyengar, Shanto, and Donald R. Kinder. 1987. *News that Matters: Television and American Opinion*. Chicago: University of Chicago Press.

Iyengar, Shanto. 1991. *Is Anyone Responsible? How Television Frames Political Issues*. Chicago: University of Chicago Press.

Jackson, David J. and Thomas I.A. Darrow. 2005a. The Influence of Celebrity Endorsements on Young Adults' Political Opinions. *The Harvard International Journal of Press/Politics* 2005 10: 80–98.

Jackson, David J. 2005b. Peace, Order and Good Songs: Popular Music and English-Canadian Culture. *The American Review of Canadian Studies*, (Spring): 25–44.

Jackson, David J. 2007a. Selling Politics: The Impact of Celebrities' Political Beliefs on Young Americans. *Journal of Political Marketing* 2007 Vol. 6, No. 4:67–83.

Jackson, David J. 2007b. Star Power? Celebrity and Politics among Anglophone Canadian Youth. *British Journal of Canadian Studies* 2007: 75–98.

Jamison, Laura. 1998. A Feisty Female Rapper Breaks a Hip-Hop Taboo. *The New York Times*, 18 January, sect. 2, p. 34.

Jennings, M. Kent, and Richard G. Niemi. 1974. *The Political Character of Adolescence*. Princeton: Princeton University Press.

Jennings, M. Kent and Richard G. Niemi. 1981. *Generations and Politics: A Panel Study of Young Adults and Their Parents*. Princeton: Princeton University Press.

Jerry Maguire. 1996. Dir. Cameron Crowe. Perf. Tom Cruise, Renee Zellweger, Cuba Gooding, Jr. Sony Pictures.

Johnson, Gary R. 1986. "Kin Selection, Socialization, and Patriotism: An Integrating Theory." *Politics and the Life Sciences* 4(2):127-40.

Johnson, J. D., L. A. Jackson, and L. Gatto. 1995. Violent Attitudes and Deferred Academic Aspirations: Deleterious Effects of Exposure to Rap Music. *Basic and Applied Social Psychology* 16(1–2): 27–41.

Johnson, Leola. 1996. Rap, Misogyny and Racism. *Radical America* 26(3): 7–19.

Jones, Janet Megan. 2003. "Show Your Real Face: A Fan Study of the U.K. Big Brother Transmissions (2000, 2001, 2002). *New Media and Society* 5(3): 400–421.

Kanner, Melinda. 2003. Can *Will and Grace* be "Queered?" *The Gay and Lesbian Review* 10(4): 34–35.

Klapper, Joseph. 1960. *The Effects of Mass Communication.* New York: Free Press.

Knowles, Trudy. 1993. A Missing Piece of Heart: Children's Perceptions of the Persian Gulf War of 1991. *Social Education* 57(1): 19–22.

Knutson, Jeanne. 1974. Pre-Political Ideologies. In *The Politics of Future Citizens,* edited by R. M. Niemi. San Francisco: Jossey-Bass.

Kraus, Sidney, and Dennis Davis. 1976. *The Effects of Mass Communication on Political Behavior.* University Park: Pennsylvania State University Press.

Krosnick, Jon A., and Laura A. Brannon. 1993. The Impact of the Gulf War on the Ingredients of Presidential Evaluations: Multidimensional Effects of Political Involvement. *American Political Science Review* 87(4): 963–75.

Krosnick, Jon A., and Donald R. Kinder. 1990. Altering the Foundations of Support for the President through Priming. *American Political Science Review* 84(2): 497–512.

Kruse, Holly. 1993. "Subcultural Identity in Alternative Music Culture." *Popular Music* 12 (1993): 33–41.

Lakoff, George. 1996. *Moral Politics: What Conservatives Know That Liberals Don't.* Chicago: University of Chicago Press.

Lambert, Ronald D., James E. Curtis, Barry J. Kay, and Steven D. Brown. 1988. "The Social Sources of Political Knowledge." *Canadian Journal of Political Science* 21(2): 359–374.

Langton, Kenneth P. 1967. Peer Group and School and the Political Socialization Process. *American Political Science Review* 61(3): 751–58.

Larson, Stephanie Greco. 2000. Political Cynicism and Its Contradictions in the Public, News and Entertainment. In *It's Showtime: Media, Politics, and Popular Culture,* edited by David A. Schultz. New York: Peter Lang.

Lenart, Silvo, and Kathleen M. McGraw. 1989. America Watches "Amerika": Television Docudrama and Political Attitudes. *Journal of Politics* 51(3): 697–712.

LeVine, Robert. 1963. Political Socialization and Culture Change. In *Old Societies and New States,* edited by Clifford Geerts. New York: The Free Press.

Leymarie, Isabelle. 1993. Rock 'n' Revolt. *Unesco Courier* 46(2): 34–39.

Liebes, Tamar and Rivka Ribak. 1992. The Contribution of Family Culture to Political Participation, Political Outlook, and Its Reproduction. *Communication Research* 19(5): 618–41.

Liebes, Tamar and Elihu Katz. 1990. *The Export of Meaning: Cross-cultural Readings of* Dallas. New York : Oxford University Press.

The Lion King. 1994. Dir. Roger Allers. Perf. James Earl Jones, Jeremy Irons. Disney.

Lusane, Clarence. 1993. Rhapsodic Aspirations: Rap, Race and Power Politics. *The Black Scholar* 23(2): 37–51.

Lyman, Stanford M. 1990. Race, Sex, and Servitude: Images of Blacks in American Cinema. *International Journal of Politics, Culture and Society* (Fall): 49–77.

Mackey, Eva. 2002. *The House of Difference: Cultural Politics and National Identity in Canada*. Toronto: University of Toronto Press.

Manufacturing Consent: Noam Chomsky and the Media. 1993. Dir. Mark Achbar and Peter Wintonick. Documentary. Zeitgeist Films.

Married with Children. 1987–1997. Fox.

Marshall, Thomas R. 1981. The Benevolent Bureaucrat: Political Authority in Children's Literature and Television," *Western Political Quarterly* 34(3): 389–98.

Martin. 1992–1997. Fox.

Martinez, Michael D. 1984. Intergenerational Transfer of Canadian Partisanships. *Canadian Journal of Political Science* 17(1): 133–143.

The Mary Tyler Moore Show. 1970–1977. CBS.

M*A*S*H. 1971–1983. CBS.

Mattern, Mark. 1998. *Acting in concert : music, community, and political action*. New Brunswick: Rutgers University Press.

McLaren, M. (2006, August 18). Punk celebrates 30 years of subversion. *BBC News*. Retrieved March 2, 2007, from BBC News online: http://news.bbc.co.uk/2/hi/entertainment/5263364.stm.

McCombs, Maxwell E. and Donald L. Shaw. 1972. The Agenda-Setting Function of Mass Media. *Public Opinion Quarterly* 36(2): 176–87.

Medhurst, Martin J., and Michael A. DeSousa. 1981. Political Cartoons as Rhetorical Form: A Taxonomy of Graphic Discourse. *Communication Monographs* 48 (Sept.): 197–236.

"Media in the United Kingdom," retrieved 13 February 2009 from www.datamonitor.com.

Medved, Michael. 1993. *Hollywood vs. America: Popular Culture and the War on Traditional Values*. New York: Harper Perennial.

Medved, Michael. 1998. *Saving Childhood: Protecting our Children from the National Assault on Innocence*. New York: Harper Collins.

Medved, Michael. 1999. TV Vice? Sex and Violence Aren't the Problem. In Daniel Shay, *Mass Politics: The Politics of Popular Culture*, edited by Daniel Shay. New York: St. Martin's/Worth.

Medved, Michael. 2001. Hollywood, Patriotism and the War Effort. *USA Today*, 20 November, 13A.

Meisler, Andy. 1995. The Man Who Keeps E.R.'s Heart Beating. *The New York Times*, 26 February, sec. 2, 1.

Mendelsohn, Matthew. 1996. The Media and Interpersonal Communications: The Priming of Issues, Leaders, and Party Identification. *Journal of Politics* 58(1): 112–25.

Meyer, Timothy P. 1976. Impact of "All In The Family" on Children. *Journal of Broadcasting* 20(1): 23–33.

Michael, George. 1987. "I Want Your Sex." *Faith*. Sony/Columbia.

Millard, Gregory, Sarah Riegel and John Wright. 2002. "Here's Where We Get Canadian: English-Canadian Nationalism and Popular Culture." *The American Review of Canadian Studies* (Spring): 11–34.

Miller, M. Mark, and Byron Reeves. 1976. Dramatic TV Content and Children's Sex—Role Stereotypes. *Journal of Broadcasting* 20(1): 36–49.

"Million March Against Iraq War," *BBC News*, retrieved 11 February 2009 from http://news.bbc.co.uk/1/hi/uk/2765041.stm.

Mondak, Jeffrey K. 1993. Public opinion and heuristic processing of source cues. *Political Behavior* 15(2): 167-192.

Moore, Stanley, J. Lare, and K. Wagner. 1985. *The Child's Political World*. New York: Praeger.

Morgan, James. 1993. The United States of Entertainment. *The Washington Post*, Magazine, 25 July.

Morgan, Michael. 1984. Heavy Television Viewing and Perceived Quality of Life. *Journalism Quarterly* 61(Autumn): 499–504.

Morse, Steve. 2004. "He's not afraid to speak out for his country Hawk? Toby Keith says he's just a straight-shooter." Boston Globe, 23 July.

Muller, Edward N., M. A. Seligson, and I. Turan. 1987. Education, Participation, and Support for Democratic Norms. *Comparative Politics* 20(1): 19–33.

Mutz, Diana C. 1992. Mass Media and the Depoliticization of Personal Experience. *American Journal of Political Science* 36(2): 483–508.

Nabors, G. *Remnants the R.E.M.: Collector's handbook & price guide*. Pittsburgh: Eclipse, 1993.

"Natalie Maines (Dixie Chick member) Bashes Toby Keith's Patriotic Anthem." Retrieved 16 February 2009 from http://www.top40-charts.com/news.php?nid=3488.

Nelly. 2000. *Country Grammar*. Uni/Universal.

Neuman, W. Russell. 1982. Television and American Culture: The Mass Medium and the Pluralist Audience. *Public Opinion Quarterly* 46(4): 471–87.

New York Undercover. 1994–1998. Fox.

Newhagen, John E., and Byron Reeves. 1992. The Evening's Bad News: Effects of Compelling Negative Television News Images on Memory. *Journal of Communication* 42(2): 25–41.

"Nielsen Music 2007." *Reuters*, retrieved 13 February 2009 from http://www.reuters.com/article/pressRelease/idUS214743+04-Jan-2008+BW20080104

Niemi, Richard G. 1974. *How Family Members Perceive Each Other*. New Haven: Yale University Press.

Nimmo, Dan, and James E. Combs. 1990. *Mediated Political Realities*. 2nd ed. White Plains, NY: Longman.

Oumano, Elena. 1996. Music and Politics: A Delicate Balance. *Billboard*, 9 November, 79—82.

Owen, David. 2000. Taking Humor Seriously: George Meyer, the Funniest Man Behind the Funniest Show on TV. *The New Yorker*, 13 March, 64.

Page, Benjamin I, Robert Y. Shapiro, and Glenn R. Dempsey. 1987. What Moves Public Opinion? *American Political Science Review* 81(1): 23–43.

Pammett, Jon H. The Development of Political Orientations in Canadian School Children. *Canadian Journal of Political Science* 4(1): 132–141.

Pan, Zhongdang, Ronald E. Ostman, Patricia Moy, and Paula Reynolds. 1994. News Media Exposure and Its Learning Effects During the Persian Gulf War. *Journalism Quarterly* 71(1): 7–19.

Pareles, Jon. 1995. Newt Age Music. *The New York Times*, 15 January, sect. 2, 1.

Parenti, Michael. 1992. *Make–Believe Media: The Politics of Entertainment*. New York: St. Martin's Press.

Party of Five. 1994–2000. Fox.

Paul, David M., and Clyde Brown. 2001. Testing the limits of elite influence on public opinion: An examination of sports facility referendums. *Political Research Quarterly* 54(4): 871-888.

Pearl Jam. 1991. "Jeremy." By Eddie Vedder. *Ten*. Sony/Columbia.

Pease, Andrew and Paul R. Brewer. 2008. The Oprah Factor: The Effects of a Celebrity Endorsement in a Presidential Primary Campaign. *International Journal of Press/Politics* 13(4): 386–400.

Perkinson, Robert. 1996. "The Indigo Girls." *The Progressive*, December, 34–36.

Peterson, Steven A. 1992. Church Participation and Political Participation: The Spillover Effect. *American Politics Quarterly* 20(1): 123–139.

Petty, Richard E. and John T. Cacioppo. 1986. *Communication and Persuasion: Central and Peripheral Routes to Attitude Change*. New York: Springer-Verlag.

Phelps, Glenn A. 1985. Hollywood and the American Voter: Images of Political Efficacy in American Movies. *International Social Science Review* 60(4): 166–175.

Philips, Chuck. 1992. The Uncivil War: The Battle between the Establishment and Supporters of Rap Music Reopens Old Wounds of Race and Class. *The Los Angeles Times*, 19 July, 6.

Poindexter, Paula M. 1980. Non-News Viewers. *Journal of Communication* 30(4): 58–65.

"Post-Punk" No date. *All-Music*, retrieved 14 July 2009 from http://www.allmusic.com/cg/amg.dll?p=amg&sql=77:2636.

Postman, Neil. (1985). *Amusing Ourselves to Death: Public Discourse in the Age of Show Business*. New York: Viking.

Potter, W. James, and William Ware. 1989. The Frequency and Context of Prosocial Acts on Primetime TV. *Journalism Quarterly* 66 (Summer): 359–366.

Powers, Stephen P., D. J. Rothman, and S. Rothman. 1993a. Transformation of Gender Roles in Hollywood Movies: 1946–1990. *Political Communication* 10(3): 259–283.

Powers, Stephen P., D. J. Rothman, and S. Rothman. 1993b. Feminism in Films. *Society* 30(3): 66–72.

Powers, Stephen P., D. J. Rothman and S. Rothman. 1996. *Hollywood's America: Social and Political Themes in Motion Pictures*. Boulder: Westview Press.

Pratt, Ray. 1990. *Rhythm and Resistance: Explorations in the Political Uses of Popular Music*. New York: Praeger.

Pretty Woman. 1990. Dir. Garry Marshall. Perf. Julia Roberts, Richard Gere. Touchstone Pictures.

Prisuta, Robert H. 1979. Televised Sports and Political Values. *Journal of Communication* 29(1): 94–102.

"Public Knowledge of Current Affairs Little Changed by News and Information Revolutions, 2009" *The Pew Research Center for the People and the Press*, retrieved 19 February 2009 from http:// people-press.org/report/319/public-knowledge-of-current-affairs-little-changed-by-news-and-information-revolutions.

Pulp Fiction. 1994. Dir. Quentin Tarantino. Perf. John Travolta, Bruce Willis, Samuel L. Jackson, Uma Thurman. Miramax Films.

"Radio Industry Revenues Continue to Slide," retrieved 13 February 2009 from http://www.bia.c om/081202_2008IIRadio4thEdition.asp.

Rage Against the Machine. 1996. "Bulls on Parade." *Evil Empire.* Sony/Epic.

Rage Against the Machine. 2000. "Testify." *The Battle of Los Angeles.* Sony/Epic.

Reynolds, S. 2005. *Rip It Up & Start Again: Postpunk 1978–1984.* New York: Penguin, 2005.

Ribadeneira, Diego. 1992. Voice of a New Generation: Hip hop Expresses Urban Youth's View of Life and Tells its Untold Stories. *The Boston Globe,* 27 July, 1.

Roberts, Donald. 1973. Communication and Children: A Developmental Approach. *Handbook of Communication,* edited by Ithiel de Sola Pool. Chicago: Rand McNally.

Roberts, Erin. 1997. The Effects of "Rock the Vote" and "Choose or Lose" on Youth Voting Behavior in the Greater Northern West Virginia Panhandle Area. Paper presented at the Northeastern Political Science Convention, 13 November.

Robinson, John P., and Dennis K. Davis. 1990. Television News and the Informed Public: An Information Processing Approach. *Journal of Communication* 40(3): 106–19.

The Rock. 1996. Dir. Michael Bay. Perf. Sean Connery, Nicholas Cage, Ed Harris. Disney.

Rohlfing, Mary E. 1996. "Don't Say Nothin' Bad about My Baby": A Re-evaluation of Women's Roles in the Brill Building Era of Early Rock 'n' Roll. *Critical Studies in Mass Communication* 13(2): 93–114.

Rose, Tricia. 1991. Fear of a Black Planet: Rap Music and Black Cultural Politics in the 1990s. *The Journal of Negro Education* 60(3): 276–90.

Rosen, C. (1992, January 25). "Some see 'new openness' following Nirvana success. *Billboard* 25 January 1992: 12.

Sabbagh, Dan. 2008. "Music sales fall to their lowest level in over twenty years" Times Online, retrieved 13 February 2009 from   http://business.timesonline.co.uk/tol/business/indus-try_sectors/media/article4160553.ece.

Savage, S. 2005. *England's Dreaming.* London: Faber & Faber, 2005.

Scarface. 1983. Dir. Brian DePalma. Perf. Al Pacino, Michelle Pfeiffer. Universal Studios.

Scheurer, Timothy E. 1991. *Born in the U.S.A.: The Myth of America in Popular Music from Colonial Times to the Present.* Jackson: University Press of Mississippi.

Schiller, Herbert I. 1976. Communication and Cultural Domination. New York: International Arts and Sciences Press.

Schmelz, Peter J. "'Have you Forgotten?': Darryl Worley and the Musical Politics of Operation Iraqi Freedom." In *Music in the Post 9/11 World,* edited by Jonathan Ritter and J. Martin Daughtry. New York: Routledge.

Schmitt, David E. 2000. "Internationalization and Patterns of Political Change in Ireland." *Policy Studies Journal* 28(4): 784–798.

Schwartz, David C., and Charles J. Mannella. 1975. Popular Music as an Agency of Political Socialization: A Study in Popular Culture and Politics. In *New Directions in Political Socialization*, edited by David C. Schwartz and Sandra Kenyon Schwartz. New York: The Free Press.

Sears, David O., and Carolyn L. Funk. 1999. Evidence of the Long-Term Persistence of Adults' Political Predispositions. *Journal of Politics* 61(1): 1–28.

Seefeldt, Carol. 1989. The Pledge of Allegiance in Public Schools. *Childhood Education* 55(1):62–63.

Seinfeld. 1989–1998. NBC.

Selnow, Gary W. 1986. Solving Problems on Prime-Time Television. *Journal of Communication* 36(1): 63–72.

Sesame Street. 1969–Present. PBS.

Shaw, Donald L., and Shannon E. Martin. 1992. The Function of Mass Media Agenda Setting. *Journalism Quarterly* 69(4): 902–20.

The Shawshank Redemption. 1994. Dir. Frank Darabont. Perf. Tim Robbins, Morgan Freeman. Castle Rock.

Shea, Daniel. 1999. Introduction: Popular Culture—the Trojan Horse of American Politics? In *Mass Politics: The Politics of Popular Culture*, edited by Daniel Shea. New York: St. Martin's/ Worth.

The Siege. 1998. Dir. Edward Zwick. Perf. Denzel Washington, Annette Bening, Bruce Willis. 20th Century Fox.

Siegel, Arthur. 1986. *Politics and the Media in Canada*. Toronto: McGraw-Hill Ryerson.

Sigel, Roberta. 1970. *Learning About Politics: A Reader in Political Socialization*. New York: Random House.

The Simpsons. 1989–Present. Fox

Singh, Robert. 2007. Anti-Americanism in the United Kingdom. In *Anti-Americanism: History, Causes, Themes*, edited by Brendan O'Connnor. Oxford: Greenwood World Publishing.

Skinner, B. F. 1974. *About Behaviorism*. New York: Alfred A. Knopf.

Smaragdi, Ulla Johnsson. 1983. *TV Use and Social Interaction in Adolescence: A Longitudinal Study*. Stockholm, Sweden: Almquidt and Wiskell International.

Soul Food. 1997. Dir. George Tillman Jr. Perf. Vanessa L. Williams, Vivica A. Fox, Nia Long. 20th Century Fox.

South Park. 1995-Present. Comedy Central.

Sportscenter. 1979-Present. ESPN.

Springsteen, Bruce. 1984. "Born in the U.S.A." Written by Bruce Springsteen. *Born in the U.S.A.* Columbia.

Star Wars. 1977. Dir. George Lucas. Perf. Mark Hamill, Carrie Fisher, Harrison Ford. 20th Century Fox.

Steyn, Mark. 1996. Bozo in the Hood: Tupac Shakur's Short, Violent, Misogynist Life. In *The American Spectator* 29(11): 56–58.

Straw, Will. 1991. "Systems of Articulation, Logics of Change: Communities and Scenes in Popular Music." *Cultural Studies* 5 (1991): 368–388.

Street, John 2004. "Celebrity Politicians: Popular Culture and Political Representation." *British Journal of Politics and International Relations* 6: 435–452.

Streich, Gregory W. 2000. Mass Media, Citizenship and Democracy: Revitalizing Deliberation?" In *It's Showtime: Media, Politics, and Popular Culture*, edited by David A. Schultz. New York: Peter Lang.

Tedin, Kent. 1974. The Influence of Parents on the Political Attitudes of Adolescents. *American Political Science Review* 68(4): 1579–92.

Tedin, Kent L. 1976. On the Reliability of Reported Political Attitudes. *American Journal of Political Science* 20(1):117–24.

Thompson, B. 1993. Right-on Rock. *New Statesman and Society*, 25 June, 22–25.

A Time to Kill. 1996. Dir. Joel Schumacher. Perf. Matthew McConaughey, Sandra Bullock, Samuel L. Jackson. Warner Studios.

Tippin, Aaron. 1993. "Working Man's Ph.D." Written by Aaron Tippin, Bobby Boyd, and Philip Douglas. *Call of the Wild*. BMG/RCA.

Titanic. 1997. Dir. James Cameron. Perf. Leonardo DiCaprio, Kate Winslet. Paramount.

Tomkins, George S. 1977. Political Socialization and Canadian Studies. *Canadian Journal of Education* 2(1): 83–91.

Top Gun. 1986. Dir. Tony Scott. Perf. Tom Cruise, Kelly McGillis. Paramount.

"Tories Plan to Cancel Tax Credits for Offensive Films," CTV.ca, retrieved 11 February 2009 from http://www.ctv.ca/ servlet/ArticleNews/story/CTVNews/20080228/credits_films_080228? s_name=&no_ads=.

Trivers, Robert L. 1974. Parent-Offspring Conflict. *American Zoologist* 14(1): 249–264.

Tupac. 1995. "Me against the World." By Tupac. *Me against the World*. BMG/Jive/Silvertone.

TupacFans—The Unofficial Tupac Shakur Fan–Site, www.tupac.com.

Valentino, Nicholas A., and David O. Sears. 1998. Event-Driven Political Communication and the Preadult Socialization of Partisanship. *Political Behavior* 20(2): 127–53.

Wald, Kenneth D., Dennis E. Owen, Samuel S. Hill, Jr. 1988. Churches as Political Communities. *American Political Science Review* 82(2): 531–48.

Weintraub-Austin, Erica, and C. Leigh Nelson. 1993. Influences of Ethnicity, Family Communication, and Media on Adolescents' Socialization to U.S. Politics. *Journal of Broadcast and Electronic Media* 37(4): 419–535.

The West Wing. 1999-Present. NBC.

Williams, Jay C. 1979. The Dynamics of the Political Movie. *Psychoanalysis and Contemporary Thought* 2(4): 593–625.

Wolfinger, Raymond E., and Steven J. Rosenstone. 1980. *Who Votes?* New Haven: Yale University Press.

Wrangham, Richard, and D. Peterson. 1996. *Demonic Males: Apes and the Origins of Human Violence*. New York: Houghton Mifflin.

Wright, Robert A. 1988. "Dream Comfort, Memory, Despair": Canadian Popular Music and the Dilemma of Nationalism." *Journal of Canadian Studies* 22(4): 27–43.

"Young People F—ing; Just Good Clean Fun," *The Toronto Star*, retrieved 11 February 2009 from http://www.thestar.com/entertainment/article/442615.

Zajonc, R. B. 1980. Feeling and Thinking: Preferences Need no Inferences. *American Psychologist* 35(2): 151–175.

Zajonc, R., and H. Markus. 1984. Affect and Cognition: The Hard Interface. In *Emotion, Cognition and Behavior*, edited by C. Izard, J. Kagan and R Zajonc. New York: Cambridge University Press.

Zillmann, Dolf. Charles F. Aust, Kathleen D. Hoffman, Curtis C. Love, Virginia L. Ordman, Janice T. Pope, Patrick D. Seigler, and Rhonda Gibson. 1995. Radical Rap: Does it further Ethnic Division? *Basic and Applied Social Psychology* 16(1): 1–25.

Index